EVERY OTHER SUNDAY

Jean Rennie fell in love with Norfolk when she
worked during the war in the American Officers'
Club as second chef. She now lives with her
husband in a tiny railway cottage, nicely
modernised, in the quiet of the Norfolk
countryside. She misses only the majestic beauty
of her Scottish mountains, and the old grey town
on the river Clyde.

Her childhood dreams of being a famous "singing
actress" have (almost) faded . . . a spark could
bring them to life again. But she is happy to sing
at Church festivals, and to act occasionally with a
local amateur group. And her writing is
compulsive, and prolific.

Stardom is not now important: her deep
happiness is.

Every Other Sunday

Jean Rennie

CORONET BOOKS
Hodder and Stoughton

Copyright 1955 Jean Rennie

First published in Great Britain 1955 by Arthur Barker
Limited

Portway Edition 1975

Revised and updated Coronet Edition 1977

Printed and bound in Great Britain for
Hodder and Stoughton Paperbacks, a
division of Hodder and Stoughton Ltd.,
Mill Road, Dunton Green, Sevenoaks, Kent
(Editorial Office: 47 Bedford Square,
London, WC1 3DP) by
C. Nicholls & Company Ltd.
The Philips Park Press, Manchester

ISBN 0 340 21837 1

This book was inspired by the late James Agate, who liked the work. And it was encouraged by an American naval officer who died in the Pacific. He said, when he had read my rough draft:

"I have just read something that is going to make you famous some day."

Fame is not my object.

I just feel that I have a story to tell, which might be interesting.

Finally, for the love and devotion which helped me in this task, I dedicate it

TO MY HUSBAND

JEAN RENNIE.

ONE

My father had two loves in his life: my mother, and whisky.

During his tempestuous early years it was always difficult to know which was dearer to him. He was gay and young and handsome, and weak, he danced and sang his way into my mother's heart. I inherited the gay laughter of my father, and, I say it humbly and sincerely, the good sense, honesty, and timidity of my mother, but not my mother's beauty.

They were married on Hogmanay night, in 1904, and on 30th October 1906, at eight o'clock in the morning, I arrived.

I was a puny, weak child, always anaemic. The only claim I had to beauty was, perhaps, my eyes. They were like my mother's—large, and deep grey.

We lived, until I was eight, in a "single-end" in a tenement. A "single-end" is just one apartment, with a cavity in one wall for a bed. This is called a "set-in bed".

Next to the bed, making the corner, was the fireplace—so easy to set fire to the bed curtains—then a gas stove, and a cupboard. Then the next wall was the long kitchen dresser, with drawers, and a coal-bunker and a sink, with a cold-water tap of shining brass. The window, just above the sink, looked on to the street, and a green park, and the railway: and beyond, the river, with the Argyllshire hills in the distant background.

Then the other wall was just blank, and we had our table and chairs there. (We didn't have any armchairs. My father cut down an ordinary kitchen chair to make it low so that mother could sit in it to nurse me and my sister, who arrived three years later.) Along this wall was a shelf—too high to reach without standing on a chair—on which was placed display china—jugs, fancy plates, precious cups and saucers, a tea service from Japan. Just a dust-trap.

There was linoleum on the floor, and sometimes a rug at the fireplace. It was all so spotlessly clean and shining, the window bright and clean, curtains always fresh, bed tidy and modestly hidden by curtains.

The lavatory was outside. It served two families. There was one on each landing.

7

We all four slept in the one bed. Except some nights when my father came home drunk and lay on the floor.

He was the finest left-handed riveter on the Clyde, and he had the finest tenor voice in all Scotland. And he could not feel a sovereign in his pocket without going into a public-house and waving, "The drinks are on me, boys."

Then they took his drink, and threw him out, and he came home.

Only now, or at least a few years ago, I can know the gradual despair that ate into my mother. He drank most when the end of the month came, and the rent was due. I think the rent was about twelve shillings a month, but that was an awful lot of money to find out of a pay that never exceeded thirty shillings a week. My father may have earned more, but my mother never got it.

She kept us clean and tidy, and well-fed. A penny bone, a pennyworth of carrot, turnip, leek, and parsley made a pot of soup that lasted for two days. We had porridge, and good stews, quite a lot of mincemeat and potatoes. I don't think we often had green vegetables or fruit, and I know we only had oranges at New Year.

Sometimes, for months at a stretch, my father would keep sober, and then mother would get material and make us little dresses and coats. I was always difficult to dress—I was all legs and arms, and so gawky. My sister was a tom-boy, and a potato sack tied round the middle looked like a model gown on her. (She still has that gift—put anything on her head and you have a model hat.)

We didn't starve, although I can remember my mother saying often that she wasn't hungry. Mothers do say that. My grandmother and grandfather nearly kept us during our young years.

My grandfather was a good, honest, honourable man who never earned more than three pounds a week in his life, and kept his little family until he had to go on the dole, and that broke his heart and his Scottish spirit; and he died a horrible, agonising death of cancer when he was sixty-nine and I was seventeen. His last words to me were, "Whatever you do, do it with a will."

Dear Grandpa, I have tried to do that. But the weakness got my father so badly that he would take blankets off the bed to pawn them for drink.

I went to school when I was five, and it was in that very

infants' class that I suffered the most terrible humiliation any small child can know. I could only have been just over five, but I remember it vividly, a lovely summer day. Whether my mother had given me a dose of syrup of figs the night before or not, I can't remember, but I wanted to go out—badly.

I raised my hand and said: "Please, may I leave the room?"

The teacher said "No."

I wriggled uncomfortably on my bottom and tried to control my bowels.

Then I asked again. Again she said "No." It was nearly dinner-time; I suppose she thought I could wait till then.

I couldn't.

I started to cry, and I couldn't control anything. When the bell rang for us to go, I struggled to my feet and, followed by the jeers and yells of cruel children, I shuffled, dirty and smelly, down the street to home. When I got across to the tenement "close" I cried, "Mama, Mama," and soon my mother had washed the filth from my legs and buttocks, and put me to bed. But with all the kindness in the world she could not so easily wash the horror from my mind. I leave it to the psychiatrists to say whether or not that would have any effect on a childish brain, but it is a fact, that until a few months ago, I was afraid—if I went into a public toilet, intending to be a little longer than just "spending a penny"— that I might be "told off". I think I have conquered that fear now.

TWO

But school was a wonderful place.

I lapped up knowledge from C A T spells cat to quadratic equations with equal ease. I had an acquisitive and inquisitive mind. I wanted to know—and to learn.

I was still weak and anaemic, and when the war came in 1914 I got a special ration of Stranraer Creamery Butter. I don't think I've ever tasted butter as good as that in all my life.

I played in the parks, and upon the hills, and paddled in the wee burn that ran beside the farm.

We drank milk straight from the cow, and we talked about what we would be when we grew up. I would be an actress—a singing actress—I said.

We gave "concerts" in the back green. We produced *Cinderella*, and variety shows, and collected money for the soldiers in hospital from the war. I sang in school. The teacher thumped the tinny piano, and told my mother: "I hope that child gets a chance. She has the sweetest voice I've ever heard, and every word is clear."

Everybody said what a sweet little voice I had, how true it was, and that it should be trained. My mother wanted it that way—she tried, so hard, but life was all against her. My father was proud of me too, but the craving for whisky was stronger than his love for me.

He went to sea sometimes. He was a fireman on board the Vanderbilt yacht, the *North Star*, in 1912; he was in Monte Carlo when I was taken to hospital with diphtheria. While he was at sea mother got her money from the shipping office, and she got it regular and sure. That was something she didn't know very much—security. I've never known it.

I couldn't do any housework at home. I was too anaemic—if I bent down I got giddy. So I used to go shopping, and I was very good at prices and calculations.

Then in 1914 we moved upstairs to a flat with a room and kitchen and an indoor lavatory. This was definitely a step up.

My sister and I slept together in the "set-in" bed in the room. And we lived there until the summer of 1929.

I grew up, long and lanky, and wanted only two things in life. To go on learning and to sing. Not impossible things to ask, surely?

When I was thirteen I passed the qualifying exam. That meant that I could either leave school or go on to a secondary school. I wanted to go on. Although my mother had gone to service when she was twelve, she didn't want that for me. She struggled and sacrificed to give me the chance she herself had never had. She told me she would have liked to go on at school, but she was the eldest of four and her father had only a very small pay. I know she was bewildered and hurt when I went to service, and was actually enjoying it, in some places.

But I got my way, and I decided to go to high school. Pure snobbery on my part, for it was only because my special friends, one a daughter of a bank manager, were going there.

10

I came home from my first day at high school with an imposing list of books which I had to get. I took my mother to the shop which dealt in school-books. I loved the smell of books and stationery.

She spent her last ten-shilling note on books, and I cheerfully let her do it. Not only my books: I had to have gym slips, white blouses and ties, with a panama hat in the summer.

I looked at the future—I was going to be educated, and I would get a position which would make mother's life easier.

Mother looked at to-morrow's dinner—and saw only despair.

THREE

So I went to the high school, with its gym tunics and blue knickers, white blouses and blue and white ties. There were train fares and books, and it seemed to my mother that I literally ate books. Figuratively, I did. I lapped up everything. We didn't get report cards in the same way as they do now, but I can remember one report card—Geometry, 100 per cent.; Arithmetic, 98 per cent.; Algebra, 82 per cent.; Geography, 75 per cent.; French, 100 per cent.; History, 60 per cent.; Drawing, 32 per cent.; Science, 40 per cent.; Latin, 80 per cent. For English, the Rector himself read my composition to the class—and gave me special mention. Maybe that shows the bent of my mind, I don't know—but I took my Higher Leaving Certificate with Honours after four years.

There was no money—my father was drinking, and in the shipyards there was just the beginning of the depression and men were beginning to dread the weekly pay packet, which may have their notices in them. And there were no paid holidays or sick pay then. My father, although a good workman, was not a steady one. However, he did get a job as assistant foreman, at four pounds ten shillings a week, with holidays paid. He was on "the staff", and went to work in a collar and tie, and a grey suit and bowler hat. At the "Fair Fortnight" he got nine pounds. Nine pounds! My mother had never seen so much money in her life. So we went down to the coast for a holiday. Miraculously, he had brought it all home, and with what mother had managed to save, she thought we'd have a nice holiday. But he broke out again— disgraced us in the street one Saturday night, and mother walked away and left us with him. I, torn between my love for my wayward father and my need of my mother, stood crying in the street. My young sister, more practical and not at all in love with my father, took my hand and ran after my mother.

I can remember scenes in my early childhood of my mother crying and holding us two in bed while my father staggered about the kitchen protesting that he loved us. She accused him of treating us to slow starvation, and cried that he had a queer way of showing his love.

I can remember vividly one evening when we were over at Grandma's. It had been a fine day in late autumn but, just before we thought of going, it started to rain. Heavy, soaking rain. My father had been having one of his bad spells, and for all we knew he was out drinking. He was not accepted in Grandma's house most of our lives. The rain got worse and mother was worrying, when came his well-known whistle outside the kitchen window. He was soaked to the skin—his boots were leaking—but he was carrying our little cloaks and my mother's coat and umbrella. I went down to the door to take the things, and cried because he couldn't come in. He waited for us and carried me home. He was stone sober. Another time, he was coming home on a Saturday night, and as he stepped off the tram (again he was cold sober) a fight was raging at the bottom of the street where he had to cross to get home. By the time he got there somebody had shouted "Police" and the crowd melted away. My father, skirting the outside of the mob, was caught. The police, never very fussy so long as they can make an arrest, anybody will do, said, "Come along, Bob, we've met you before," and yanked him off to spend the night in jail. They ought to have known better. He was not a fighting drunk. He was a friendly drunk, and all the world was his friend.

He stood one night, about midnight, at the fountain near the bowling green, singing, "I have heard the mavis singing his love song to the morn...."

A policeman came along and said, "Come on away hame, Bob—whoever heard a mavie singing at this time o'nicht?"

Two or three times my mother sent him away. And he

always begged to come back. Always she went to him and found him in some rat-infested hovel near the docks, coughing as though he was near the end—weeping tears of genuine remorse, and swearing that he would never touch another drop. And the dear, fine heart of her would melt, and she would think of us, and take him back. But always he spoilt things for her. At a social, or a wedding, or a concert, or meeting—always he would get drunk and make an exhibition of himself, in a perfectly gentlemanly way. He was self-educated, and meticulous about manners. I think the psychiatrists would say it was repressed dramatic instinct. But it needn't have been repressed.

In his youth he met Harry Lauder. Harry was just beginning, and he recognised my father's voice was far superior to his, good as Harry was. He could have worked with Harry, as a team, but there were two reasons why he didn't. One was genuine stage-fright; the other was—the old enemy, whisky!

My father died, aged 81, in 1957, with not an enemy in the world. But he was inclined, subconsciously, to dramatise everything, as I do.

I've come a long way from the fact that I wanted to sing; a fact that I knew and recognised when I was six. Somebody told me, recently—if you have a singleness of purpose, a real desire for something, if you concentrate on that one thing, you'll get it. I could not know then what the years would do to my "singleness of purpose".

FOUR

September 1923. A "Former Pupils'" dance in my old school. I had been given a dress—a lovely navy blue, heavy crepe-de-chine dress, with side panels, by my dear cousin Lucy (the rich one) and it had been taken out and ironed very lovingly and carefully by my mother. Then, in the afternoon, she thought she would get it out of its tissue paper (we had no wardrobes, and clothes just hung on the doors, except for a big cupboard in the lobby, and this dress was far too precious to put in a dark cupboard with other things), it had been folded away in its box.

13

When my mother went to the box, it was gone.

I know now the shock she must have had. It was only a few minutes later that my father came in. Meantime mother had gone across the lobby, in tears, to her sister-in-law. My mother was worn out with worry, and heartbroken that I couldn't go to my dance.

"Aye, she'll go to her dance," said Aunt Mary. "Wait till I get that brother of mine."

His feet were heard stumbling up the stairs, his uncertain key in the door.

"Oh, Mary—I've done a terrible thing—a terrible thing..." and he sat at the table and sobbed.

He had got half a crown for my lovely dress—and it was very easy to get drunk on half a crown then. My mother nagged him—it is difficult not to nag when you are subjected to constant shocks and nerve-racking scenes.

Aunt Mary was a brick. She was always broke herself, but she managed half a crown.

"Give me that ticket, Bob." She shook him.

"Oh, Mary—I've done a terrible thing to my Jeanie."

"Aye, I know—you should be ashamed of yourself. Give me that ticket."

So I got my dance frock, and went to the dance.

But in the spring before this I had got *work*! At first I had not known how to start. I knew so little of any value. I could sit on a cushion and sew a fine seam, but I couldn't *do* anything. I tramped round the shipyard offices—I was taking shorthand, typing, and book-keeping at evening classes. I answered advertisements—I saw the manager at one big factory.

"Aye, I'm sure you're a good lass, but I'm no' takin' on anybody the noo!"

My mother used to work in "The Mill"—a famous woollen mill. She went with me to see the foreman she used to know. He sent her to the foreman of another department.

Yes, I could start on Monday morning, eight till five-thirty, eight till twelve Saturdays, at ten shillings a week, and there would be threepence off for insurance.

I was thrilled. I would be able to try to pay back my mother for all she'd done for me.

Mother wasn't so happy. She knew the mill. "I wanted you to get an education"—her voice was faltering and weak

14

—and tired of the struggle. And yet, there were so many years ahead of her, of more struggle.

So I started at the mill.

It was a good three-quarters-of-an-hour walk from our end of the town to the mill, high up on the west hills. I walked—there were no buses then—and we all sometimes ran the last few minutes so that the gate wouldn't come down on us. I walked up six flights of stairs, to the top of the "Flats"

My work was making long hanks of wool into the nicely twisted hanks you buy in the shop, putting them into bundles of six, or eight, or sixteen, and wrapping them up in paper parcels. I learned to make beautiful parcels. We made tea in the morning, and lunch time, and afternoon, in unspeakable cans. We brought sandwiches from home and, sometimes, when we worked overtime, we would have permission to send out for pie and chips, or maybe just chips. We worked till eight o'clock and got two and sixpence extra.

I was still writing to a French girl who had been corresponding with me in high school. I could still write and speak fluent French then—I was just seventeen. One day I was reading Mademoiselle Madelaine's last letter to me and, having brought some paper, I was writing to her in reply, in French.

The girls (having no respect for privacy!) asked what was that. With perfect innocence, I replied: "A French letter." It was many years before I understood the hoot of glee that gave me a rather loose (to put it mildly) reputation round the mill.

But I was very silly, at the usually very silly age. I never could feel content, I was always reaching for something better.

Then one day I was going up, or down, I don't remember which, in a lift with some parcels under both arms. We carried three or four in each hand, by the strings, and each was two pounds; two under each arm, and we had to go down two flights, along a connecting passage to the packing department, and sometimes down to a basement—it depended on the wool we had packed. Half-way between two floors the lift stuck. It was one of those hand-working lifts you pull with ropes, and another girl had been pulling. I was stuck with my parcels. We started to shout. I do suffer from claustrophobia, but I always try not to give in to it. I hate all these isms and phobias and nerves as an excuse for everything.

15

But we both got a wee bit frightened in the lift, and I'm sure we cried a bit.

Eventually one of the men got it working for us, and we were taken up to safety. Then for some reason I was sent for by the manager.

He asked me what had happened. I told him that all I knew was the lift wouldn't go, and we got a little frightened. So he sacked me—for "Incompetence, Inefficiency, and Insubordination."

My poor mother! Just a few weeks of getting nine and ninepence regularly from me and then that stops. Why? I don't know. I did my work—I always do—I had fun the same as the other girls; I learned most of my dancing in the mill. But I certainly did not deserve those three epithets.

Since those days I have been able to meet that same gentleman on his own social ground, and I was able to give him back that memory. He didn't remember at first—but he had the grace to apologise, and he was very hot under the collar. But his apology was too late—he took nine and ninepence a week from my mother when she needed it—no apology can wipe that out.

So there were a few more weeks of unemployment. As I had only paid Health Insurance, there was no unemployment benefit for me. So my mother sank her pride and went to see that gentleman's wife. She used to work with her in another part of the mill—only the other woman had the sense to marry for position—and saw that it was attained.

But the outcome of it was that the gentleman would give me another chance. I was sent to the hosiery department, and special orders, where I packed large sacks with the orders that came in from all our many branches. My pay was fifteen shillings a week and it was nice work.

That lasted right into the spring of 1924.

On the 1st December 1923 there was a dance in the mill club-house. I wore the blue dress which I had worn in September at the high school dance. This was a better dance—these working boys and girls were real. My school friends had been nice, but I was beginning to feel differences already.

In my schooldays I often used to walk along the West End streets, and I would see the little servant girls in their caps and aprons cleaning the steps or the windows, and I know

16

my nose went literally in the air. (Perhaps that's why it's still turned up!)

One couldn't, of course, acknowledge that these creatures were just like oneself. One would never descend to cleaning doorsteps! The Rector would be horrified! Top in French, Mathematics, English, History, etc.? Unthinkable that one could even contemplate any menial task. And as for cap and apron!

FIVE

Now the Depression was making itself felt all over. I didn't know anything about world economics, or politics. But it seemed that people weren't buying so much wool or knitted garments. It seemed silly, because maybe they needed them but they hadn't the money to buy them. So it was February 1924 when I was "suspended"—the polite word for "sacked" —because of redundancy.

This time I did get unemployment benefit. Six shillings a week.

My father took a ship to Australia—he was three months going out—and I believe the voyage of that little ship made history.

He was four years in Australia and sent my mother four pounds in all those four years. Sometimes he worked, sometimes he didn't. When he did, he drank; when he didn't, he starved (no new thing for him) and slept on the beach.

Like the time he went to Canada. He sent us glowing letters about the job he had, and that he had put down a deposit for our fares out. My mother sold a lot of her furniture (she had gathered some nice, quite plain things) and then came the news that he was coming home— broke.

He'd had good jobs, and drank himself out of them. One night he entered a competition for singing in a variety show. He sang "Mary of Argyle" and brought the house down. Only absolute starvation gave him the courage. He won sixty dollars, and that gave him, and a couple of his cronies, the first meal (and drink) they'd had for nearly a week.

The management offered him a constant engagement, but

he turned it down. Don't ask *me* why. The *chances* that man has had! Chances that I would have given my ears for! And *never* got.

Well, he came home, with only the rags he stood up in, and the same from Australia.

The spring of 1924 dragged on till May.

I kept writing to the pitifully few jobs advertised in the local paper, and went constantly to the library for more opportunities in the bigger papers. Then one day there was an advertisement for a third housemaid in the Highlands.

I hadn't any idea what a housemaid was. Vaguely, I thought she might do housework. And I never had done any housework—I was never strong enough.

Well, I wrote that I had had a good education (more of a handicap than an asset, as I found out), a good home training(!) and I was willing to learn. I enclosed a reference from my minister.

And, glory be, I got the job! With minute instructions about what I must wear, when and how I must travel, and where I would be met. And my wages would be eighteen pounds a year, all found.

I can only vaguely imagine what my mother must have felt. All that time, and all those books, and all my education —I know she was inarticulate—but I can see now the hurt in her eyes, that after all that, her daughter, her eldest, gawky, clever, talented daughter, was going "into service", as she herself had done at the age of twelve—without education.

I felt it a little, and I tried to understand. I tried to tell her that it wouldn't be very long—that I'd get a better job after a while.

I didn't know then.

My greatest horror was the knowledge that *I* would now have to submit to the badge of servitude—a cap and apron.

So, on a clear May day, my mother, my aunt, and I sailed on the little *Comet* to Tighnabruaich, where a groom in a dogcart met me, and drove me twelve miles across to the shores of Loch Fyne.

My mother left me at the pier.

She said, "Be a good lassie now, and dae whit's right."

There were tears in her eyes, as I started on the long road that only ended in 1940—a sixteen years' sentence.

18

SIX

I came to Ballimore, Argyll, a grandly beautiful Highland castle, with towers and battlements and all, standing high on the hill on the shores of Loch Fyne. I don't remember the exact moment of arrival at the back door, but I do remember walking along a seemingly endless red-tiled corridor. I heard the sound of scrubbing as I went along and I saw a young girl on her knees scrubbing energetically, and seemingly enjoying it. I caught a glimpse of what I afterwards found was the scullery. It was down two steps, and it had the same cheerful red-brick floor. Rounding a corner, I saw the kitchen —a wide, gleaming place, with a long spotless white table down its middle, big windows, barred with railings, like parks, spiked at the top. It looked so clear and clean and friendly. And there was no one in it. I was taken along the passage, right to the end, where I was put into a room with two single beds.

I was introduced to Jessie, the second housemaid, with whom I was to share the room. She was a nice-looking girl, slim and petite, fine-boned, and with smooth skin and silky brown hair. I thought she was lovely, and wished I were like her. She was slim, I was skinny; she was graceful, I was gawky. I found out later that she didn't wear corsets—she never needed them, so I threw away mine, with disastrous results.

Then it seemed that tea would be ready soon.

"You needn't change yet, Jenny. I've done the tea for to-day, but that is your job. You can change after tea."

Jessie took me along to the "hall"—the servants' hall— where we ate and sat in our leisure time, which was never very long at a stretch. She picked up a hand-bell and rang it furiously, then took me along to the lovely kitchen. She took me to the big kitchen range, all hot and glowing, with three great big kettles standing on it, boiling quietly and cheerfully.

She showed me how to make the tea in a great big teapot, and fill a large jug with hot water. She put them on a tray, and the whole contraption looked as big as herself, as she led me back to the hall. This time the table, laid with a white cloth, was occupied.

Only, at this meal, the cook did not appear. She had a cup of tea taken to her in her room, and only appeared at six-thirty, when she started getting the dinner ready.

At the cook's place there were a lot of cups and saucers, milk and sugar, and we each had a small plate and a knife. The table was loaded with cut bread, two large plates of butter, two dishes of jam, a plate of home-made scones, and a large fruit cake. The kind of cake that I had only ever seen at New Year, and we knew as "bun". I watched very closely what the others did, because we had always had "something to our tea" at home, which meant a knife and fork. And I thought, privately, that this was a very poor show for a big house.

But I watched how they put a lump of butter on the side of their plates, then a great spoonful of jam, and they used their own knives to spread the butter thick on the bread, and then thick with jam. So I did the same. There was some talk round the table in which I could not really join because it was mostly about our employer, the owner of this lovely castle and the miles of land around it. It did occur to me at the time to wonder how the land belonged to him when it was all part of Scotland, but I couldn't ask, of course. There was also, I remember, a great deal of talk about "when I was with Lady ———", "when I went to Paris with the Duchess of ———". I couldn't join in that either.

Then we started on the scones, with more butter and jam. And then—I saw it for the first time, but not for the last: butter—*and* jam, spread thick on the lovely fruit cake—and, to add to my horror, some of it was left on the plates, and, of course, put out to the pigs at the home farm. I nearly choked with anger at the wanton waste. I could remember so many hungry children—and here was good food being contemptuously pushed aside. And I must be allowed to say, here and now, that in all the sixteen years that were to follow, I never met a single domestic servant, male or female, who was at any time satisfied with the food served to them.

But I had to swallow my anger, and we went back to our bedroom to "change". Now I felt the real feel of a black frock, a little white apron, and a white muslin cap, with black stockings and shoes. My mother had turned me out well. I had three morning "wrappers", but the humiliation of them was awful. They were old ones of my mother's, and the only concession she had been able to make to modernity was to shorten them a little. But they had mildly leg-of-mutton sleeves, and they were tucked here and there, and buttoned very much up to my neck, so that I had to wear a collar. I was laughed at quite a lot over those dresses. And I was horribly sensitive, and hated being laughed at.

When I had changed I went with Jessie to clear the tea and wash up, which I did in the scullery. I found Maggie there, peeling potatoes. It seemed to me a funny time of day to be peeling potatoes, but I didn't say anything.

That earned me the reputation of being "stuck-up". I wasn't. I was frightened and shy, and not very sure what I should say to people.

Tea things washed up, we could go for a walk, or do some mending, or write letters, till dressing-time, at seven o'clock. As the letters wouldn't go out till next afternoon at three o'clock, I decided I'd write to my mother when I came back, so Jessie and the kitchenmaid and I went for a walk. We went through a deep wood, which had a downward path and brought us on to the pebbly shore of the loch.

It was about 5.30 in the evening, and the purple hills against the golden sky would have held me speechless with their glory if I had been alone. But, as always in my life, just when I see or hear a thing of sheer loveliness, it is snatched away: just when I get the door open on the scene which I have dreamed of since I could dream—someone slams it in my face.

The purple hills and the straggling farms dotted over the hillsides, the faintly lapping waves on the pebbly shore—the far glimpse of another castle stronghold across the loch—all had to be left. The kitchenmaid had to be back by six, so we went with her. I was too new and too shy to say I'd like to stay and look.

So we went back.

Jessie and I went to our room and put on our caps and aprons again, and Jessie helped me put my few belongings away. Then I wrote a letter to my mother, and soon it was seven o'clock, the hour when I was to be initiated into the mysteries of being a housemaid.

I don't remember the exact way from our kitchen corridor into the house beyond. I can remember a narrow passage

21

with a baize door at the end which led into the front hall, because it was on a shelf in that corridor where reposed the grog tray, from which the butler had taken the whisky he handed to me at six o'clock one morning to wake me up!

I don't remember how I got to the bedrooms, but here we were, and I followed Margaret meekly. We took a dustpan and brush with us, and a duster, into the bedroom belonging to the eldest daughter of the house. There was the Laird and his Lady, two daughters and a son, a lady housekeeper, and some visitors.

Margaret showed me how to pick up bits of ash and paper and things from the carpet, to draw the curtains and shut the windows. To shut the windows and draw the curtains on the glorious sunset over the purple hills seemed to me sacrilege, but it seemed that the "gentry" didn't have time to look at sunsets.

We straightened the room and then Margaret moved to the massive wardrobe. She opened the doors wide, and there were hung dresses and coats and costumes, enough to take my breath away. She dug out a black lace dress and laid it across the bed. Then she looked at the other side of the wardrobe and chose from dozens of pairs of shoes a black satin pair, and put them on the floor beside the dress. She went to a drawer and took out a long black slip and some other black underclothes, and from another drawer full of stockings she selected a pair which she examined very carefully before she laid them, with the foot tucked in, across the bed with the other clothes.

I was full of questions, and some I managed to ask, but mostly I just wanted to touch and look at the lovely dresses in the wardrobe.

Why did she put out that dress? Why not another one? Why couldn't Elspeth—well, Miss Elspeth then—pick her own dress? Suppose she didn't want that one, suppose she wanted a different colour—she'd have to get out all her own things then?

"You ask too many questions, Jane—we've got to do it—it's our job."

We lit the fire and made sure it would burn up, and that was that room done. We had several more to do, and we had to hurry apparently. It seemed the dressing-gong would go soon, and we must be out of the bedrooms and be ready to go into the drawing-room and other rooms.

In each room we did the same things. Margaret did unbend sufficiently to tell me that you get used to what the ladies wear, especially when they're alone. When there were visitors, or very important visitors anyway, perhaps they preferred something different, in which case they usually told Margaret during the day. But usually it was the same old black frock.

"Just to eat their dinner?" I asked.

"Yes, of course."

"Wouldn't it taste the same in the dress she's wearing now?"

But to that there was only an impatient, "You ask too many questions, Jane."

Since then I have learned a lot, and I know the delight of dressing for dinner. But I didn't, then.

Then I heard the deep reverberating tones of a gong just as we'd got back into the dining-room passage. Margaret and I stood with the butler, who was putting finishing touches to the dining-room table. He went through into the front hall, and after a few minutes, he came back and nodded to Margaret.

"They've gone up," he said.

Margaret gathered me up, dustpan and brush and duster and all, and we went to the drawing-room.

The same performance as the bedrooms—bits gathered up, papers and magazines straightened, cushions plumped up and put in their proper places. Firesides swept up and dusted, and fires made up. There were two fires in the great white drawing-room, both blazing high.

Then we went to the gun-room, but Margaret just looked in and said, "No, that's all right. Come on, billiard-room."

The billiard-room was just that, and nothing more. Two large billiard tables filled the whole length of the room, and stacked under the tables till they were almost pushing the tables up, were newspapers—I think every *Glasgow Herald* and every *Scotsman* that had ever been printed.

Here, too, there was a huge fireplace, with a blazing fire, and we had to tidy up here as well. The same in the front hall, curtains and windows to shut out the still loveliness of the evening.

We were still scuttling round when the gong rang through the house again, and we had to pick up our brushes and dusters and run quick.

Apparently we mustn't be seen. It was to be assumed, I suppose, that the fairies had been at the rooms.

However, it was now eight o'clock, and I was feeling hungry and tired. We went and put our dustpans away, then went to the servants' hall, where we got out a bag of linen and Margaret showed me how to darn tablecloths and patch sheets and things. I had learned how to patch at home, and I could darn socks and stockings, but I had never darned tablecloths before. But I enjoyed it.

I have a precise, tidy mind, and I like every stitch even and straight, and every darn a perfect criss-cross of thread or wool.

Then when we'd been sitting about half an hour, Margaret said we'd have to go upstairs again.

"What for?" I asked.

"To put away the things," was the answer.

"What things?"

But Margaret was too impatient to reply, so I had to follow her again.

There seemed to be no end to it, I thought.

"No end to it?" said a whisper from the future.

"You wait, my girl, you've only begun...."

We toiled up the three flights of stairs again to the same bedrooms which we had tidied so nicely just over an hour before.

It didn't seem possible that one woman could make such a mess when all she had to do was step out of the clothes she was wearing, and scarcely needing to move, step into the other ones put ready for her.

It is true that one of the ladies of the house made no kind of a mess at all. You'd scarcely know she had been in the room. But the other one—she hadn't used any of the things we'd put out for her, and so they had been flung anyhow all over the bed.

Drawers were open, powder was spilt lavishly all over the place, stockings, shoes, underwear, all flung anywhere.

Margaret said nothing. I said plenty.

But what was the use—we were "supposed" to do all this —we were paid for it, after all, "They" were "gentry". I still couldn't see any real reason for this wanton destruction.

We tidied up, then we had to turn down the bed. We took the eiderdown off, and then the silk cover, which we folded very neatly. Under the silk cover was a white patterned cover

24

sheet. This we had to make sure was folded over the blankets, at the top, with the top sheet coming right over both blankets and cover, so as to prevent the least touch of blanket coming into contact with the fair lady's skin. Then, having put that straight across the bed, we turned down one corner, and very carefully turned in any smallest sight of blanket, so that it was a perfect triangle.

"Now we'll go and have supper," said Margaret.

Oh! so we were to get supper! That was something new, and I was really hungry.

SEVEN

At nine o'clock, with the sound of the bell still ringing in my ears, we sat down to supper. In the same order as tea-time, but this time there were no teacups on the table. Instead there were tumblers, and jugs of water, and places set with knives and forks, and dessert-spoons, just like dinner-time.

I think we had cold meat and fried potatoes and some kind of pudding. Whatever it was, it was all very new to me, and I ate up every scrap.

It was now I saw that important person, the cook, for the first time. She sat opposite the butler, a vast mountain of a woman in spotless white. When I came to know her afterwards, she was a gem of goodness, honesty, and generosity. But at first, at work, she was rather frightening.

Well, we had supper, and, when it was over, young Maggie, the scullerymaid, cleared away the things and carried heavy trays of dishes into the scullery. I would have liked to help her but I was told I mustn't.

Then, apparently, we had to go upstairs again. This time with bottles.

"Bottles? In this weather?"

"Yes. They never use them, but they never tell us to stop them, so we must put them in."

That, I supposed, is one of the intelligent things which I was supposed to admire in "Them". So at ten o'clock we took bottles up and put them in the beds. Curtains drawn, windows shut, hot-water bottles. God almighty! The joys of being RICH!

25

I was aching with weariness. But it seemed the evening wasn't over.

"Did I dance?" asked Margaret.

"Dance? Oh, yes!"

"Well, some nights we go over to the gardener's bothy and have a wee dance. Sometimes we just have a cup of tea and a sing-song. Would you like to come?"

"Oh, yes—when is it?"

"Now. As soon as you're ready."

"Now? But we're supposed to …"

"Yes, we're supposed to be locked in by 9.30, but if we didn't make our own fun here, we'd never get any."

And I, who came from a big shipbuilding town, heartily agreed.

So we changed out of our caps and aprons quickly, and into an ordinary frock. Then we went along the passage and met Maggie and Ella, and wonder of wonders—the cook!

Yes, there she was, with a coat over a dark dress, all ready waiting.

We all trooped out of the back door, we three house-maids, the cook, kitchenmaid and scullerymaid, and James, the young red-headed footman. I think I fell madly in love with him, until I met Donald, the keeper, in his kilt, playing the pipes.

The butler saw us out and locked the door.

It seemed that the procedure was that he kept the door locked until his "Lordship", the Colonel, had been on his rounds, and then unlocked it for us.

Well, we went to the "bothy".

We crossed the lovely lawns at the back of the house and into a wooded thicket; through that and out to a clearing, where there was a long low building lit by oil lamps and seemingly divided into rooms. It was not unlike the pictures we had seen of a western shack in American cowboy films. We went into one of these rooms, which had a long wooden table, and along one wall wooden tiers of benches, like the benches in the fo'c'sle of an old ship. There were wooden benches and wooden chairs, and there were tin mugs of tea. Donald played his pipes and David his fiddle, and we danced.

Oh, the lovely lilt of the Highland dancing! Oh, the "Hoochs!" and "Heys!" and the laughter. It went on till about two o'clock in the morning. And I was no longer tired.

The boys saw us back to the house, and there was much

giggling and kissing, and it was all very sweet and young and lovely. It was for me, anyway. It made the long day's work seem worth while. I was new, and rapidly popular with the boys. I was different, and I was an excellent dancer.

We got back uneventfully, and were up at six-thirty next morning.

I had to "do" the gun-room, the front-door steps, and the billiard-room. I liked doing the front-door steps, because the front door faced directly on to Loch Fyne, and it was so lovely. I could gaze at it to the full while I was polishing brasses. I didn't dislike the gun-room either. It was always very muddy, and the floor had to be polished every morning. I didn't mind that, because I could see results, and I used to polish until the wood felt shiny and soft to my cloth. And it looked so good and smelt so rich after it was done.

But the billiard-room! It was a long dreary room with nothing soft or lovely about it. The first morning I did it I naturally picked up the priceless rug at the fireplace, took it outside and swept it. I was surprised to see a half-crown lying on the floor beneath it. It was a heavy rug and the half-crown wasn't at the edge, it was right in the middle. I thought nothing of it, however, and put the half-crown up on the mantelpiece.

I learned more of the mysteries of being a housemaid during the day. The beds, the "slops", the carpet sweeping, the dusting. I gradually learned whose job was which, and that one must not do anyone else's job. Not even to help them. So nobody helped me.

But I must get back to the billiard-room and the rug. A few days later I found, when I lifted the rug, a pack of cards spread out face upwards, all over the floor.

I was extremely annoyed, because it takes time to pick up a pack of cards all spread out on the floor. I know I said something very rude, but my mind was, as yet, completely innocent of any double-dealing, and I still thought it had been carelessness. So I picked them up and put them on the mantelpiece.

During the day I mentioned it casually to Margaret. Her face set in angry lines.

"God! She's still at it, is she? The old ———!"

I looked my surprised questioning.

"That's to make sure you lift the rug every morning," Margaret said. "And if you don't, *I'll* get the trouble."

I told Margaret about the half-crown.

This time she called the old —— something worse.

"That's to make sure you're honest."

I burst into tears and I wanted to go home. That anyone should question my honesty in such an underhand manner was even worse than an insult, it was unthinkable.

Well, I watched that rug and, sure enough, in a few days a pack of cards was spread out face upwards under it. I was early—I had rushed over my steps and gun-room to be sure of the billiard-room.

I looked at the cards, and at something else—a half-crown in the middle of the floor. She's doing it thoroughly this time, I thought.

I hurried along to the butler's pantry.

Yes—he had some glue.

I took the little bottle and, very carefully, I smeared some glue on the half-crown and pressed it on to the floor. I quickly turned each card over, with its back facing upwards, and left them. I managed to smear a few and left them stuck to the floor. Then I did the rest of the room and went on with my day's work, not without fear, for already I had been warned of the awful consequences of "not getting a good reference", and I was a wee bit scared of what my mother would say, because she would never have dared to do a thing like that.

There was nothing said, at least not to me. But I know that that marked the beginning of my doom. But as long as I was there, there was never again anything under the rug.

Now I know I am not original in what I did. I know that kind of thing went on for years before I went to service, and that the glued money usually cured it, but branded the servant as a rebel, and that was a dangerous thing to be in 1924.

Life was not all work, however. I was having fun and lots of boys. Playing the footman off against the gardener, and the keeper against the piper, with all the farm hands for miles around who came to the Highland dances, and liked me.

And, too, I was eating. Eating such food as I had never dreamed existed, and masses of it too. And I didn't realise I was putting on weight until one day somebody called me "Fatty."

Me! "Fatty!" My school nickname had been "Skinny-ma-linky long legs". But the trouble was I began to put on weight in all the wrong places. Round my sit-upon and hips, waist-line and tummy.

There was no other reason for it, only the wonderful Highland air, the abundance of food which replaced the energy we used in work and in play. But I must forestall any thoughts that there may have been another reason why a girl of seventeen should put on weight in awkward places.

I was, as yet, a virgin. And for many years after that, too.

Certainly I kissed in the moonlight, and enjoyed every minute of it. And most certainly I basked in the feeling of being wanted by every attractive boy for miles. And, *most* decidedly, I learned to deal with any who had further ideas. I wasn't interested yet.

We had to take our fun as we could. We had no real "time off", unless the two hours from after lunch till four o'clock tea-time, and the hour after that could be called "time off". And when there were visitors we were not always sure about getting even that.

We worked hard and played hard when we got the chance. We ate masses of the very best of food, milk, butter, home-made jam, cakes, and scones; meat, vegetables; and puddings, the contents of which I did not even try to guess.

Two events stand out in my memory of that first job. One left a physical mark which is with me yet, and the other a searing memory of petty spite and injustice.

One afternoon, after my morning's work (and probably the evening's dancing), I was sitting in the servants' hall. I was tired and had just sat down for half an hour before getting the tea for the lady housekeeper. (I think I have forgotten to mention that that was one of my duties. She had her breakfast and lunch in the dining-room, but her tea and dinner she had on a tray in her sitting-room. She was neither lady nor servant, and so was despised by both.)

The schoolroom bell rang.

The schoolroom was now converted into a sitting-room for Miss Elspeth. It was about 3.30 in the afternoon. My legs and back ached and I thought I'd doze off for a few minutes.

But the bell rang.

I straightened my cap and apron, buttoned my shoes, and ran upstairs.

I knocked and went in.

Miss Elspeth was sitting in an armchair in front of the fireplace, with her feet touching the fender. She was smoking, and on a small table beside her chair was one of those great big boxes of matches.

"You rang, madam?" I said.

"Yes. Light the fire."

Without moving her backside off the chair she could reach the fire, which was all ready laid and had to be guaranteed to light. Without moving her body at all, by just a shift of her fingers, she could light a match.

I lit the fire—and was inwardly seething.

But it had to be inwardly.

One evening in early September we went out as usual about ten o'clock to go over to the bothy. The butler locked the door and we knew that he would faithfully unlock it again when the Colonel had been his rounds.

We stepped quietly over the lawns, and as we moved off into the little thicket I tripped, possibly in a rabbit hole, and turned my ankle. It was painful, and I hobbled a bit, but we got to the bothy. But I didn't dance. I felt a queasy sickness, and I just sat there, not knowing that my ankle was swelling while I sat.

It was more painful soon, and I wanted to get back to go to bed, but I couldn't go, of course, until everybody went.

So about one o'clock we left, and as I stood up and put my weight on my foot the rush of sickening pain came right over me and I fainted. When I came to I was outside, lying on the soft grass, with them all standing more or less patiently round me.

Eventually I was half-dragged, half-carried across the lawns to the back door, which was just down a few steps. The footman ran ahead to open the door. He turned the handle and then stood and looked at us stupidly.

"It's locked!"

"Locked? Can't be! Try it again."

But it was locked. Bolted and barred.

James went round in stockinged feet to the butler's window, but that gentleman was so thoroughly asleep that a whisper could not wake him, and a whisper was all James dared attempt, because two floors above was the Colonel's bedroom window.

So there we were, wrongdoers, being punished.

Barred kitchen windows—no possible entry—or was there?

The bars ended in spiked railings, like those in a public park, about eight inches from the top. The tops of the windows were open.

Have I mentioned how small and slight Jessie was? And how I admired her neat little figure?

Jessie volunteered to crawl through the eight-inch wide gap. Even now, thirty years later, I still feel the shudder of fear I felt when I was told what was being done. The pain in my foot was appalling—I was cold and miserable, I was afraid for Jessie, and I shared the common fear that we would all be found out.

Jessie was handed up by the boys, who stood below. Perched on steady shoulders, that slight body wriggled through, slowly and carefully—the least slip might have impaled her horribly on those wicked spikes.

But presently there was a bump and a subdued shout. Jessie had landed on the kitchen dresser. She ran round to the back door and soon had it open. Quickly I was bundled in. Ruthlessly, my foot was plunged into cold water. I was violently sick, and was being scolded all the time, just as though I'd wanted this pain, and as though it were my fault that we were locked out.

We never found out the mystery of the locked door. The butler was horrified, and told James he should have thrown a brick at him, or anything at all, to wake him. He had locked the door at the usual time after we'd gone out and, as usual, listened for the old man (the Colonel) doing his rounds, and, when he'd gone, he had opened it again.

Whether the old man had been uneasy as to whether he'd been round, or whether he suspected anything, we don't know, and we couldn't, naturally, question the Colonel on that point. We were never questioned about the evening's outing. I was commanded, with awful penalties, to make no mention of my injured ankle. As I could only drag one foot painfully after the other, and as the injured one was swollen to twice its size, it was not easy to hide it. But I had to say that I had tripped and fallen down the kitchen steps; and I did, to save us all from being sacked. But it didn't help *me* any.

That rude cold water and cold-water bandage was the only attention my foot ever got, for I had to be on it every day. I have a permanently swollen ankle, not too bad when I am at rest, but swollen and black and shapeless if I stand too long or walk very much. I never breathed a word about where we had been, but somehow it got out. Not only had I been threatened but I had given my promise not to tell, and that was sufficient for me.

31

I became quite a good housemaid but I never became a good servant, and a week after that night's outing I was sacked.

I had dared to question the Divinity of "The Gentry", and as such I was suspect, because I was "different".

My mother and my aunt met me at the pier.

I could tell my mother was angry, but I couldn't help being sacked. I did nothing wrong. At least, no more wrong than anyone else had done. But that wasn't what made my mother angry—and I know now that her anger was mostly fear. She rushed me to the doctor, who asked me a very awkward question about regularity.

I said "No."

At that my mother nearly fainted.

I was taken to hospital for an examination, which all left me rather bewildered and awkward. The same question was asked and I gave the same reply.

When I was dressed again and went to my mother I was surprised to see her looking happier and relieved, but with tears in her eyes. I was still completely ignorant of all the fuss. My mother took me to the best restaurant in town for tea before we went home.

I didn't know for many years afterwards that my mother had been afraid I was going to have a baby. The doctor who had examined me had assured her that the temporary irregularity was only caused by the sudden change of climate, food, and environment, and that her daughter was still the good girl she had always been.

But I was home, and unemployed. And the tiny kitchen of our old tenement looked small after the big, airy, barred kitchen of the castle. The whole town looked greyer than usual; there were more men at street corners, and the men who were working had fear in their hearts, for they knew their turn must come.

The voice of the shipyards was muted. But dances went on, and I danced right through that winter.

My mother got a job as a laundrymaid in a big house in the West End. It meant that she had to live in, and she was up early in the mornings to do big washings, all by hand. And as if that wasn't enough, while her washing was drying out in the big green at the back of the house, she had to do house work. Her wages were three pounds ten a month, and that kept us going, with my sister's wages, about fifteen shillings a week, from the mill.

I went to evening classes for shorthand, typing, and book-keeping, and also another class for singing. But it was choral singing, and I'm never good with a lot of voices. I can't hear myself, and it seems such a futile waste of time and energy.

I gathered a little of typing, and a smattering of book-keeping, although I thought privately that it was all very silly, and unnecessarily complicated. I was full of questions about things I couldn't understand, but nobody would answer me, so I just went on not understanding them.

But shorthand just would not penetrate. I tried. Oh, I *did* try. My brain was active, young, and intelligent. There seemed no reason why I couldn't learn shorthand, but I couldn't.

Somehow the winter passed.

I missed the good food I had been getting and I reverted to my listless, anaemic state. But I didn't lose much weight, for some unaccountable reason.

I went on answering advertisements—for anything. I wrote countless letters: went to see managers of shops, works, offices. So many times I've done all that in the years.

There was nothing.

I did not, of course, get any unemployment benefit. Having been a domestic servant, you were not supposed to be out of a job, and anyway there was no Employment card, only the Health Insurance card. So, no benefit. We managed without going to the Assistance Board, or as we knew it then—the Parish Relief.

Then the winter had passed and spring came, and still I sang and poured my heart out, and my voice was very sweet. Completely untrained, but natural and clear. And sometimes my mother would snap at me to shut up. I knew it was because her nerves were stretched to breaking-point with worry. But she snapped at me once that I should go out and sing in the streets and try and earn some money to pay for my keep. She had sacrificed to send me to high school and now I was walking about like a lady, and singing—as if I had something to be happy about.

I tried not to eat for a whole day, but youth does not take kindly to starvation, and I had my tea with the rest. But that had hurt me. I only sang because I couldn't help it—it was as natural as breathing.

33

And then one day in April came a letter.

I thought it was a reply to one of the letters that I wrote constantly with ever-decreasing hope. But it was from my cousin Sheila.

"DEAR JEANIE,

"I know a cook who wants a scullerymaid..."

Every time that day in April twenty-nine years ago comes back to my mind I can remember vividly my feelings and impressions. Remember, I was nineteen—I was educated, with an acquisitive mind and a not very strong body, although stronger than it had been. I had ideas and ambition—and, among other things, I had written to the famous Birmingham Repertory Company to ask if they would give me a start.

They replied that they needed people with "experience". How was I to get experience, until I could get in to get experience? No one has ever answered that question.

But Sheila's letter....

I took it into the front room and sat with it, looking out of the window, but not seeing anything.

"I know a cook who wants a scullerymaid..."

Stupidly, the famous lines came into my mind, and stayed there—

"I know a bank whereon the wild thyme blows."

I just sat and suffered. Because I knew now what a scullerymaid was. She was the lowest form of human life—the butt of every other servant, a servant of servants, and the universal whipping boy.

And I, at nineteen, was to start on that—when most girls (in service, that is) start at the bottom about fourteen and have worked their way up a little bit by nineteen.

I read the rest of the letter through tears—I was to get £24 a year, and we would be three months in London and nine months in Yorkshire.

Come now!

London! Surely there I could perhaps get a better job, perhaps a job in an office—go to evening classes, keep up my languages. Why, of course! Here was Opportunity, in the humble guise of a scullerymaid!

I was to write to Mrs. Preston, which I did, and finally, on the 4th of May 1925, I set off again.

34

EIGHT

The day grew hot, the trains were dusty and stuffy; somewhere I must have taken the wrong train, and I landed in Harrogate about six o'clock on a lovely May evening. I don't remember much about Harrogate, except that I have an impression of a large green lawn, with lovely flowers making a big garden, and backed by a large red building. I think I remember a glimpse of a blue sparkling sea, but I may be wrong; I only saw it from the station.

The weird jabbering of the Yorkshire porters fell strangely on my ears. I had never heard anything but the broad dialect of the west of Scotland.

I had been travelling since eight o'clock in the morning. I was tired and dirty and hungry, my face was grey, and my eyes were like dirty grey saucers with weariness and misery. And I wanted my mother.

At last a porter took pity on my dirty face, and showed me where to get a cup of tea, and then where to get the train to Ripon. But it took a long time to get there, and it was nine o'clock before I saw the name on the platform.

I was left on the platform, alone and frightened. Presently an official of some sort came over and asked if I was for S——. I said yes, very thankfully, and he led me outside the station to where the inevitable small pony and trap were waiting.

A very annoyed man and his equally annoyed wife were sitting in it.

He barked at me.

"You're very late."

"Yes ... I'm sorry. I got on the wrong train."

"Well hurry up now—don't stand there, get up."

The trip through the lovely Yorkshire moors in the gloaming was too soon over; it was nine miles from the town.

It was almost dark, a soft velvety starry darkness, when the pony clattered into the cobbled courtyard, where a great chestnut tree stood in the centre, its leaves a brilliant green in the friendly light from the kitchen windows.

I was led through a door, along a passage, and into a kitchen on the right.

The new scullerymaid had arrived.

The kitchen was not so big as the one in Scotland, but it had the same kind of things—the big coal range, now nearly cold, the red-brick floor, white scrubbed tables and long dressers.

A girl in a blue cotton dress and white apron came forward and held out her hand.

"I'm Alice, the kitchenmaid," she replied.

"I'm pleased to meet you," I replied.

Just then a short, fairly stout figure in white came into the kitchen from another door. She seemed severe and unsympathetic, but she came forward and said, "So you're Jenny. What happened? Did you miss your train?"

I must have mumbled something.

"Never mind. You'd like a cup of tea? Yes. Alice, see that Jenny gets a cup of tea, then get to bed, and show her what to do in the morning. Don't be late, Jenny. Goodnight."

And she went back to the mysterious regions she had come from.

Alice poked the fire into a blaze, made sure the kettle was boiling, and made a pot of tea.

"Would you like a hot bath?" she asked suddenly.

I was suddenly aware of the tiredness of my body, and visions of lying full length in the warm luxury of a bath made me answer with enthusiasm.

"Oh, yes! I would, please."

"Well, have this tea, and come up to the bedroom and get your towel and stuff. Then I'll take you up and you can have another cup of tea when you come down. Here's your candle."

Candle?

She handed me a candle in an enamel holder, with a box of matches beside it. She lit her own, then mine, and I followed her back through the scullery passage, across to where a door opened on to a short flight of stairs. Up we went, shading our candles, and into a room at the left.

There were two rooms up here—the one on the right belonged to the cook and the other to Alice and me. I wondered momentarily when *I* would have a bedroom of my own.

Two candles were a very poor light for the bedroom, but Alice showed me my bed, the inevitable washstand and crockery, and two towels over a chair-back. We gathered up the towels and soap, she helped me find my face flannel, and then she took me, with her candle, back downstairs, through the kitchen, and out of the other door, through which Mrs. Preston, the cook, had already come to see me.

Out here it was another world. It was well-lit, although the passage was grey stone, and I could hear voices and laughter round to my right.

Alice led me up a flight of steps and through another door, baize-covered.

This gave me a momentary glimpse of still another world. It had that same indefinable smell that the rooms and passages had in the castle in Scotland, although here it seemed to be even more pronounced, and softer. It was a smell that I've never forgotten—a conglomeration of rich carpets, velvet hangings, polished floors and furniture, especially when it is polished with bees-wax and turpentine, instead of manufactured polishes. It also has a hint of ladies' lovely dresses, of perfume, powders, and silks—in short, it is the smell of generations of luxury and easy living, and is unmistakable.

But we had to hurry through this green-carpeted luxury and scuttle through yet another door, and up more stairs. Not carpeted, these, but linoleum-covered, leading to a linoleum-covered passage.

Well, it seemed we were here at last.

Alice opened a door which showed me a dimly lit place that looked like a laundry. All over it was hung with aprons, small and large aprons, vests, caps, stockings, knickers, petticoats, dusters, tea-towels—a conglomeration of everything, and all very damp. The clothes-horse, on which a lot of them hung, completely hid the bath. But Alice pushed it aside and I saw the bath—a hideous, chipped, grey thing, nakedly jutting out of one wall.

Alice left me, and I locked the door behind her. I turned on the hot-water tap and a faint trickle of water ran out. Slowly, I took some of my clothes off. Then, suddenly, for a few minutes, there was a great gush of hot water, so that I had to turn on the cold. That didn't last long, though, and very soon it dwindled to a trickle again. So, with alternate tricklings and gushings, I eventually got a bath half full of tepid water. I didn't know whether I ought to be up here or not, and whether I should find my way down.

Timidly I opened the door, when I had dressed completely again, and, having a quick sense of direction, I found my way through the luxury, back down to the passage leading to the kitchen. The brown teapot was still sitting on the hob, and my cup and saucer, with milk and sugar, were on the table. I poured out another cup of tea—I was hungry, but there didn't seem to be anything to eat.

I found my way up to the bedroom, then I asked Alice where was the lavatory. She said it was out at the passage to the back door, but there was a "thing" under my bed.

I was quite horrified.

At home those "things" were only used in extreme illness, extreme age, or for children. But my three months as a house-maid had certainly shown me that the "upper classes" were not always so fussy about their personal habits. Now it seemed as if English people were all like that. I have known them to go *past* a lavatory to get to their bedrooms to use one of these things.

I refused to consider it, and put on my coat and went downstairs and up to the back door.

Alice was asleep, with her candle out, when I got back. I got into bed, and I must have been asleep before I put my head on the pillow. Just a minute later, the fierce jangling of the alarm clock strode into my dream, and it was six o'clock.

NINE

It is not going to be easy to describe the days that followed. To give that first day in detail is not possible, because it was a frightful jumble of fires, vegetables, dirty saucepans and dishes, greasy water, vegetables, rabbits, scrubbing floors, polishing, dusting, vegetables—more vegetables....

But I must give some idea of the ideal day.

First job then, was to open up the damper on the donkey boiler, clear it out, and, if necessary, re-light it. This was nearly always necessary, although it was one of those that the manufacturers said should never go out. It was a devil of a thing to light, and it burned coke. The sulphur fumes from the coke when I opened it up to stoke it (when I remembered), well, it's a wonder I have any lungs left.

All right, given that the boiler is merrily started, red hot, heating the water for baths (and everything else), by that time Alice had a kettle boiling and we had tea. That morning tea was lovely. Then Alice took me along, with brush and dust-pan, to the servants' hall. This room I had to sweep and dust every day, once a week scrub it and polish it, then set the table for breakfast for the servants.

At seven o'clock I had to go and "call" Mrs. Preston, the cook. This "call" was an elaborate business. It wasn't just a case of knocking at the door and saying "Seven o'clock, Mrs. Preston." Oh no. It involved a tray, set with teapot, hot-water jug, milk and sugar, cup and saucer, and small plate of bread and butter. Then I had to take up a can of hot water for her to wash in. This was placed in the bowl on the washstand. If the bowl had been used the night before, as it usually was, it had to be emptied into the slop pail, the fresh hot water stood in the bowl, and her face-towel put over it, to keep it warm. So that meant I had to take a clean wiping cloth with me for the bowl. As I only had two hands, this was quite a balancing act. The tray of tea, can of boiling water, and a small damp cloth.

Then it had to be at seven a.m. *Not* one minute to seven, or one minute past seven, but—seven.

I should, by this time, have the hall done and be ready to start the front-door steps, and then do the gun-room. It was a very strange thing, I thought, that when I had been third housemaid the front door and gun-room had been my job. Now I was scullerymaid they were still my job. But I enjoyed doing the gun-room and front-door steps. Only here the gun-room really did want "doing". It was muddy and untidy, and I just loved getting all the mud off and leaving the floor and side cases all mellow and polished, with that lovely smell all round.

By now it was eight o'clock. Theoretically. All this while, remember, I still had to be flying in and out to see to my old "donkey", and perhaps it wouldn't be burning, and would have to be lit all over again.

Then I had to be washed, and my apron clean, my cap tidy, to take in the breakfast and ring the gong.

All this while Alice, too, had not been idle. The kitchen range was a symphony of black and silver and red. Two kettles purred contentedly on the sides, an earthenware coffee percolator stood in its tin of water, with a saucepan of milk. From the kitchen came a lovely smell of coffee, tea, toast, bacon, eggs, fish, scones, and on the dresser there was a large ham on a dish.

I am giving an ideal day—on paper. It hardly ever worked out quite like that.

I took the breakfast in, on a large flat dish, with nine hot plates. (It must have been cold before they got it.)

Alice came with me and showed me where to put them.

The dish and plates went at the head of the table—for the butler.

Alice said, "Hm. Somebody showed you how to set a table then."

"Yes, the butler at my last place showed me."

The teapot, hot water, etc., were put at the opposite end of the table for Mrs. Preston.

"Where do we sit?" I asked innocently.

Alice almost jumped out of her skin.

"We don't come in here! We have our meals in the kitchen. You'd better get the table set for us."

Something else to be done "before breakfast".

Mrs. Preston swept through the kitchen, dressed in spotless white, gave us a dignified "Good morning", and went to her breakfast.

Alice and I scurried around and got a little table set, in a kind of way. We had a white cloth, it's true, but it was a farcical scramble.

Alice had to keep her eye on the stove, her coffee, her scones, and I had to be sure my "donkey" was still working.

So we gobbled whatever there was for breakfast, and then took our cups of tea and ran round the kitchen getting our jobs done.

"Hurry up and get ready for prayers," said Alice suddenly.

"Prayers?" I echoed stupidly.

"Yes, we go alternate mornings. Mrs. Preston has to go every morning. Get your cap straight. Is your apron all right, are your shoes clean?"

It was about fifteen minutes to nine. Mrs. Preston came in and looked at the stove, asked Alice one or two things, and then said something about "prayers".

"No, Jenny's going this morning. I've had too much to do. I haven't got my scones made yet."

"You do go to church at home, don't you, Jenny?" Mrs. Preston asked me.

"Oh, yes. Nearly every Sunday. I used to go to Bible Class too."

She nodded.

"Church of Scotland, of course? Yes. You will find the English services a little different, but come along. I'll show you where to go."

We went round the passage in the direction of the servants' hall, but at a door on the left, that I had noticed but thought it was a cupboard or something, stood a weird collection of people, waiting, as if they were waiting for a cinema to open. There was a young lady dressed in an ordinary dress, a navy blue cloth of some kind. There were three others, one elderly and hatchet-faced, one a little younger, but surly looking and grim, and a young one—big and fat and vacant looking, with small light blue eyes in a big red fat face. But the terrible thing about the three of them was that they were all dressed in eye-shattering pink dresses, with long morning aprons and caps. I've never seen such a pink—before or since. It was ghastly.

Mrs. Preston went to the door, to be ready when the bell rang. Then I saw George, the footman.

We had certainly had young James, the footman at the castle, but he had never been dressed like this. I'd never seen anybody like this. He wore a striped waistcoat, yellow and black, with a coat which seemed to be entirely covered with brass buttons, and it had a tail, which was also covered with brass buttons, all highly polished.

Then there was a man dressed in a black suit, with a tail coat. This was Mr. Carter, the butler.

Then there was me.

A little bell rang, and Mr. Carter opened the door and stood to let the ladies pass.

Mrs. Preston first, in her dignified white, then Miss Bentley, the lady's maid, in her superior ordinary dress. Then the three boiled lobsters—honestly, I could think of nothing more like that awful pink—and lobster is a *nice* colour.

Then I was ushered in, followed by Mr. George and Mr. Carter.

And there we were in the dining-room.

This was a lovely room. I can only now recall the dull red patterned carpet, the dark panelled walls, and a table set in the middle with a white cloth, gleaming silver, and flowers.

At the head of the table sat Sir John with a Bible in front of him. Opposite us, in our chairs which were set in a semi-circle, was an exactly similar semi-circle, and there was there

41

a beautiful elderly lady, an even more beautiful young lady, and three young gentlemen.

Sir John started to read, while we all sat very silent.

Then, having finished reading, he closed the Bible and said, "Now Let Us Pray".

On this command everybody in the room, except Sir John, stood up, did a smart right-about turn, and knelt down in front of their chairs. And I had to do the same.

I was furious.

I had never knelt in the church in my life and I didn't see that I was any the worse for that. I didn't shut my eyes or bow my head—I glanced quickly to my right, and George gave me a terrific wink through his outstretched fingers over his open eyes!

That put "Prayers" in their proper perspective!

My next time at prayers was the Sunday, and I didn't even mind when Sir John read out for his lesson "Six days shalt thou labour and do all thy work, but the seventh day is the sabbath of the Lord thy God—" he took a deep breath—"in-it-thou-shalt-not-do-any-work-thou-nor-thy-manservant-nor-thy-maidservant———" and he gabbled those last words just as quickly as he could. From what I found out later, he should have said, "Six days shalt thou labour—and the seventh day thou shalt work harder than all the rest of them put together."

That's what he *should* have preached.

Well, that was prayers, Heaven help us.

We filed out and went back to work, each one of us swearing in our own way about the waste of time and the rush it would now be to get breakfast in. For Sir John seemed to get an appetite from prayers and demanded his breakfast on the stroke of nine.

George came and collected the breakfast, and got time to give me another wink! So it seemed there might be some fun to be had even here.

But the day wore on for me in a welter of dishes, greasy water, stoking the "donkey", peeling potatoes.

Alice cleaned down the kitchen tables and swept the floor, made up the fire, and put a white cloth on the little table where we had our breakfast. She put a book, an ordinary exercise book, on it, with a pencil. Then she and Mrs. Preston seemed to be rushing about frantically: Alice shouted at me because there wasn't a clear inch of space in my

42

scullery for her to put her board on, and it seemed she had to work out here while her Ladyship was in the kitchen.

But she didn't help me to clear away any of the dishes. She didn't show me how to stack them, or even how to get a bath full of water which wasn't all greasy scum. I'd never met hard water in my life, and I'd never seen such a muddle as this in the lovely kitchen on the shore of Loch Fyne. There, young Maggie seemed to have always lots of lovely hot lather, and I would have enjoyed getting dishes clean. But when you consider that every piece of china used in the dining-room, servants' hall, kitchen—saucepans, kitchen tools, and vegetables—all came to this one sink, and *that* one of those old-fashioned stone sinks, big and shallow, I don't know really how I ever got through it. The fact is, I lived in a greasy, chaotic muddle.

I was hot and sticky, and my black stockings were getting stuck to my feet. I had to wear a sack apron over my white one, and even that got all wet. (I can do it now, in an *evening dress!*)

Then—a voice in the kitchen, and Alice shut the door quietly, and came and hissed at me: "That's her Ladyship. She'll want to see you."

So I waited, trembling, not daring to move a spoon, for fear it would make a noise. I was quite tidy, but almost unconscious with fear, when Mrs. Preston's voice at the door said:

"Jenny. Come here. Her Ladyship would like to see you."

Alice whispered: "When she says 'Good morning,' say 'Good morning, my lady'."

I nodded, too sick to answer.

I had never *seen* a real live Lady, let alone talked to one. I was astonished to find she was just made like everybody else.

I found myself at the little table, with Mrs. Preston on my right.

"This is Jenny, m'lady," she said.

"Ah! Yes. Good morning, Jenny."

"Good morning, m'lady," I whispered.

"Now, I hope you're a hard worker and an early riser. Mrs. Preston will teach you, but we must all learn to take the rough with the smooth. Sometimes I'm *so* tired at night, I *cannot* sleep.

"We were glad to see you at Prayers this morning, Jenny. We do feel that five minutes of our time is not too much to give to God. That will be all, Jenny."

Mrs. Preston gave me a nudge, and I tottered out to the scullery, where I stood trying to fight rising waves of anger, disgust, and nausea.

She had patronised me! Talked down to me. Did I work hard? Did I get up early? Give five minutes to God.

I'm forgetting—it's just coming back, as I feel the bitterness of that moment. She asked me when I had left school.

I told her, "I left high school in 1923, but I was supposed to go to University."

She coloured with anger.

"University?" As much as to say, "How dare you, a servant, go to University?"

"What were you going to take at University?"

"Languages. I was going to be a French teacher."

"And why didn't you?"

Very simply, I answered: "There wasn't enough money. My father's out of work."

At that she smiled. All was well again in her world. The lower classes had no money.

"Ah! well. That's what comes of flying too high. You must learn, Jenny, to be content with that station in life to which it has pleased God to call you. You work hard, and you'll get on."

Not a word about my dreams of academic brilliance—not a word about the sorrow of my mother, who struggled and saved to give me a chance—not a word about whether I'd wanted to do anything else—if I had any other talent.

No, she'd got a cheap scullerymaid, and if my dreams were thrown in the dustbin, then it was the "station in life to which——".

Her second son, a lad of about fifteen, got the shock of his life when I carried on a conversation with him in fluent French, until *he* had to give up. We hurled some Latin at each other, but we soon gave up. He was a nice boy—he loved coming into the kitchen, to see if he could pinch some hot scones.

I make no apology for the bitterness in this page. It must be remembered that I got the tail-end of the era when a domestic servant was something that crawled out of the nearest drainpipe. And cooking was considered "low". I got the end of that, up to the war, in 1940.

The bitterness went deep—so deep, that it will never really go. Unless perhaps this writing it down will move it out of my system. It only really comes when I look back, as I must do now. I'm a very happy person, as I hope you will find through these pages.

But the bitterness *will* creep in—sometimes.

TEN

Her Ladyship gave her approval, or otherwise, to the menu which Mrs. Preston had written in the book, and then swept out.

Mrs. Preston opened the door and called.

"Come on, Alice, she wants apple pudding for lunch. I told her I couldn't get it done in time, but she just sneers as though it was my fault. Look at the time—eleven o'clock, and not a thing done...."

And so she went on.

It was the maddest piece of humbug I've ever known, this kitchen looking as though nothing was ever done in it. I learned, many years afterwards, on the very highest authority, that it was ordained that way because it enabled a Lady to say to her friends:

"My dear! It's the only time I see my kitchen looking even presentable—if I looked in five minutes later it would be a shambles! And I *must* see a clean kitchen at least once a day!"

What impertinence!

The gardener had been in. He hadn't left any apples. Not surprising. It was May, and there weren't many about. But he had some.

That meant that someone—it should have been me— would have to go up to his house and ask him to bring some in. It was extremely doubtful if he would do this. As I didn't know where to go, Alice went.

So I had to chop suet, and grease basins, and put big steamer pans on. Meanwhile, who's going to do my potatoes? And all the other vegetables that seemed to be necessary? And keep the fire up?

Me.

Alice came back, panting.

He'd bring some, but he wasn't sure when.

I went back to my scullery.

45

Somehow, Alice made a cup of tea, and they called me to come and get mine.

Thankfully I took the big cup of tea and went to sit down in the chair in the corner where our black cat, "Sooty", lay, curled up asleep.

"Oh no, Jenny! We don't have time to sit down—you take your tea into the scullery and drink it there. Have some cake or something."

I took two huge buttered scones—"Here, put some more butter on them," said Alice—and went back to the sink, where I stood and wept tears of disillusionment into my tea.

I think the apple pudding was a failure. It was bound to be, knowing what I know now. It didn't go on to cook till after twelve, and lunch was at one o'clock.

So that, ever after, her Ladyship could taunt Mrs. Preston with the fact that she couldn't make apple pudding. *And* she did, too.

But I know she could, because I tasted the one that she left boiling till tea-time, and it was delicious. Certainly she couldn't make something in forty-five minutes that takes two and a half hours to cook. But you couldn't convince her Ladyship of that.

She wanted apple pudding, and if you don't produce it, you can't make it.

Well, that day went on. I got through the washing up, although I left one or two burnt pans to soak. I finally got my scullery floor scrubbed about four o'clock.

The whole house seemed perfectly still. I got a chance to look through the bars of my window and saw the lovely tree, with the sun glinting on it, and its branches rustling in the little May breeze.

I was looking at it, entranced—it was so lovely, the green leaves against the cloudless blue sky—when Ellen, the third housemaid, came in to fill her kettle. She "did" the afternoon tea, as I used to when I was third housemaid.

"What are you staring at?" she demanded.

"That tree. Isn't it lovely?" I was almost afraid to speak, lest a word should spoil the lovely stillness.

She hooted derisively.

"Tree! Good heavens! I never notice them!"

I believe it was the fashion just at that time to belittle all natural beauty—it was "the thing" to treat artificial things as real and beautiful. Anything different and you were "soft".

46

She spoilt the beauty of the day.

I went to my bedroom and flopped on my bed—unmade, just as it was when I got out of it.

"You should do that immediately after breakfast," said Alice, "and Mrs. Preston's room, too."

"And what about Prayers? And the fire? And the washing-up? And..."

"You should be able to get it all done," said Alice smugly, without telling me how.

I should have brought up a can of water to wash my face. I would have dearly loved to put my feet into a bowl of hot water. My black stockings were sticking to my feet. But——

"Hurry up, you've got to be downstairs by four-fifteen," said Alice.

It was just that time then. I wiped my face, I combed my hair, I put on a clean apron, and I went downstairs.

The evening was a repetition of the morning.

More potatoes, more vegetables, more pans, tins, spoons, and, worst horror of all, sieves—wire and hair sieves.

I also met, for the first time, copper pans. They are the loveliest things to cook with, and when I went to my next "place" I took a keen delight in seeing my pans shining along the kitchen shelves, and often took one down for cleaning, if it had got a little dim. I will tell you about the cleaning of these pans later on.

But here I didn't have time to clean them properly or take a pride in them.

It was just one glorious, heart-breaking muddle day after day, and I cried myself to sleep with sheer weariness most nights. If the station had been even at the Lodge gates I would have gone home.

But, young as I was, the thought that kept me going then, as it did all through my life, "I can't go—there's no work, and I must send some money to my mother."

This was not as easy as you would think.

We should be paid on the first of the month. Some months it was the ninth or tenth, and it has been the sixteenth before we were paid.

I did hear tell of a kitchenmaid who went on strike till she got her pay, on the sixteenth.

She got her pay, and her month's notice.

To any tentative enquiries by Mrs. Preston, her Ladyship would reply with such infinite boredom that "Really—Sir John has so much to do—the servants think of nothing but money!"

So that between not knowing when we'd be paid and not knowing when we could get off to go even up to the village to send some home, even if it was only a pound out of my two pounds a month, it always seemed as though we were working for nothing.

ELEVEN

The days settled into a routine and, very gradually, I fought my way out of the muddle. Very gradually, because nobody showed me the right way—only the hard way.

I learned to pluck and draw a chicken.

Not without suffering. Just after lunch one day Alice brought me a white feathery chicken, and said, as she flung it on the floor, "She wants that for dinner."

I looked at it in horror.

"Haven't you ever done a chicken before?" Alice snapped.

"No," I whispered feebly.

"Good God! I don't know how I'm going to get time to show you—all right, leave it there, I'll start it for you anyway."

Some time later, as I was trying to get rid of the greasy, scummy water, she came back.

"Look, it's quite easy, see—" and she started plucking out—"only be careful you don't break the skin—keep it like this—see?"

So I started it, very slowly and fastidiously. It must have been painful to watch—it's even painful to think of that first time, when I think of the speed I attained later.

But it was finished eventually, only I hadn't noticed that Alice had been upstairs and washed and dressed. It seemed she was having a half-day off.

I was still hot, and tired, and greasy and feathery. My nose tickled and my legs and feet were weary.

Alice came in, and snapped again.

"Good God! Haven't you got that thing finished yet?"

I said meekly that there was an awful lot of feathers on it.

"Well, I've got to go out. You'll have to set the table for Mrs. Preston. You know how to do it, you've seen me. And keep the fire up. Finish this bird and then go and get washed, for heaven's sake! Look, I'll cut it for you."

Skilfully, she cut it just above the parson's nose, and forced it open. Then she said:

"You can draw it—just put your hand in and pull—I don't want to get messed up again. Cheerio. Have a cup of tea ready for me when I come in."

And off she went.

Gingerly I put my hand into the chicken and drew out something wet and clammy and horrid.

Then I fainted.

When I recovered, the chicken was still lying gaping—it had to be done. I was violently sick after I got it all emptied out, but that, too, I had to get over as best I could. Nobody came near me—it was my job, and I had to do it, sick, or faint, or well—it didn't matter in the slightest to anybody.

Mrs. Preston came down to go to her tea, and saw me still trying to clean up the mess of the chicken.

"Haven't you washed yet, Jenny?"

"No, Mrs. Preston. I've been doing the chicken, and I was sick."

"You should have had that done ages ago, and it's no good being sick. You'll just have to learn to do these things. That's your job. Now get your face washed, and see that the fire is kept up."

That evening was a nightmare.

I did manage to get my face wiped, but I didn't have any chance to do my feet, and I hadn't any clean underclothes. So I put some of my clothes to soak in a bucket, in a lather of soft soap and soda, which was all I had to wash up with. But it was four or five days after that when I got time to do them, and they were nearly sour.

TWELVE

These are isolated incidents in the welter of scullery life.

I was feeling well, although never very strong—a healthy young animal who worked, ate, and slept, and, of course, danced.

That was our only chance of recreation.

We were thirteen miles from town, with not a hope of getting there. Except once a month, on an afternoon, we were sent, alternately, leaving at two and returning at 5.30. In the big, open red Daimler. It was lovely.

Theoretically, we went once a month. That is, I should have gone every second month, but I was there thirteen months and I only went once.

So three hours, once in thirteen months, is hardly conducive to taking evening classes or looking for a better job. And the job I had, had many compensations.

I could eat whatever I liked, and I certainly did! After the first few mornings Alice and I discontinued the farce of sitting down to breakfast or dinner, so that, eventually, the only meal we sat down to was tea.

The only time off we really had was alternate Sunday mornings and afternoons.

Sunday morning "off" meant from after breakfast until lunch time, and as going to church was essential, it wasn't really time off. In my case I had to have my potatoes done and other vegetables, as well as the "rough vegetables", which had to be done every morning. These rough vegetables were just about half a dozen carrots, two or three onions, turnips if in season, leeks and celery, and some sprigs of parsley. If I had all these done, as well as the breakfast washing-up, and the donkey fire was burning, I might get upstairs by 10.15 to be ready to walk a mile and a half up the hill to the village church for eleven o'clock.

I found the English service very different but rather nice, and once I got used to it I got quite emotional about it and was almost considering deserting my Scottish Presbyterianism for the English Church. Until one Sunday evening I was sitting in the village church, and at the prayers I just sat there because I was enjoying it, and I didn't feel all that wicked in not kneeling.

I got a violent dig in my back.

I turned round and glared—it was the lady's maid.

So I just went on sitting, and that finished me. I might have come to it gradually, of my own wish, but I will not be bullied into it.

It doesn't matter very much now anyway.

But church on Sunday mornings was a "must". And I sat there half-asleep and tried to think of the service and about what my scullery would be like when I got back. Then the helter-skelter down the hill, and the scramble back into cap and apron, and the endless round of greasy dishes.

But there was one thing which I lavished love and attention and "elbow-grease" on. That was my two taps, hot and cold. They were originally brass, but they had got corroded with months of neglect. Gradually I got them clean and gradually clear.

And soon the words "Jenny's taps" were synonymous with anything extra specially clean. I made it my last job every afternoon, even if I had only a minute to wash and get changed for tea. They glittered like gold in the gloom of the grey scullery. I was very proud of them.

It was while I was polishing them one afternoon quietly that I heard the first bit of spiteful gossip that was a dig at me. I have told you how I arrived that first night, weary and tired, and frightened and shy, and terribly homesick and wanting my mother. And how Alice asked me if I'd like a bath....

I heard voices in the kitchen and I knew it was fat Ethel, the third housemaid, and Olive, the second housemaid.

The voices rattled on and I caught a phrase—I was too intent on my taps to bother about anything. But the words "and she'd better keep her eyes off George—he's mine" caught my ears, and that sixth sense I've got told me they meant me. The reply came:

"Yes. But what about the first night she came here? Two hours late, and then marches in here and demands a hot bath, if you please!"

There was a sniggering laugh and some rude noises and then footsteps.

Ethel, with her kettle, came into the scullery.

Fear and horror kept me silent. My heart was thumping

and I was all in a cold sweat. I know I should have tackled them, but I was afraid. I had only been there a short time, but already I knew the fear of a bad reference, and couldn't know how far these girls could influence my life. I knew they'd been there a long time, a few years that is, and the new servant is always wrong.

So fear of consequences and, yes, fear of people, kept me quiet.

Ethel just filled her kettle and went off, her fat red face redder and fatter than ever, and I heard frantic whisperings.

As for George—well, it was true that George had been paying me quite a lot of attention; he had danced with me in our little dances in the servants' hall on an occasional Saturday evening, and once he had waited for me at the back door and kissed me good-night. It was very nice.

There was also the gardener's boy, and the chauffeur, and a boy from the village who had a motor-bike. I was always popular with them. I was new and different, a good sport and a good dancer. There was nothing else—I still had plenty of time.

But why one or the other of those two girls should have called George "hers", I don't know.

Sunday afternoons off were the best, and Jack, the boy who had a motor-bike, took me one Sunday afternoon to see Fountains Abbey.

It was a glorious summer day, and for a few brief hours I could forget cap and apron and that I was a servant. We stopped for tea at a little place and then we went to church.

I had to be in at nine o'clock.

Just when the summer evening is getting lovely—that last breathless daylight—I had to be inside, and all I could see from my bedroom window was the wall of the kitchen garden, and from my scullery window a patch of sky and my lovely tree in the courtyard. But I couldn't linger in the courtyard in the hush of a glowing summer evening or go for a walk even in the kitchen garden.

One Sunday morning it was Alice's morning "off". There seemed to be less washing-up than usual and somehow I had everything clear.

I made every opportunity I could to go into the kitchen, partly because I was lonely and partly because the kitchen was lighter and brighter than my scullery. And I sometimes collected dirty dishes and pans and took them away to wash up.

This morning I went in to help Alice, who was rushing frantically about, swearing at having to go to church when she had so much to do.

I made up the fire for her and swept the floor—I liked to see the fire glowing and a nice tidy fireside.

I looked round the table and took some dirty spoons and things into the scullery. I came back, and going, as I thought, helpfully along the table I saw on her board a little heap of white crumbly stuff: it looked as if she had swept it to one side and intended to wipe it into the bucket.

So, to help her, I wiped it off the board into a plate and smartly dropped it into the pig bin, which stood near the donkey fire in the scullery.

In a few minutes there was a howl of sheer agony from the kitchen.

"*Where's—my—horse-radish?*"

It was such a scream that I went in, wondering.

"Horse-radish?" I asked innocently.

"Yes. I got it ready and I was just getting my sour cream —where is it?—" she thumped her board—"I left it just here."

Suddenly enlightenment.

"Oh! Do you mean that funny white stuff that was on the corner of your board? I put it out."

"Funny white stuff!" she shrieked. "You put it out! I'll show you just how funny it is—get you out to the gardens and find Mr. Grey and ask him for some more, *if* you can find him, *if* he'll give it to you, *if* he hasn't gone to church. Then come back here and scrape it *and* grate it and you won't find it so funny! Go—get it out!"

Finding Mr. Grey was one thing. Asking him to work in a Sunday morning was another. He called me all kinds of a fool and worse for daring to disturb him on a Sunday morning.

Shuddering with fear and impatience, I followed him meekly, while he went to the kitchen garden and got some lumps of this queer-looking plant that I had called funny white stuff.

I rushed back to Alice and showed it to her.

Then I said, "Aren't you going to church?"

53

That brought another tirade—how could she go to church when she had to do all her work twice because of damned silly scullerymaids who didn't know horse-radish when they saw it—she would tell her Ladyship that was why she wasn't at church, and much more in the same strain.

"Well, get it done, and grate it—don't stand there looking soft."

The tears caused by the horse-radish hid the tears from my heart. I wasn't yet immune to harshness or punishments—I was still "soft". But all I had thought of was to help Alice—I did so like to help anybody.

It was the same drastic lesson and cure as in everything, but I never forgot horse-radish.

Everything in the larder was so tempting, to someone who had never seen such a plentitude of food. I brought in the tin of sardines for the savoury and, after a great deal of struggling with a silly little key which broke, I finally got the tin opened. In all innocence, I asked what dish I should put the sardines into.

"For God's sake don't move them out of the tin!" Mrs. Preston shouted.

"They must go in in the tin, and they have to be left in the tin so that Sir John can see how many are left."

So I had to let the succulent little fish lie in the tin till the next time they were asked for. They were usually sent in for breakfast, still in their tin.

THIRTEEN

Then one day came exciting news—we were going to London!

But it wasn't just a case of "picking up a handbag and suitcase and be off".

Household linen, saucepans, dishes, kitchen knives and spoons, all had to be packed in great big hampers to take with us. We were to be there, I think, about six weeks.

The best of the whole affair was the fact that for a complete day we'd be sitting down! And just to sit down was our idea of Paradise.

But our work in the kitchen was increased threefold. The normal routine which was always chaos (at least it was as far as I was concerned—I just couldn't get out of the muddle), and in addition the packing—"We can't pack these, we'll need them for dinner to-night; we can't spare that, we'll need it to finish off lunch," so that most of our kitchen utensils had to be packed after dinner on the last night.

Then on the Day we had to make sandwiches for everybody.

"They" wouldn't pay for lunch on a train. Not when they could have sandwiches made by their staff, who would have nothing to do for a whole day anyway.

Thirty years have dimmed the details somewhat, but I know that we did sit for the whole day, and were just as tired when we got to London.

But for me it was thrilling and exciting. The crowds and the lights and the traffic, the taxi from the station to Eaton Square, our arrival about 6.30.

Then, as we had had a long day's rest, we couldn't expect any more, so we had to get dinner ready for eight o'clock.

I was shown my scullery, and I could have cried.

It was a place which was obviously an afterthought, put on as an extension. It was about four feet wide and about ten feet long. It had a shallow stone sink, the same as in Yorkshire, and the donkey boiler in a little cubby hole beside it. It had a window, but it was dark and grimy with years of dust, and it looked on to the door of the coal shed and the lavatory. The light burned all day and it was airless and cheerless and spotlessly clean.

But not for long.

I thought a day's rest would have made me feel better. But I was more tired than ever, and no matter what went wrong it could always, somehow or other, be traced right back to me.

Everybody was irritable—Mrs. Preston especially so—hampers had to be unpacked and a dinner got ready, "They" were too tired to go out.

I had to light the donkey fire and make sure that it would go, for baths; I had to get potatoes and vegetables done for dining-room and servants' hall, and get the washing-up done.

The water had to be hot—Sir John would not eat his dinner unless he had a bath.

Missing saucepans, coffee percolator, knives, dishes—

55

somehow or other it always transpired that I was the last one to have handled them—so everybody's wrath was hurled on my unfortunate head. Every scullerymaid got that; if you had any sense you took it philosophically and shrugged it off. I didn't. I fought it, as I've fought everything—injustice, real and imaginary, large and small, and untruths and exploitation. It hurt me, it all went so deep.

But at last the long day was over and we could go to bed.

The kitchen and butler's pantry and servants' hall, of course, were downstairs, below ground level. The ground floor was usually the front hall, library, and dining-room, sometimes a morning room and a cloakroom. The first floor, the drawing-room. Second floor, best bedroom, dressing-room, with perhaps tucked in between the ground and first floor, a boudoir.

Then the third floor was other smaller bedrooms for the grown-up family, and spare rooms; and the fourth floor was the nursery floor; and the fifth, or attic floor, was the servants'.

A room for the cook, a room for the head housemaid, a room for the second housemaid, and a room for the scullerymaid and kitchenmaid. Only the second housemaid travelled with the family. The head was either a temporary, for the season, or a permanent housemaid-housekeeper.

The butler and footman had rooms in the basement.

There was no lift. Even if there had been we wouldn't have been allowed to use it. The housemaid had to carry buckets of coal up to the nursery floors, if the day was cold, all the way up four flights of stairs. In winter, of course, the house was central-heated up to the nursery floor. *Not* the servants' floor.

This general lay-out fits most of the London houses, with minor variations.

The back staircase came up to the second floor, and then you had to go through a door and bang on to the front staircase. We had to be very careful in case we were what was called "caught" on that main staircase if we were going up to wash in the afternoon. We mustn't be seen. And if we committed the unforgivable sin of being seen on the staircase going up, it added to the extent of our sin if we had slipped off our cap, or carried our shoes to rest weary feet on the thick pile carpet.

We had to listen for voices as we gingerly opened the door,

then rush like mad, but silently, upstairs to the safety of our bedrooms.

Well, on that first night, the housemaids had made our beds.

The rooms were large and airy and had electric light, one naked bulb at the window, with the switch at the door, and the beds on the other side of the room.

Weariness tugged at my bones, but that indescribable atmosphere which is London in May conquered it.

I hung out of the window—mercifully it looked on to the front, on the Square—and I saw the cars passing, with men and women in evening dress, I heard gay voices, and from somewhere I heard dance music, and my feet ached to dance.

Completely enthralled ' and strangely comforted by the thought that I was in London and would soon find a better job, I went to bed—I didn't even wash—and was asleep before my head hit the pillow.

FOURTEEN

In London there was never any question of regular "time off". No whistle blew at 5.30 to signal the day's work done, no clock card to punch at eight o'clock, and no chance of being "quartered" if you were late.

You started at about six o'clock in the morning and *never* later than 6.30, and if you could get "finished" by three, then you had a whole hour to get washed and cleaned up and maybe wash stockings or your hair, or mend things.

"Finished" meant the lunch things all cleared away and washed-up, tables and dressers scrubbed down, and scullery floor scrubbed. The kitchenmaid scrubbed her floor first thing in the morning.

Here, there was a coal range, too, but it was only a small thing: it couldn't have burned more than one hundredweight of coal a day. But there was also a gas stove, so that it made life that little bit easier. The only concession to London life was that we bought bread for the staff and for cooking. Bread for the dining-room had to be made. And there were no Prayers. Apparently God didn't need five minutes of our day in London!

But when all these things were done, in addition to having vegetables prepared for the dinner and any poultry plucked, drawn and trussed, it meant we were free for that limited time. The kitchenmaid had to be down to get the drawing-room tea, to cut very thin bread and butter, put out cakes, biscuits and scones, all home-made, and then she was free, till 6.30.

I had to be there, theoretically, to get our tea, Alice's and mine, but we never sat down to a spread tea—we might squat on a couple of chairs, with our cups of tea at the end of the kitchen table, and eat till we were full, but we only rarely sat down to breakfast and dinner, and never supper.

I wanted to go out—I wanted to see all the London that I'd heard and read about—But the days and the nights were full. Miss Marguarita had come up to be Presented and that meant a great many dinners and dances.

It also meant, occasionally, that "They" went out to dinner. But they took good care that if Sir John and her Ladyship went out, Miss Marguarita was at home for dinner. Or if Miss Marguarita and young Master John and Master Edward were out, "They" would be in; and there was the nursery and Nanny.

It was only twice, I think, that they were all out for dinner, but there was always the staff to feed.

And although they grumbled about their food, *always*, they would hurry away from wherever they were, in Town from theatre or pictures, or even visiting friends, to be back for supper. And it had to be there.

In the country, if we did go out, we had to be in at nine. In London we had a concession till ten. I tried to argue about that.

It was supposed to be for our own interests. I couldn't see that if anything was going to happen to me, it couldn't happen just as easily at ten minutes before ten, as ten minutes past ten.

But again that showed signs of thinking, and I was told not to be cheeky. Rules were rules and had to be obeyed.

Then came the night before Miss Marguarita was to be Presented.

She was a girl of wonderful beauty, of face and figure, and she was almost the exact age of myself with, possibly, a few weeks difference.

There was to be a dinner party and dance, and a breakfast

58

at four o'clock in the morning. I don't remember what night it was, but I do know that we were hard at work for three days before it.

My little scullery got chock-full of dishes and pans; nobody could find anything; Mrs. Preston stormed at me, Alice stormed at me, the butler raved at me because I'd broken one of his best dining-room plates.

I can only remember a chaotic nightmare, until just before nine o'clock on the night of the dance. On that day we did get upstairs to wash—we hadn't for three days. And on that day the ban on being "caught" was lifted. We were free to move upstairs at our convenience.

I had cleared away most of the rubbish—the heat in the scullery was intense—and I tottered upstairs in stockinged feet and minus my cap. I didn't meet a soul.

I had a can of hot water with me and I had a new pair of light cotton stockings.

My black ones were stiff and smelly, and I hated them.

My underclothes were not much better, and I had too much on anyway; I had never experienced such heat, and my mother had always insisted on woollen vests and sensible knickers, as well as corsets and a petticoat.

I had the bedroom to myself and I stripped. Very quickly I washed myself all over and put on a thin vest and knickers, but no petticoat, corsets, of course, since that first scare my mother had been adamant about them. I put on light stockings and thin shoes, a clean dress and apron, and went downstairs.

With a wildly beating heart—for this was indeed rebellion—I went fearfully downstairs to the gloom of the basement.

But I felt so well. Clean and spruce and tidy, and ready for anything—except more trouble. I reached my scullery without being seen, and found it stacked all over—benches, dresser, draining-boards, sink, and floor—with more and more dirty things.

Mrs. Preston had tried to tell me to keep on top of my washing-up, not to let it get on top of me. I felt, as I said, fit and well and clean, and I got started. Some instinct must have shown me the right way, because I very soon cleared the lot.

There was one more blessing. We hadn't brought so many copper saucepans so that the washing-up water didn't get so sandy.

Copper pans were cleaned with two mixtures, one for inside and one for outside. The inside mixture was soft soap and water and sand. I can't remember the quantities now, but I think it was equal. Soft soap and a little water boiled together in a big old pan, and then it was thickened up with handfuls of sand until it was soft and pliable, and it was used with the hands to rub round the inside of the pans.

The outside mixture was sand, flour, and vinegar, with perhaps a squeeze of lemon juice. It was not boiled, but was kept in a basin beside the sink, or under the sink.

What these two mixtures did to my hands and nails over a period of three years would have to be seen to be believed. But no matter what I did, the sand seemed to permeate everything. And with only one sink it was no easy task to make sure that it was entirely free of sand.

This particular evening it seemed that the dinner and supper were all ready, and Mrs. Preston asked me if I would like to come along to the servants' hall and see the supper things laid out. I was delighted, of course.

Two big trestle tables covered with white sheets were laid along the walls. On them were silver dishes and glass dishes of the most exquisite, colourful looking—could it be *food*—I wondered!

I stood absolutely astounded.

I knew Mrs. Preston was a good cook, but I had never realised the extent of her skill. I don't know now all that was there because I didn't know then all of it. I remember, though, tiny slices of pink salmon, all beautifully decorated —it wasn't a bit like the tins of salmon we used to have at home. Then I was told it was fresh salmon. That didn't make it any easier to understand.

But that first Presentation dinner must have made a very strong impression on me, for when, many years later, I came to do a Presentation for a princess on my own, I remembered the general lay-out and I modelled it on that. Thank you, Mrs. Preston, you said I'd thank you for it some day. And I have, many times.

"I wish I could do things like that," I said.

"You will learn, Jenny, if you learn the bottom first."

She was very tired, but I realise now, very proud. She'd had a little help from Alice—Alice was a good hard worker and a good staff cook, but she was no artist.

She'd had no help from me, because I hadn't known or

understood that she needed all these pans to cook these lovely things, and I hadn't always had them cleaned for her.

"You mean you used to be a scullerymaid?"

"Certainly. It's the only way to learn."

I had an artistic sense, and I would have dearly loved to decorate those delicate little patties filled with chicken *chaudfroid*. But I didn't even begin to know what it consisted of. It looked so easy when she did it, but I didn't even know how to hold a palette knife.

No, clearly I had a great deal to learn.

Suddenly we heard a Voice and a step on the stairs from the front hall.

The butler stuck his head in the door—"Her Ladyship!" he mouthed at us.

"God Almighty! What the hell does she want? Get back to the kitchen Jenny, quick, and for God's sake put your cap on!"

I just managed to skirt the door as she swept in, in a gorgeous evening gown—I think it was grey, but I'm not sure.

"Ah! Mrs. Preston. I just wanted to see the supper—I shan't have much chance when it comes up. Yes, why isn't Jenny wearing her cap? Ah, yes, very nice—very nice, Do you think this is a little too pink? Still, it's all very nice, Mrs. Preston. Carter!"

"Yes, m'lady?"

"You will see that the staff have what they want for supper."

"Certainly, thank you, m'lady."

And having graciously given her permission for us all to taste the lovelies and administered her edict in respect of my cap, she went upstairs to face her guests for the evening's dancing, eating, and drinking.

FIFTEEN

I was sent to bed when the dinner was over and I had had my fill of the dainty food for my supper.

When I went up to call Mrs. Preston at seven o'clock next morning as usual, she had only been in bed an hour, and, judging by my scullery, I knew she had been busy. Breakfast at 4 a.m. for nearly a hundred people was no small task.

I was tired too; we had had three days practically non-stop, but we still had to go on churning out more and more food. I used to wonder where they put it all.

"But," her Ladyship says plaintively, "I only have the *tiniest* bit of chicken on my plate, and only *one* little potato, and the *teeniest* helping of French beans, surely you can't be tired preparing such a *little* meal?"

Two excuses we were never allowed for anything: you hadn't time or you were tired. You had all the time on the clock, and you got plenty of food, so you mustn't be tired.

It's true we got plenty of good food, and I was beginning to acquire a taste for richer things, that I'd never tasted before. Like coffee, and chicken in a thick creamy sauce, and aspic jelly, salmon and cucumber, strawberries and cream, french beans, fresh garden peas, and I ate everything I saw. To say nothing of tasting the contents of every saucepan and mixing bowl that came out to be washed.

The housemaids, on the other hand, had to be content with what was given them, and although it was good it was never plentiful—enough, but not too much, and not very exciting.

SIXTEEN

The day after that Presentation dinner was a quiet one—two breakfast trays upstairs for her Ladyship and Miss Marguarita, and breakfast in the dining-room for Sir John and the two boys.

Lunch as usual, but only the family, and an early dinner, and a light snack on a tray for Miss Marguarita.

That being so, Alice had the afternoon off.

Quiet? Compared to the last three days, yes, but still plenty to do. Although, there was a lot left over from the party which could be used up and it made it a little easier.

About six o'clock the butler came and whispered to Mrs. Preston. She nodded, and started taking her working apron off.

She turned and said to me: "Look after the stove, Jenny, I'm going to see Miss Marguarita in her Presentation gown."

I think my face must have been a study in eagerness. I know my mouth and eyes were wide open, and I must have moved forward, and somehow found the courage to speak, stuttering:

"Oh! P-p-lease, could—could I come?"

She hesitated.

"Well—I suppose so—but only for a minute. Are you tidy? Put your cap straight. Come on."

Trembling in anticipation of the glory of a wonderful sight, I followed her.

Up the stairs, to the holy of holies, the front staircase, and then a discreet knock on a closed door. It was opened by Miss Bentley, the lady's maid.

Mrs. Preston whispered hurriedly, and Miss Bentley and she disappeared inside. In a moment Miss Bentley came back and beckoned me in to the bedroom of this most fortunate young lady.

I can see her now.

She was utterly lovely.

In gleaming white satin, that seemed to be crusted with glitter, but not all the glitter on her gown could dim the light in her lovely eyes. So proudly, but so daintily, she wore her three white feathers at the back of her head.

Her eyes met mine, and I know I looked all the love and longing I felt, for I did love her. She was a very sweet girl.

We looked across the artificial gulf of money and, foolish creature that I am, I felt my eyes fill with tears and my head fill with impossible longing. Some day——

Then she spoke, a little shyly, to *me*!

"Would you like to see my curtsey, Jenny?"

I could only nod, stupidly.

And she curtseyed, with infinite grace and beauty.

That is a picture that I shall carry with me till memory goes.

Whatever is good or bad about it, whatever the difference —and there was only one—between Marguarita and me, she was a very dear, lovely girl, and it may be that I shall meet her again.

This time I shall *not* just stand and gawp at her.

I shall remember how lovely she was—she in the white feathers of Service, I in the white cap of servitude.

Later on we went to see the cars with the debutantes along the Mall, to the Palace, but none of them looked so glorious as my young lady.

SEVENTEEN

Soon, too soon, it was time to go back to be ready for the "twelfth"—"The Glorious Twelfth".

The old routine went on—visitors came, and that meant more work, and the summer days called, but so did my scullery.

One night, it was late in July, I went to bed about 11.15 and, of course, went right off to sleep. I was roughly shaken, only fifteen minutes later, but I thought it was time to get up.

Mrs. Preston was saying, "Jenny—Jenny—wake up—wake up at once."

When I did wake up she stood over me till I dressed, at her command.

"Now come downstairs—no, put your cap and apron on properly."

Fully dressed, cap and apron, and rough apron for work, black stockings and shoes.

I knew what it was, my guilty conscience told me. A copper pan that Alice had used to make milk pudding in, burnt almost through. I had left it to soak under my table, to make it easier to clean in the morning.

It took me an hour and she sat in the kitchen, grim and silent, while my tears helped to wash it.

At half-past twelve I took it to her, clean and shining.

"Put it on the shelf. Good-night, Jenny."

It was a drastic cure, but I never left another pan soaking.

I was in the scullery again at six-thirty in the morning. I was sick, homesick, angry, rebellious, weary, and frightened, confused and worried all in one go.

What could I do?

Leave?

What else was there?

A scullerymaid is a scullerymaid anywhere, and the conditions could have been worse. In many ways Mrs. Preston was kind, and she was certainly clever. Sometimes she would talk kindly to me: she said I was stubborn and lazy, and she wanted to help me to get on.

Stubborn I was, but lazy I never was. Awkward, forgetful, erratic, up in the clouds one day, down in the depths the next

—temperamental—feeling always a square peg in a round hole, and resentful of it. And every natural talent and longing for self-expression crushed. Dancing was the only means of escape—and I danced every minute I could.

Another incident stands out.

It was my Sunday afternoon off and I was going out with the boy with the motor-bike.

Just after lunch Alice brought me two rabbits.

"Skin them before you go, and put them in a bowl of water in the larder."

(I had by this time learned to skin rabbits and I didn't mind the "innards" now at all. So that by the time I came to learn to do a hare, I was quite immune to "innards".)

Well, I skinned the rabbits, put them in a bowl of water, said to myself, "Now I'll just take up my hot water and then I'll put them in the larder."

Of course, scatter-brained Jenny, thinking about Jack and his motor-bike, forgot all about the rabbits.

Until I got back that night.

It was with a sickening horror that I saw the two bodies in the water where I had left them.

Bodies, did I say?

Skeletons!

Two poor little skeletons, every scrap of meat gone.

I thought the cat had had them; in my guilty agony it never occured to me that Sooty would scarcely nibble all the meat off and then kindly return the skeletons to the water! Or else that he would calmly wade into the bowl and have a watery feast!

I scarcely slept a wink.

In great fear I faced the wrath to come next morning.

Calmly, Alice took the bones from the water and put them in a pan; she came to the sink and ran cold water over them and washed them.

With seeming indifference I asked, "Were the rabbits all right?"

"Rabbits? Oh, yes. Mrs. Preston just wanted the flesh: she cut it all off to make rabbit quenelles."

She cut it all off!

My crime had not even been discovered!

I shook a fist at Sooty.

"You wait—next time I'll see that I put them where I'm

65

told, and the thought of you eating them won't worry me—you cat!"

Sooty said "Miaow," and shut his eyes again.

EIGHTEEN

Then came a blow.

Alice was leaving on the first of September.

It wouldn't be easy to get an experienced kitchenmaid during the shooting season, and it would be "the Twelfth" in a few days' time. On the other hand, a girl from one of the outlying farms would like to start in the scullery, so wouldn't it be a good idea to make Jenny kitchenmaid? She's a smart, intelligent girl, and she seems to have a nice sense of making things look nice. Perhaps she's in the wrong environment (oh, how true!), she may be excellent, given a little encouragement and teaching?

"No!" said Mrs. Preston. "I haven't time to teach a kitchenmaid in the shooting season."

But she had to give in.

It was so easy for her Ladyship to say she couldn't get a kitchenmaid, and if she had, she would have had to pay her £36 a year. She could pay me £28 a year. It was £4 a year more than I was getting, but it was still £8 a year less than an experienced girl could get.

I thought Mrs. Preston was being unkind. But she knew what a shoot was, and how much she should be able to depend on her kitchenmaid. I didn't.

I could only see the end of greasy washing-up, of donkey fires, front door steps, and servants' hall.

But the "Glorious Twelfth" came, and I soon knew about shooting. My gun-room! Mud and heather and feathers—mostly mud.

Then the grouse started coming in, then snipe and woodcock, more rabbits, and now hares. And, from the first of September, pheasants, and in October partridges. Now I had the lot.

So, on the first of September, I became kitchenmaid.

NINETEEN

My kitchen range didn't burn, nor the steels glitter as brightly as when Alice did them. But then I found the answer.

The flues.

I had never seen Alice do them, but I had seen the long-handled rakes she used to get to the soot that collected in all the sides and bottoms of the range.

So on a Friday morning I had to be down early: it was really best to be in the kitchen by 4.45. First the fire had to be cleaned out in the usual way, then the round top plates at each side on top of the ovens, where soot collected. That had to be swept down so that it would fall into the space at the bottom.

Then the sides, and finally the bottom. I pushed in the big rakes and got masses of soot out. The crooked "spade" of the rake got into the corners at the back, and when I could hear it make a clanking sound against the sides and back I knew it was cleared to the front, and most of the soot out.

The little door to the flue at the front was about three inches deep and about six inches wide. The flue was the whole length and breadth of the ovens at top and bottom and each side.

This particular range had two ovens at the top and two at the bottom—two each side of the fireplace, with a plate-rack between the top ovens.

I wasn't really satisfied with the soot that the rake pulled out, so I got down on my tummy and pushed my hand and arm in as far as it would go. I felt rather like Alice, putting her hand out of the window of the White Rabbit's house.

But this was lovely. Handfuls and handfuls of lovely soft black soot, my fingers scraping into the corners to get every last particle out.

Oh, yes! This was much better than taking the innards out of a chicken!

I was black to the elbows, my cap was dirty, my face was dirty, and my sack apron was filthy.

But I was happy—I had reached the bottom of the stove, and it was all *clean*.

A hurried wash in the scullery and a clean cap and white

apron, and the fire to light, and the floor to scrub, and the coffee to put on, and the staff breakfast...

Mercifully Mrs. Preston came down early and did the breakfast for me. She also had to show me most of the rest of the day's work.

I know now it was not easy for her, but it had all looked so easy when Alice had done it. I was awkward and gawky and I just didn't know what to do.

The only things I could do really well were setting the table for Mrs. Preston and myself, keeping the fire up so that she always had a hot stove, and keeping the floor clean.

Setting the table was one thing my tidy mind really enjoyed.

The long white scrubbed table lay parallel with the stove and Mrs. Preston worked on the side nearest the fire, I opposite her. We each had a big thick wooden board to work on, and between the two boards there had to be put an oval deep tin, with a section on one side for flour and the other side in two sections for salt and pepper. It had a lid on each side and a handle across the middle. Beside that, a heap of enamel plates and another pile of basins of all sizes.

Then along the centre of the table a dish of margarine and lard, a basin full of sugar, a basin of eggs, and one or two lemons.

On Mrs. Preston's board had to be put her special small knife, a clean tea-towel, and clean net-cloth. Beside each board there must be a collection of knives, her steel, spoons, palette knives, spatulas, wooden spoons, whisks; suspended by a nail in the cupboard door was a pile of small squares of kitchen paper and larger sizes of greaseproof paper.

This had to be set in the morning, then everything cleared away for her Ladyship's visit, then set again.

Then after lunch it all had to be scrubbed down and set again at 6.30.

I learned to read the menu, but as the days and weeks passed it got more and more obvious that I was a complete failure. I just couldn't cook. I was erratic and undependable. I would forget so much.

I can still remember one day—another drastic cure.

I had put in a rice pudding for the staff dinner, and promptly forgot all about it. I was much more interested in all the exciting things Mrs. Preston was making with oranges and lemons and gelatine and eggs and cream.

She asked about the pudding before she went in to her dinner.

When she saw it I was ready to sink into the floor with shame and horror. It was just a bit of black skin and every vestige of rice was burned up.

Timidly I asked what I should do.

"Do? Do? I'll tell you what you can do. You can carry that pudding in and apologise to Mr. Carter for having spoilt his dinner. And perhaps if they all complain to her Ladyship I'll get a decent kitchenmaid. Come along."

She stalked along the passage. I followed behind her, burning up with resentment. I had not yet learned to take blame when it really was my fault.

And, dear lady, she didn't know she was advocating United Action!

The thin wedge of Trade Unionism—that dreadful Thing that was not even mentioned!

Half-way along the passage I let my wounded and guilty feelings go, and muttered, half-hoping she would hear, half-hoping she wouldn't: "You rotten old bitch!"

She turned on me and almost shook her fist.

"Yes, I know I am, but you'll thank me for it some day!"

She was so right—I have already acknowledged that.
I never burned another rice pudding!

TWENTY

Meanwhile Molly, the new scullerymaid, was showing me up with a vengeance. Not only could she cope expertly with all the game that flowed in but she took in her stride the washing-up and the donkey fire; she even found time to come and help Mrs. Preston!

Which made me feel very small and unwanted and jealous, and consequently unsure of myself, and so stupid. Sometimes I just didn't know what to do next, and yet it seemed there was so much to be done.

One day we were sending the lunch out in a hay-box. We had potatoes baked in their jackets and two big basins of steak and kidney pudding—one for the "guns" and one for the beaters. The "guns" pudding was in a china basin, and it was very finely cut into very small squares of meat and kidney, with onion and chopped parsley, it had been cooking since six o'clock in the morning. The lunches went out at eleven-thirty.

The beaters' pudding, about the same size, was in an enamel basin and was not quite so dainty! But they were both good and well cooked and wholesome, the same meat and kidney was in both.

I had to take the grubby pudding cloths off the top and wipe round the basin, and then put a clean napkin over it, tie it round the top, and then knot the four corners together over the top to make a sort of handle. I did all that.

Then I picked up the china basin *by this napkin handle*, which was only loosely tied, and carried it across in the direction of the hay-box.

Of course the inevitable happened. Smash on the floor went basin, pudding, gravy, and all.

I must have broken Mrs. Preston's heart—I should have thought that would have been the last straw. The beaters' pudding had to go to Sir John and his guests (the "guns") and the beaters had to have a cold leg of lamb. *They* didn't feel very kindly disposed to me either.

Although I could read the menu I was never sure what *I* ought to do and what Mrs. Preston would do herself.

For instance, when I saw Baked Ham on the menu I should have know there must be served with it Cumberland Sauce. But not only did I not know that, I didn't know how to make Cumberland Sauce. So Mrs. Preston had to show me—that took more of her time.

However, I was not always dumb and stupid. Some days I was really crisp and efficient, and I truly did start *every* day by saying, "Now, *to-day*, I'm not going to make *any* mistakes *at all*."

But I just had not got the groundwork knowledge to be able to build from it, and, sure as fate, I would do something silly. Then she said I sulked.

It wasn't just sulks. It was a kind of queer blankness that seemed to shut down on me—it seemed to make me quite immobile—I know now it was nothing more or less than my old enemy, Fear.

How I must have aggravated her! She certainly had no

time to teach a kitchenmaid during the shooting season—I doubt if she would have had much time at any season, but shooting was definitely the worst.

She was so tensed one day over all my failings—she had asked me to do something and I had forgotten it—she gave me a violent push and I sat down with a gasp and a howl in the coal bucket.

I didn't speak—I was too full to speak—and at any time I hate to lose my dignity. I got up and walked out of the kitchen and up to my bedroom. I just sat there and suffered; maybe I cried, I expect I did, but I wondered how long I could stand it, and, worse thought, and one which has haunted me in every job I've ever been in—How long will they keep *me*?

Remember, I'd been sacked three times: the first time because I showed some signs of being human, the gentry were not ready for that yet; the next time, in the mill, for no reason that I could find—probably bad temper that morning; and the third time for redundancy, due to world economic conditions.

So my own failings and shortcomings were very real to me; I never had any sense of security—sort of "I shall stay here for ten years"—as many people had whom I met. That fear of being sacked went very deep and is still with me.

When I went back down to the kitchen she was kindness itself—the incident was never mentioned again, and she tried sometimes to talk to me, to tell me that I had the makings of a good cook, that I should try to remember things, and I assured her I did try. Sometimes I threw her kindness back in her face and sneered at her. I was a nasty little beast at times.

Then I'd be sorry and I'd go to her bedroom at night and apologise.

But I was a cross she had to bear—until the next London season.

TWENTY-ONE

Mrs. Preston put on her menu one day "Baba of Rum".

We had about twelve people in the dining-room; it was a very strange thing, but during the whole of my career I always managed to go to the places which were the visited— I never went to any family which did the visiting, thus leaving their servants free.

Only once in the thirteen months I was there did they go away. That few days when I first went there. So we had visitors for the shoots, visitors for Christmas, Easter, Whitsun, London season, hunting—any and every excuse for visiting the house I was working in, even the humble "week-end".

So this dinner party of twelve was quite usual, from August till December. (This was what her Ladyship meant when she had said "…the rough with the smooth!")

I watched Mrs. Preston closely after we had started work again when her Ladyship left the kitchen—I wanted to see this "Baba" being made. I heard Mrs. Preston say to her Ladyship, "Will you ask Sir John for the rum, m'lady?"

And she was assured that the rum would certainly be forthcoming.

Several times during that day Mrs. Preston asked Mr. Carter if he had orders to get her a glass of rum. (She had other cooking wines in the kitchen—sherry and port and marachino—but no spirits.)

It came to dinner-time, table set, and, I omitted to tell you, at the extreme end of the table a white cloth had to be put on for a dishing-up cloth, with spoons, etc.

The queer, soft yellow mixture lay in the bowl and Mrs. Preston was nearly in tears.

The butler came in, looking triumphantly mournful.

"Sir John says he can't spare the rum, but you can have a bottle of ginger-beer if you like!"

I thought she would never stop.

She stormed and raved and cursed and blasphemed, and it all came back to *my* fault *somehow*.

The storm passed, and she calmed a little.

"I know—if he won't give me the rum, I'll get my own back on him. I'll give him sweet omelette, and he hates it, and he won't have any pudding at all! Jenny, throw out that Baba!"

I lifted the basin of yellow stuff to take it away, then I realised it was about seven-thirty and I had to make up the fire, get the plates hot, and get everything ready before eight. So I laid it down again.

At two minutes to eight Sir John appeared at the kitchen door carrying a large glass of rum. He looked so tall and handsome and distinguished in his evening suit, and he smiled, such a sweet smile.

"Here you are, Mrs. Preston. I hope I'm in time. I'm sure it will be the loveliest Baba we've ever had."

And he went away.

The gong rang for dinner.

I looked round for the Baba I was to throw out—the basin was empty.

I didn't know Mrs. Preston had transferred it to its tin and it was now in the oven, baking.

It was fear of the consequences if she had openly defied him by sending in something he particularly disliked. And although she was a superlative cook, still she may have seen the writing on the wall and known that in a very few years she and her kind would be ten-a-penny. Also, she was not young then—she must have been about forty-seven or forty-eight; she was a widow, with a family of four, almost all grown-up, *and none of them in service.*

That took some accomplishing.

And her early life and training had been hard, much harder than mine seemed to be to me. When she was young, not only did they have to go to church, they had to wear bonnets to church and sit in the servants' pew.

Kind, motherly soul, she did try to make something of me, but I seemed to be filled with a perverted sense of independence and obstinacy that wasn't me—it wasn't that I didn't know she was being kind, when she was. I was ashamed of myself, but I was too weak to own up to it, so I was resentful of what I dared to call her "preaching".

I am glad and thankful, though, that I was able to visit her at her home when she retired, and we could laugh over those times, and I could thank her sincerely.

TWENTY-TWO

I rubbed vigorously and joyfully with my emery paper at the steels on the grate. The fire glowed red between the bars and already the ovens were hot for the scones. My first scones had been little round grey lumps of leather, but now they were really getting better.

A huge crock of dough stood on a chair beside the stove, covered with a white cloth.

My first batch of bread made entirely on my own; set to rise after we'd finished work last night about eleven o'clock.

And last night I had done the whole of the game course *alone*!

A brace of pheasants, which I had trussed myself, a dish of sprouts—each sprout dry and separate and green—a dish of potato crisps, all cut by hand and fried, and really crisp, served on a folded napkin. A sauceboat of good gravy, another of bread sauce, and another of brown breadcrumbs.

I was very happy. I was learning, and, to me, the acquisition of knowledge was always a joy.

So this brisk November morning I stretched up and polished the plate-rack between the two ovens—I felt warm at my right side so I moved a little. It was still warm, so I looked down, and nearly got my face burned.

I screamed and dropped my brush and ran. The passage had a door at each end, one leading on to my courtyard, one to the gardens and the side of the house, where was the gun-room and the butler's pantry. The rapid movement fanned the little flame on my dress, and by the time I reached the back door the whole side of my dress was in flames, and my hair was singed. Shrieking, I ran from one end of the passage to the other.

I don't know how or what made me think of it—I picked up a heavy bass mat at the back door and held it to my side. George came running to me and helped to beat out the flames. By this time Mrs. Preston had come down in her nightdress, and Mr. Carter had followed George.

I didn't faint or anything but I was very shaken. Mrs. Preston led me up to the bedroom and helped me find a clean apron and dress and underwear. My clothes were burned right through to my skin, and to this day there is a small white scar about an inch long and a quarter of an inch wide on my waistline at the right side.

I went back to work, shaken or not.

Ever after, whenever I put on a clean dress and apron, I was greeted with the cry:

"Hello, been another fire?"

TWENTY-THREE

Swiftly the days drew in to preparations for Christmas. Again we were to have visitors.

I had to make extra bread for breadcrumbs for the Christmas puddings. There were about fourteen pounds of raisins to be stoned. Cake tins to be greased and lined with paper, basins to be greased, and, horror of horrors, I had to peel onions—little, tiny onions for pickling—by the pound!

At home Christmas passed almost unnoticed, except for hanging up our stockings when we were children. New Year was our time, and it seemed to me that Christmas was being made an excuse for a lot of eating, when I had thought it should be a religious festival, if they wanted to keep it at all.

Then one day in casual conversation I heard Mr. Carter say to Mrs. Preston: "When is the pig being killed?"

"Next week, Mr. Carter."

Mr. Carter turned to me and said, casually, "Of course, that's your job, Jenny."

"Me? You mean—*I've* to—to *kill*—a—a *pig*?"

Mrs. Preston looked at me in astonishment.

"Certainly! It's a kitchenmaid's job. I've never had a kitchenmaid who couldn't kill a pig."

I was white with fear and horror.

"But I couldn't! I couldn't! I can't kill *anything*!"

"Don't be ridiculous and soft, Jenny. It's your job and it's got to be done."

For five days and nights I suffered. I scarcely ate and I lost weight rapidly. I was frequently sick, and I had nightmares in which a gang of pigs chased me with knives and rolling pins, and many other confusing dreams.

I got no comfort from anybody.

Whoever I asked agreed, with surprise at my asking, that it was certainly my job.

The day before the pig-killing I went up to the bedroom in the afternoon. I really couldn't spare the time, because work was just nonstop, from 6 a.m. till 10.30 or 11 at night. But I felt sick and weak, and I lay on my bed and cried.

When I went down again, and when we started dinner, Mrs. Preston said, "Don't you feel well, Jenny? You've been very quiet."

I dared to murmur that I felt sick, about the pig.

She looked puzzled for a minute, which should have warned me.

Then she said, "Oh, the pig! Oh, yes, I've had a talk with the farmer, and I told him you were not very strong, and he said he'd get two of his men to do it, if you'll make them a nice jug of cocoa. But they'll want to bring it in here to cut it up. So have your kitchen table nicely scrubbed."

"You mean—the pig—on my nice scrubbed table?"

"Certainly. You're very lucky—now get on with what you're doing."

Still they kept up the cruel joke until after the pig was killed.

But to me the horror of a bloody pig, dead, on my table was infinitely less than the horror of sticking a knife into an animal.

I slept a little better that night and I enjoyed what little food I did have.

Whether my mind was slightly unhinged, I don't know. I know I can still feel the terror of that week of dreadful anticipation. But nerves were not allowed in those days (except to people like her Ladyship and daughters of ladies), and if you can't afford a nervous breakdown, you just don't have one. You just keep on.

The next morning, after her Ladyship had been in, I didn't make any move to set the table, and suddenly Mrs. Preston said irritably, "What about my table, Jenny? I've got to start work."

I stammered, "But—what about the—the pig———" I swallowed. "I've made the cocoa."

Again that puzzled look crossed her face.

Then she burst out laughing and ran out to call Mr. Carter.

Together they stood in the kitchen and howled with

fiendish glee, as Mrs. Preston pointed helplessly to my specially cleaned table.

"She believed it all the time! Oh, good heavens, what a joke! Ha, ha, ha——"

And the whole horrible five days' suffering was dismissed in those cruel laughs.

I suddenly didn't care whether the table got set or not. I walked out of the kitchen and up to the bedroom and flung myself on the bed.

There are some shocks that go too deep for tears. I was a shy, sensitive, highly strung, nervous girl—only I never had time to give way to shyness or nerves. But I just lay there shivering, completely stunned and blank.

Perhaps I was wrong to feel as I did. I should not have been so easily taken in. But I was so truthful and honest myself—I claim no special credit for that, it was the way I was taught—I was new to the ways of the English country people. I had no means of knowing of any precedent. And the whole rotten hoax had been carried out with such seeming truth.

I suppose I had a minor blackout, I don't know. Perhaps my brain refused to accept any more hurt and shut down on me, I don't know, but suddenly there was a shout from below.

"Jenny! Do you want to come and see the pig killed?"

That was the crowning horror.

To go and watch the animal—and then I heard stamping of feet in one of the outhouses in the courtyard, shouting of men, and, above it, the frightened squeals of a pig.

And then it stopped.

I went down to the kitchen.

Mrs. Preston was working at a half-set table. I made up the fire and finished the table.

The big jug of cocoa was gone—the men were apparently enjoying it after their bloody task.

Time and work are great healers, and it was not long before, superficially at least, I put the thing out of my mind. But I never joked about it, and anybody who did try to joke with me about it met with such a stony look that it soon died as a subject of conversation.

But I carry the scar in my mind yet.

Later on that day I went out to the outhouse to see the pig.

There it was, cut up into hams, and sides, and the head. Seen like that it had no terrors for me.

And soon we were busy making sausages, and lard, and pork pies.

The sides were sent away to be cured into bacon, but the head gamekeeper cured the hams himself, down in the bottom larder.

Down there one day I was watching him, and I talked to him about the ham, and asked him what he was doing.

Then I gingerly put a finger on the ham.

Without a word of warning he slapped my arm and then he slapped my face.

Then he started raving at me—"silly bitch" was the mildest term.

I ran up to Mrs. Preston and later on he came up and told her. He apologised for losing his temper, and Mrs. Preston explained to me that a woman's hand could be dangerous to fresh pork while it was being cured, and Mr. Garret had told her she must keep me away from that ham. He watched it very carefully, but apparently no harm came to it.

For which I was very thankful. I had had quite enough trouble.

TWENTY-FOUR

So it came to Christmas.

When the winter days came in, quite apart from the fact that the normal working day was about seventeen to eighteen hours, seven days a week, there was just no point in having an afternoon or evening off. We were one and a half miles from the village, which had only a church and some cottages. Maybe it had a pub, I don't know. I had never been in one, except just once in "Dirty Dick's", and I wouldn't have gone there anyway. We were eleven miles from Ripon and had no means of getting there.

So that the only time off we did get, when the winter came in, was alternate Sundays. And, in actual fact, there was no point in staying out on a cold Sunday evening when you could be in in the warm.

We in the kitchen, that is Molly and I, were not allowed

in the servants' hall, so it was really just as well that we were busy.

Eventually all the cakes were made and iced, and I learned a bit more; the puddings were made and steamed, and stacked away in the store cupboard.

On Christmas Eve there was to be a tree in the front hall, and her Ladyship would give us all our Christmas presents. She usually gave us a dress length. I thought that would be very nice.

So, after an early dinner on Christmas Eve, we all trooped into the front hall—Mrs. Preston in white, Molly and I in our print dresses and cap and apron, black stockings and shoes. The housemaids in black and white, and lace caps; Miss Bentley in a nice dark dress; the butler in his evening suit; and George in his wasp waistcoat and his tail-coat with brightly polished buttons.

We stood awkwardly huddled together in one corner; Sir John came forward and led Mrs. Preston to the tree, which stood ten feet high, and glittering in the opposite corner.

We all thawed a little at Sir John's patronising joviality as he shepherded his servants to partake of his Lady's bounty.

The youngest son, Master Edward, shyly handed each one of us a parcel with a murmured "Merry Christmas."

Sir John made a little speech, which we all acknowledged with sheepish giggles, in which he thanked us for our service during the past year, and spoke of the nobility of service in a gentleman's house, ". . . they also serve who only stand and wait"—with a sly look at Mr. Carter and George, whose faces were stony—and now to the high spot of the frolics.

Snap-dragon.

Mrs. Preston and Mr. Carter left the hall, and in a moment came back, Mr. Carter carrying a big oval silver dish, a big flat one, almost as big as a tray.

It was piled high with almonds and raisins, and it was placed in the centre of the table in the front hall, on a big square of green felt. The fruit and nuts seemed wet and were glistening under the lights.

Sir John put a match to the dish and all the lights were turned out. The little blue flames leapt among the fruit as the brandy burned. Somewhere among that pile was a sixpence, and we had to put our hands in and grab a handful of the fruit and nuts.

George got the sixpence.

Then the fun was over and we went back to our kitchen to open our presents. I hugged my parcel tightly, dying to open it.

What would it be?

Black velvet? I did so long to be sophisticated in black velvet!

I opened the parcel.

There, in its hideous glory, was a length of that awful pink cotton—a length sufficient to make a morning dress—for work.

Not a piece of material for a dress for the very rare times I was off and could dress up. Not a dress to dance in—just the one thing that mattered to her Ladyship—work; the nobility and the privilege of working for her, dressed in hideous pink, for about threepence an hour.

I never made it up and I never wore it. I don't know what became of it.

Next morning Sir John asked George for the sixpence! George just looked at him in amazement, then fished in his trousers pocket and threw a sixpence on the floor of the dining-room and walked out.

He nearly got the sack, but good footmen who would live in the country were scarce.

TWENTY-FIVE

Christmas Day, 1925.

I was in the kitchen at six o'clock and had the puddings on boiling by seven. The ovens hot and the bacon cooked by seven-thirty. Mrs. Preston came and helped me with the eggs.

The mince-pies were made the day before, with delicious puff pastry—Mrs. Preston had done it all herself, although I had been able to help her make the mincemeat, chopping suet and nuts, putting apples and raisins through the mincer; weeks ago we had done that, and then we had "fed" the big jar occasionally with brandy.

On this day Molly and I were to go into the hall for dinner.

Turkeys were ready. I had helped with the chestnuts and bread sauce; our own home-made sausages, and it was really a fairly easy morning.

Prayers, of course, as usual, but only the family went to church in the car.

Lunch went into the dining-room at twelve-thirty and ours was to be at one-thirty. I wondered why Mrs. Preston was so insistent on clearing everything away as we used it.

"Clear the table, Jenny. Sweep the floor, Jenny. Take those things out to be washed. Get that away to the larder...."

Then the great moment had arrived.

George had set the table, and he carried in the turkey, while I supplied him with roast potatoes, sprouts, bread sauce, and gravy.

The stove was clear, except for the steamer which held our pudding. The fire burned brightly. Molly's scullery was clean and her donkey fire was bright too.

"Now," said Mrs. Preston, "we can really enjoy our dinner."

She was dressed in a nice dark red woollen dress, not in uniform.

We went along, and the room was really a picture. I hadn't seen much of it since my promotion; Molly had kept it nicely, and the floor was polished, a bright fire burned, there was no dust anywhere, and the table looked lovely. White cloth, silver spoons and forks, ivory-handled knives (all dining-room stuff), glasses, holly and mistletoe, and decorations.

And smack in the middle of the table, a bottle of port!

Dishes of sweets and nuts and fruit on the table too; and we were to have time to enjoy it all, for, according to time-honoured custom, the "gentry" were pledged to give us this hour (one hour in the whole year) and not ring a single bell.

So Mr. Carter joyfully carved turkey, and I tucked in and ate everything in sight—all sorrow forgotten. Except that I knew my mother wouldn't be getting a dinner like this.

But Mrs. Preston gave me a little pudding and I bought a chicken, and dressed it myself, and sent them home to mother. So I knew she would have that for New Year anyway.

And every year after that, wherever I was, until she died, I sent my mother a chicken and a pudding for Christmas. *Always* one of the household puddings—we called it our "perks"—and well we deserved it.

It was a wonderful dinner.

And when it was over Sir John and her Ladyship came

along, and drank a glass of port, and said that theirs, too, had been a wonderful dinner and quite the best pudding Mrs. Preston had ever made. (He had said that every Christmas for eight years!)

Now I saw why Mrs. Preston had insisted on clearing up.

When we went back to the kitchen there was only some food to put away, and Molly only had plates to wash.

No scrubbing to-day, and only a little bread and butter to cut for tea, with the Christmas cake. (And it was also quite the best Christmas cake Mrs. Preston had ever made!)

Now there was a whole evening with practically nothing to do. And that was just plain awful.

A cold supper—turkey, ham, pork pie, Russian salad, trifle, and jellies (home made).

Too tired to walk—unthinkable to wash dirty stockings on Christmas day, although God knows they needed it! A letter home, yes, and a lie-down on the bed. Perhaps iron my dress for our little dance to-night in the hall.

Yes, it was a very pleasant, happy day, and I was fairly content—for a little while.

TWENTY-SIX

Spring came and I had been there nearly a year, and there was talk of our going back to London.

This time I was determined to make an effort to get a better job. We were talking one day, Mrs. Preston and I, and she asked me what I thought of doing. I didn't know she was leading up to give me the biggest shock of my career, so far.

I said I wasn't sure.

Then she said, "I think you should go back to the scullery."

I gaped at her.

"Back? To the scullery? What for?"

"You've got the makings of a good, really clever cook. But you've got no grounding, and you need that for your career as a cook."

"But I don't *want* a career in service!" I shouted. "I want a private life—I have a soul——"

She looked at me severely.

82

"You are not allowed a private life, or a soul, in service, and once you're in, you'll never get out."

"Oh, won't I?" I said.

She shook her head.

"No. You won't."

The train to London said the same thing, "You'll never get out—you'll never get out—never—never—never get out—"

"I will—yes, I will!" I whispered fiercely.

"No, you won't—you won't—you won't," said the train gleefully.

Then one day in London, this time we were in Princes Gate, she came and said to me, just after lunch, "Jenny, put your cap on straight, see that you're tidy. I've got someone to see you."

Meekly, all the fight knocked out of me, I followed her to the servants' hall.

A little man with a small black moustache and twinkling eyes shook hands with me, when Mrs. Preston said, "Well, Mr. Brunet, this is Jenny. I've told you about her."

"Yes—she is tall, is she not?"

I felt excited. He was obviously French.

"Yes, and she is still growing. She will be a good girl, I know, but she does need a proper grounding. She was promoted to the kitchen too soon."

He nodded, and then he nodded to me.

"You would like to come to me—be my scullerymaid, yes? We go to Scotland soon."

"Scotland? Oh, could I go home for a wee while?"

He smiled.

"Yes, we could see about that."

Mrs. Preston said, "All right, you can go now, Jenny. I'll make the arrangements."

Thus my future was disposed of. Why didn't I make more fight? Why did I meekly submit? Why doesn't the elephant hop lightly from twig to twig?

I saw one day in an evening paper an advertisement for a cashier for a confectioner's shop. I went, and rather timidly asked about the job. A man gave me a sum in mental arithmetic, which I added up smartly as he gave it. Then he asked where I lived, and I said the number in Princes Gate. He looked rather surprised, and then asked when I would be free. I said I'd have to give a month's notice.

"A month? Why, people usually give a week. Where do you work?"

I said, "I'm in service."

He repeated, in a *very* different tone to the one he'd been using: "Oh—in *service*?"

Then, "Just a minute."

He went into a wee sort of office and talked to someone.

Then he came out.

If he had had a pair of tongs he would have used them.

He said, "No, I'm afraid you wouldn't be quite suitable."

So I walked out.

I was neat and clean and tidy. I was young and healthy looking; I was educated and intelligent, and I had met up to his requirements as regards everything else.

I went away burning with indignation and shame.

As for my dreams of being an actress!

Well, to begin with, I had made one attempt and had been told they wanted "experience", and I had no idea where to start again. I didn't know anything about agents, and it was quite out of the question to attend any audition, even if I could have had the nerve to face such an ordeal, even if I had known about such a thing. And no kind person ever heard me sing and wanted to give me a chance in the theatre.

No, it looked as though I would have to be content with that station in life to which it had pleased God to call me. Although why He should be so almighty pleased about it, I don't know.

Well, if I had to be a cook, I would be the best cook that ever was. And if the way to learn to be a good cook was to go back to the scullery for a "grounding"—"whatever you do, do it with a will"—then back to the scullery I would go.

So I took a deep breath, and went back.

The arrangements had been £28 a year, plus 2s. 6d. a week beer money, and 2s. 6d. a week washing money.

Mrs. Preston put me in a taxi and I arrived on a June afternoon at the basement of a big house not far from St. James's Palace, the London home of the Duke and Duchess of Roxburgh.

The new scullery maid had arrived—again.

TWENTY-SEVEN

A wide wooden corridor, almost as big as a hall, leading to steps, down which were big glass doors leading into the kitchen.

A big kitchen—bigger than the one at Loch Fyne, but red-tiled floor and white scrubbed table were there, with a big range all along one wall, and at one end a gas grill, at the other a huge gas oven, big enough to hold four men!

Along the window a dresser and two white tiled sinks and draining boards; along the other wall, shelves with lots and lots of lovely copper pans; then through an archway, and larders on one side, "chef's bedroom there" on the other, then into my scullery.

Oh! What a joy to work in here! Not one—not two—but *five* sinks! Two great deep wooden ones on one side and two white tiled ones and a deep iron one on the window side.

Only one disappointment—the windows, while big enough, were high up so that I couldn't see out, except when there was a procession from the Palace we could stand on the kitchen dresser.

And the same red-brick floor, and simply dozens of big, sensible white tea-towels—I was allowed seventy-two a week.

In Yorkshire I was grumbled at if I dared to send *four* to the laundry, and I had to keep them clean myself.

I looked round—no donkey fire. The second kitchenmaid asked me what I was looking for, and I said "The 'donkey'— hot water?"

"Oh, we have nothing to do with that, the odd man keeps all the boilers. You'll have plenty of hot water. Now come and have a cup of tea, and then you can change."

First she took me up to my room, whch she shared with me. It was up a little wooden staircase leading off the big parquet-floored corridor, and there were two rooms at the top. One on the left was Gladys's, the head kitchenmaid, and the one on the right was Barbara's and mine.

Gladys and Barbara were sisters. Both were completely capable, efficient, kind and helpful, but quite cold and distant and indifferent at the same time.

Barbara showed me my bed, and said, "You do these two rooms in the morning, Jenny. You're used to that, of course."

I said, "Well I used to—when I was scullerymaid, but I've been kitchenmaid for about nine months—and——"

"Yes, but you're scullerymaid now."

And that was that. I made up my mind I wasn't going to be hurt. One of the very first layers of steel that I had to build around my heart so laboriously during the years.

We went down to tea. Across the end of the big kitchen table, but much lower, because the table stood high enough to have a raised block all round it, was another white scrubbed table, with a white cloth on it, dainty cups and saucers, bread and butter, dainty little biscuits and buns, and jam.

Barbara talked quite nicely. I tried to appear quite at my ease, but I made an awful ass of myself. I was really still smarting about having come "down" again, and trying to cover it up with cheap bravado.

After tea, when I had washed up the cups, Barbara took me upstairs again and said I could unpack.

So I did, and changed into my print dress, cap and apron, and black shoes and stockings, and went down. Barbara was sitting at the table sewing.

I sat and wrote a letter to my mother, and then I asked Barbara what she was making.

"Knickers," she said. "We make all our own underclothes. Do you do any sewing?"

"No, I never had any time at my last place, but I'd like to."

"Well, you'll have plenty of time here, so if you like to buy some stuff, I'll cut it for you and you can sew them."

And she was quite right. I did have time, and I did make knickers, nightdresses, and cotton dresses for work, and even a little summer dress to wear when I went out.

I didn't know then that the next one and a half years were to be the happiest and the most rewarding of all my career. Or that I was to bless for always the decision to go back for a "grounding". For that I did get, most thoroughly.

Just before Barbara got up to set the table for work, she said casually, "Oh, you needn't wear a cap in the afternoon, you know. And you can wear light stockings if you want to. Chef doesn't mind."

86

"Oh, that's lovely. Shall I take it off now, then?"

"Yes, put it upstairs, and then I'll show you how to start."

Gallons of hot water, tins of soft soap, as much as I wanted, dozens of clean towels—what a joy my work was!

I was a little scared of Chef at first—I always treated him with the greatest respect, and he was the same with me. I had to call him "sir", and I was never allowed to dawdle, or stand and watch him in the kitchen. So I used to walk slowly round, looking for dishes to wash, to get every opportunity of seeing how he worked. The first thing I noticed was the calm, the complete absence of chaos. I had never seen a chef, and at first he had seemed funny, with his check trousers, white coat, and big white cap.

That first night Gladys did not appear. It seemed she was having the night off. So, after dinner was over, I was called to set the supper table, and the three of us sat down to supper.

Supper? More like a dinner!

By nine-thirty I was all cleared and washed up, and now I had some leisure on my hands, I didn't know what to do with it.

I was puzzled, because the kitchen was completely isolated —no housemaids came in for kettles, only the footman and hall boy, an odd man, and the under-butler who brought the silver.

There were only two in the dining-room, the Duke and Duchess, and they had a butler, a groom-of-the-chamber, an under-butler, three footmen, an odd man, a steward's-room boy, and a hall boy. Five housemaids, chef, head kitchen-maid, second kitchenmaid, and scullerymaid. Four laundry maids, a housekeeper, and two stillroom maids, and I don't know how many gardeners and gamekeepers.

When I had quite finished I was looking helplessly about the kitchen, and Barbara was sitting sewing.

She said, "Do you want to go out, Jenny?"

"Out? At this time of night? It's a quarter past nine!"

She smiled.

"That's not late. You can go for a walk if you like. Or go to bed early, or sit here, just as you like."

"What time do we have to be in, then?"

"I expect Chef would like you in by eleven, but Gladys, of course, comes in when she likes, and I do, too."

Eleven!

A walk in the cool of a June evening in London, but then it would mean I would have to dress, and I couldn't be bothered. I realised I had had some excitement that day, and I felt a little tired. And oh, the luxury of feeling tired, and being allowed to feel tired, and getting time to feel tired!

"No, I think I'd like a cup of tea, and I'll go to bed early. What do I do in the morning?"

"I'll make some tea. You scrub this floor with me, before breakfast, then you set our breakfast, and then it's just ordinary scullery work, which you know. Now we'll have a cup of tea."

I asked her about the housemaids, and their tea, and hot-water bottles, but Barbara told me there was a stillroom.

"What's that?"

"It's the housekeeper's job. It's a small kitchen place where they do the teas and coffees, toast, scones, bread and butter, make jams and cakes and everything. We only do the actual meals."

"You mean we don't have to do coffee and scones for breakfast, and things like that?"

"No, nothing like that."

"Goodness! There can't be much to do."

She smiled.

"You'll find you'll have plenty to do. Chef likes everything clean."

That didn't worry me at all. I could keep things clean—I liked them that way, too—if I had half a chance.

And the thought of all that lovely hot water!

Next morning Barbara and I started the floor about six-forty-five. First, I had to light the two fires that fed the long stove, then I went to the far side of the kitchen and scrubbed the floor.

Barbara made a cup of tea and, as before, I drank it while I was scrubbing. I'd leave it on the dresser, scrub a bit, two or three stretches, then have a drink, then off again.

By the time I had finished, Barbara had the breakfast cooked, and Gladys came down. I set the breakfast, and Chef came in.

Then we four had breakfast together, and with time to sit down and enjoy it!

The Duchess's breakfast tray went up with the menu book.

There was no nonsense here about clearing away everything so that it looked as though no work was done. This kitchen never looked as though anything was being done, because the work was so skilful and orderly, that Chef scarcely moved from his board, except to the stove.

No surgeon was ever better served by a theatre sister than was a chef, or a cook, with a skilled staff.

Whereas a surgeon had to say "Scalpel", and "Clips", and other things that he wanted, Chef's wants and needs were anticipated, and everything was there for him.

Chef showed me how to read the menu, and he was very thrilled when he found I could speak a little French. At best, it had been schoolgirl French, although my vocabulary was extensive and fluent, but it had got a little rusty—but I knew what "Pommes de Terre" meant, and I knew what "choux-fleur" meant.

I had to read the menu to find out what vegetables to do. I did a great sinkful of potatoes first thing after my big basin of rough vegetables. He was very pleased when I had that ready for him on the first morning.

If the Duchess was to be out to dinner, she would put a line right through the meal suggested. Because the Duke would not dine alone.

Perhaps they were to be out to both meals, then a line was drawn through the whole day. And on those days our work was definitely easy. Chef went away for the day, sometimes, and perhaps Barbara would take the chance to clean out a cupboard, or I would do some extra scrubbing in the larders, which I had to keep clean.

But for the first time I could plan my work to please myself. I had nothing to do outside the kitchen premises, except our two bedrooms. Barbara did Chef's room.

So I could perhaps say, "I'll do this to-day, and that will make it easier for to-morrow," or "I'll leave this for to-day—I can do it in a day or two".

But my scullery began to take on an atmosphere of being cared for and attended to. Chef and the two girls were very good about the copper pans. They would use, as far as possible, any that had got a little discoloured on the outside, so that they would come in for cleaning, and they always looked shiny and golden on the shelves.

But there were big ones, too, stock pots, nearly half my height—the biggest of them reached from the floor up to my waist. It was not easy to empty it. Chef and Barbara used to carry it in together and dump it on the floor. Then, somehow, I, had to pick it up and empty the bones and bits into the pig bin by myself, and then get it washed and cleaned, inside and out.

But I did it, somehow. Perhaps I'm feeling it now.

We had occasional little parties, when Chef and Gladys would bustle about all day, and I had to keep going too. But there was never any heartbreaking clutter of dishes and pans and everything. I only had the kitchen utensils and the vegetable dishes and meat dishes from the servants' hall.

I learned to do the ice-cream. Chef showed me how to set the ice-pail, with crushed ice—it came in a block, and I had to whack it down myself—and freezing salt. Then Chef would get the custard in, and I would get settled on a little stool and turn a handle till it was so stiff I could scarcely move it. Then I'd call Chef.

To his strong hands it still moved easily, so he just said, "More!" and walked away.

At last it would be done to satisfy him and the ceremony of taking out the movable spatula which kept the cream stirring, would begin.

He scraped it clean with a palette knife, laid it on a plate, and showed me how to "bed down" the finished ice-cream.

The accumulated water in the ice-bucket was poured off, the can staying in the bucket; it was built up again with more ice and salt, the cream in the can covered with a buttered paper, and firmly lidded; that then covered with a thick folded white cloth, the whole lot lightly covered with ice, and that covered with a sack.

Then, and only then, was I allowed to carry off my prize, the inside "arms" of the whip, which still had lots of ice-cream attached. And proudly and triumphantly I carried off my "perks", to make a pig of myself in the scullery! And *such* ice-cream!

So I got very fast over the "bedding down" of the ice-bucket.

And, of course, at the end of the evening, there was always some ice-cream left.

I soon tasted Peach Melba (with *real* Melba sauce, not raspberry jam), ice-cream with *hot* chocolate sauce, which I first thought impossible, but soon knew how nice it was.

Yes, I had plenty of work and I had plenty of food. Good food, luxurious food, and I ate everything.

I learned how to work neatly and quickly, how to dovetail one job into another—I mean, while I waited for one thing to be done I would prepare something else.

And I watched Chef closely at every opportunity. Mrs. Preston had warned me, wherever I went, not to say in effect, "Oh, that can't be right, Mrs. Preston didn't do it like that." She said that everyone had their different ways, and my best way was to watch the different methods as I went on and pick the best of them for myself. So I did.

I saw many, many ways of doing things, but I never met any better than Chef's and I never have in all the years.

TWENTY-EIGHT

As the summer days passed I began to feel a kind of pride of achievement. Our little domain was so compact, and so calm and orderly, with no hysteria or screaming panic.

If there was to be no dinner, that is, if both the Duke and Duchess were to be out, it meant only the staff supper, so that we could go out.

Only one stayed in, either Gladys or Barbara. Barbara was engaged to one of the footmen from the Duke of Norfolk's, and he used to come in and visit her. We never had any full time off, but there were quite a lot of nights without dinners—sometimes no lunch either—so we got out quite a lot.

Then, too, we were paid *regularly* and promptly on the first of each month, and my pay was £2 6s. 8d. a month. On top of that there was this 2s. 6d. a week beer money and 2s. 6d. a week washing money.

The beer money was a relic of the olden days when cooking was done over big open fires and the cooks and scullions got very hot and thirsty. The custom had never been withdrawn.

The washing money was a relic, too, of the old days. Now

there was a laundry which did our aprons and Chef's white coats and caps, and for our personal washing we used the household soap.

So that meant a clear pound a month extra on my wages! £3 6s. 8d. a month! I was rich!

I sent thirty shillings home, kept myself in clothes—cheap ones, of course, and probably all wrong, but I was learning to make things.

Mother had always kept me clean and kept my clothes clean. But I'd never had to do very much for myself, and my thirteen months with Mrs. Preston had been such chaos that, when I looked back, I knew what they meant when they said had there been a fire every time I put on a clean apron or dress.

I blushed inside me for shame.

Barbara taught me a routine of washing and ironing and mending. She cut out things for me in a fine white cambric, and I made them cheerfully by hand. But I never saved a penny, except when I had something specific to save for.

It would be very nice and very conventional if I could say I'd saved two and six a week all my life, and I've got a nice little pile in the Post Office now. Well, I never did.

I made several attempts later, but somehow there always seemed to come a rainy day and it got used. My money went in fripperies. In silly things that I saw in Selfridge's Bargain Basement. It went on the pictures and, very occasionally, a theatre.

I went visiting my cousins at various times, and visited other servants' halls, too, all over London.

Of course, London, to me, was the area within Kensington Gardens, Knightsbridge, Hyde Park Corner, Victoria, Belgravia, The Palace, Westminster, Piccadilly, Oxford Circus, and Marble Arch. If there were suburbs outside of these, I was much too snobbish to know them.

But I was really well-off and happy, and, in a way, a little more content. Not completely, because I still wanted something better, but I was *learning*—always learning something new, and that, to me, was the supreme joy.

The first morning after breakfast Gladys came to me and gave me five shillings.

"What's this for?" I asked.

"Your taxi fare."

"But it was only two and three, and I gave the man sixpence."

She just smiled.

"You keep that, you can probably use it."

I could! But I thought it was very funny.

TWENTY-NINE

Towards the beginning of August we were to go back to Scotland and I was to get home for just a few days, so that I would be in time for the Glorious Twelfth again.

Goodness! Here was a whole year gone—I was nearly twenty and still a scullerymaid. Once again a summer had passed in London without my making any real effort to get something "better".

But that one attempt to get into a shop had hurt me so much. And now I was *interested*. There seemed to be more to this cooking business than constant panic and chaos, and fighting for a glass of rum.

Floors Castle stood on a slight hill overlooking the border town of Kelso on the River Tweed. Such a lovely castle, such miles and miles of grounds, such glorious country.

Another big kitchen and a big, fresh scullery, with a large table, and three sinks.

The kitchen stove was a great big affair, right in the middle of the floor! We could walk right round it, and it had a polished steel bar round it, waist high, so that one didn't get blacked or too hot by leaning over to get a saucepan or anything.

Our bedrooms were up a short flight of stairs, just off the kitchen and along a passage. Big, airy bedrooms and our bathroom.

Chef's rooms were on the other side of the castle—it was shaped like the three sides of a square; the middle block was the castle proper, where the Duke and Duchess lived; one side was the kitchens and staff quarters, with the laundry at the back; the other side was the stables and the groom's quarters.

Chef had his rooms there—a little flat, I believe. He was married, and his two daughters lived there with their mother. One of them had just started work in a bank.

Not in a kitchen.

Grouse, rabbits, hares, chickens, ducks, geese; then pheasants and woodcock and snipe and partridges. I did them all.

Only, to my very pleasant surprise, I was told to keep my
rabbit skins and hare skins. As I often had about two dozen
rabbits in a week, with occasionally a hare, I soon found the
reason for this.

An old travelling packman came round every week, and
for each rabbit skin he gave me fourpence and for each hare
skin a shilling. But they had to be very nicely skinned and not
broken.

So I was *really* well-off!

As always, we had visitors, and shooting lunches out—
and we had once, as a visitor, the then Prince of Wales, for
the local Agricultural show.

When he went, he left a sum for tips for everybody. I got
ten shillings—the first and last tip I ever had in service. With
the ten shillings I put two and sixpence and got a camera—
a square box-camera, which is still functioning!

Christmas was coming, and preparations were lavish and
plentiful.

We were within walking distance of the town and I went
constantly to the shops, to the pictures, and dances.

And then came the Wireless!

This new machine was installed in a big room, down near
the stillroom. This room was big enough for dancing, and I
don't know what its purpose was. Maybe a recreation room
for the men-servants. I think perhaps there had once been a
billiard table in it.

Anyway, when I heard the music of a dance band my feet
led me straight to it. Actually, I was not allowed in here but,
grudgingly, the footmen—most superior, supercilious fel-
lows!—let me come, because they knew by this time I was
the best dancer.

But the first footman, snootier than the others, decided I
must not come, and he told me so in insulting tones, that I
was only a scullerymaid—this room was for themselves and
the housemaids, not for low creatures like me—"Get back to
your pots and pans in the scullery——"

Mostly I was meek and mild and timid, but I turned at
that.

I stood at the door and looked at him, then I said, quite
loud enough for them all to hear:

"Well, anyway, a lick out of the scullerymaid's pots is

94

better than a lick out of the housemaids' pots any day!" And I ran away, scared to death at my temerity, but secretly pleased.

He knew very well I meant those "things" to which I had such a rooted objection. He and his kind used them in their bedrooms, with a lavatory next door, and the housemaids had to "do" their rooms.

I thought it was quite a triumph. But he always hated me after that.

They complained sometimes that their cabbage wasn't green. So one day Gladys said, "Bring me your cabbage when you're ready to cook it, Jenny."

I had a gas stove in the scullery to cook my potatoes and greens, so when the water was ready I told Gladys, and gave her the cabbage in a big bowl.

"Where's your soda?" she asked.

"Here." I showed her the tiny piece, about the size of a very small cigarette-end.

"I'll give them something to grumble about," she said. "Give me the jar of soda."

She chose two lumps, both about the size of a walnut, and dropped them in the water with the salt and the cabbage.

It was green, all right!

But there was a terrific rush on the toilet paper the next day, and many groans of pain! Nobody complained again about their cabbage not being green!

THIRTY

We were to have a staff dance at which the Duke and Duchess would be present. Of course, all the refreshments would be prepared by—the kitchen staff.

So for two days we were hard at it, all four of us, and Chef was in the kitchen at 5 a.m. and lit the fires himself! But now I *knew* what I was doing. I could see things forming as I went about, and I was even allowed to make the jellies! Out of packets, it's true—it was not yet time for me to learn how to make jelly from fresh oranges and lemons, and gelatine and sugar and whites of eggs.

But I was allowed to help, even allowed to make up the

fire, and Chef saw that I knew how to do that, even if he had cakes in the ovens. I got my bucket of coal ready, opened the top very carefully, then, with my poker, I pushed the hot fire to the oven side, so that the temperature wouldn't be reduced, and then very carefully put in the coal.

He turned out dozens of sausage rolls, mince pies, chicken patties, jellies, trifles, eclairs, and iced cakes.

As well as preparing for Christmas. When he was making the puddings he sent me down to the larder (there were three or four larders—one was the game larder, hung with dozens and dozens of birds) for six dozen eggs.

Six dozen! And they all went in the puddings.

Our staff dance was lovely.

The Duke and Duchess did come down, and the Duchess danced with Chef, and the Duke with the head housemaid. They sat a while and chatted, but the most I can remember about it was the Duchess's lovely plain silver shoes, like bright steel, with high heels.

I was determined to have a pair like that one day.

I did—one day.

She smoked a lot, in a long cigarette-holder, and her evening dress was, of course, in the current ugly fashion, short and shapeless, but beautifully glittering, and I liked anything glittery. Evening wear always made a bigger impression on me than any other dresses.

I sang, in my usual little nervous way, "Danny Boy", and there were quite a few of them had tears in their eyes.

We all got some lovely presents at Christmas, and among them I got a lovely pair of blue moccasin slippers from Gladys and Barbara.

Always, in the kitchen, we had the best of food and, of course, there was also always plenty left in the pans to "taste", but the staff meals were never very exciting or, indeed, too plentiful. The pantry staff, that is, the butler and his footmen, always had plenty, because they usually finished off anything that was left over in a dish.

There had to be always enough on the silver dishes to leave something over, and it was very seldom anything came back, except perhaps what was left of a whole salmon, or game, or joint, like a saddle of lamb, but cutlets and vegetables and sweets very rarely came back.

But the housemaids were the worst off. They were dependent entirely on what we sent from the kitchen, and Gladys and Barbara, while their skill was unquestionable as regards doing dining-room meals, were not too keen on putting themselves out for the housemaids. In fact, a permanent state of war existed between the two sides of the house.

The housemaids were jealous of the good things *we* always had to eat, but at the same time they considered themselves very much above us in the social scale, and they certainly wouldn't have lowered themselves to do any of my kind of work.

And cooking was a very "low" occupation indeed!

But as I remember, I used to do fried potatoes every night for supper, with a variation sometimes of bubble and squeak, and occasionally, on a Sunday night, baked potatoes in their jackets.

Their meals were ordinary and unimaginative, while what went into the steward's room was a feast. I don't think this was anybody's fault. It was the custom and, really, after what I learned about housemaids on board wages in Yorkshire, I must confess I lost a great deal of sympathy for the tribe.

But although I was, as I said, comparatively happy, I still felt the driving in me for something better. Kind as Chef was, he was a strict disciplinarian. I started to sing softly at my scullery window one day. He called in a voice of icy steel:

"Jean!"

"Yes, sir?"

"Quiet!"

And that was all.

I never dared to sing again.

And yet, one Sunday morning I was doing two pheasants. He used to come in with the game or rabbits in his hands, throw them on the floor, and say, casually, "To-morrow", or "Dinner", or "Now". And I would leave them or start them straight away, according to the above instructions, and how my work was progressing.

This Sunday morning, early in the year, he had brought the two pheasants in and thrown them on the floor and said, "To-night".

I put them on my table, and went to get some old newspapers to take the feathers, taking a few feathers off the breast first. I'd noticed they looked rather bloated about the necks, and they had certainly hung quite a few days. When I got back, *those pheasants had moved!*

Gingerly, I pulled at the feathers on the neck, and the skin came away in my hands....

Certainly I had seen maggots before, had even enjoyed throwing them on the hot stove and watching them wriggle before they were swept into the flames.

But this teeming, crawly heap of obscene life was something I'd never seen before, or since. The entire neck, from head to crop, was moving—even in the bird's mouth. The whole area of the back and tail end and legs was a filthy mass of these heaving dirty monstrosities, some about an inch long.

I screamed and ran in to Chef.

Gladys and Barbara were not there—I think they had gone to church.

I gasped: "Chef!—those pheasants! They're horrible—they're walking—they *moved*! I can't touch them—they're absolutely *walking*!"

He raised his eyebrows and his eyes twinkled.

He picked up his sharp knife and rubbed it on the steel which he wore at his side from his belt, as he walked in front of me to the scullery where the horrible things lay.

"Well," he said conversationally, "it is a nice Sunday morning, perhaps they like a little walk, yes?"

With about two slashes on each bird, he cut away the breasts, cleanly and decisively.

"There," he said, as he threw the bodies on to my paper, "put them out—I've got all I want," and away he went, with the four little pheasant breasts in his hand.

Hastily I smothered the horrors in lots of newspaper and put them out to be collected by the old man who tended the garden boilers, and incinerator, and laundry fires, and things like that.

Yes, I was learning fast!

I used to watch Barbara as she peeled potatoes for the dining-room, how she cut them round and round, till they were all exactly the same size and shape. And how tenderly she watched over them as they boiled. Clearly there was a lot more in cooking than just sticking things in a pan and letting them boil. So, with my usual tenacity and determination, I watched everything that was done, as far as I could, and thought, "There won't be much wrong with my cooking if I do it like this."

THIRTY-ONE

Soon we were back in London again, and soon there came the biggest day of that London season.

We were to give a dinner party, which, although it would not be a very big affair in numbers, was to be the very highest in quality. The Duke and Duchess were entertaining Their Majesties King George V and Queen Mary.

I know now all the things that were done beforehand, but all I knew then was that for about three days I simply couldn't keep a copper saucepan on the shelf for five minutes —as fast as I put them up, they were used.

Late one night, about eleven-thirty (and we'd been at it solidly for three days—all of us—only stopping to eat, and a quick wash and go to bed at night), Chef brought in his biggest copper stockpot, the big chap that I've already told you about. He emptied it into the bucket for me, and I didn't look at it, I was so tired. I bent over my sinks and didn't say anything.

He put the pan on the floor beside my sink, then he said, in his funny clipped French way, "You *can* leave that till the morning."

I looked up, and the memory of the night I was dragged out of bed to clean a pan came back.

"No, thank you, sir—I'll wash it now."

And I did. Washed it and cleaned it, and put it back at the end of the stove. Then I went to bed, at twelve-thirty, and was in the kitchen again at six-thirty.

But I was *clean*, and everything round me was clean—my scullery looked, as Mrs. Preston once said it should look, "so clean that the Lord Jesus Christ Himself could come and inspect it".

So the Great Day had come at last. It was not to be thought of that *I* might catch even a glimpse of Their Majesties, and it just so happened that I could have done. Everything was timed to a minute—the Royal car arrived and the King and Queen were welcomed—but a certain lady who lived two houses away, on the same side, just a few steps, kept them waiting twenty minutes before she deigned to walk next door. She was the wife of a *very* famous brewer.

So while Chef was stamping anxiously about, afraid of his lovely dinner being spoiled, Their Gracious Majesties waited on the pleasure of the woman next door.

So that I *could* have been up to see them but we didn't know that.

But I did see the dinner table set—with gold plate, and crystal, and silver, and priceless flowers—I only got a glimpse.

During that day Chef had had another chef in to help him, and as I cleared away the copper pans I went into the kitchen as often as I could to get more dirty dishes and pans. I couldn't find any.

I pottered about, and thought that a Royal dinner party seemed to make much less work than an ordinary dinner.

It was too early to set the ice-pails—I had two to do to-night. My scullery was all clean, all my towels spread out ready for the onslaught, but no onslaught came.

I had had the job of doing the peas for the dinner. *Two sacks* of peas, but as I did them I had to separate them and pick out the smallest, full little peas, all the same size, but very small. Not the little sort of not-yet-formed peas, just the very tiniest, but *all uniform* and all fully formed.

Chef got a little woman in to help me in this job, but she didn't take enough care with the sizes and Chef put her on to the washing-up. But she didn't do that to please me, so Chef sent her away after lunch. Chef announced himself satisfied with the peas and then asked me *if I'd like to cook them*!

What a triumph!

Well, I did, and, bless him, he only looked at them once—he trusted me—and I felt there never could be a man like him.

The potatoes, too, Barbara had to pick out the very tiniest, although *she* cooked *them*.

Then suddenly the mystery of the missing saucepans was solved.

They were all stuffed under the kitchen table!

There was a shout: "Jean!"

"Yes, sir."

"Here."

I ran in.

He pointed—"There."

And the twinkle was in his eye again!

I soon cleaned them and then started on my ice-cream.

When I went into the kitchen again I thought I was seeing

things. There were *three* chefs there and two other women who, I was told, were cooks.

And I had to keep things clean for the lot of them.

My own Chef, the chef who had been in during the day, who went away shortly after tea-time, and another chef—rather older, light-haired with a fair moustache and fair skin, heavily built—with a name that is famous.

I am proud that for a short time I had the benefit of his teaching, and saw its results.

He looked at my ice-cream when I thought it was ready—I had had to give a wee while to both pails—and he, too, turned the handle easily in his strong hands. So "More!" he said.

But soon it *was* ready, and I performed the exciting ceremony that would give me my "perks".

I thought the day could hold no more excitement. I went into the kitchen and was motioned to keep away from the dresser.

There was Chef, standing on the dresser with white paper spread out all over the floor in front of him. In one hand he held a rolling pin and in the other one of those things that make holes in biscuits.

Gladys stood close to his feet and held up to him a copper pan; he dipped the biscuit-marker in the pan and waved some light feathery stuff over and over the rolling pin—some of it fell on the floor but most of it stayed, making silvery tinsel threads across the rolling pin.

On the other side stood Monsieur Saulnier, the big chef, and occasionally he would take some of it off the pin and lay it on the table.

The whole thing only took a few minutes while I stood and gaped. That was the first time I had seen spun sugar.

But that wasn't all. Tremendous activity in the kitchen, a quick undoing of my ice-cream pails, and a quick whisking noise from the kitchen. Voices, imperative, sure and confident—I went back, timidly.

More surprises.

One of the ice-creams I knew had tasted different, but I didn't know what it was, until Chef had put some tiny little cubes of fresh pineapple in it before I packed it down.

And now! The pineapple ice-cream was inside a pineapple, and, what was this, surely not meringue? But people couldn't eat raw meringue?

101

Quickly—sugar—fold it in. Gladys goes to the oven—goodness!—no!

Quick! MY PINEAPPLE ICE HAS JUST GONE IN THE OVEN!

It's not possible—my mouth and eyes wide open—as Gladys stood with her hand on the door and then timed it to a second. Charles, the under-butler, came in his solemn dignified way and placed his tray at the end of the table.

Gladys opened the oven and took out the golden-brown-topped pineapple.

Monsieur Saulnier brought a silver dish of plain ice-cream.

Chef took another pan, ran something out of it in a straight line on to his marble slab, dropped the pan, and picked up the yellow line and tied it in a bow of golden satin ribbon—only it wasn't ribbon—it was sugar, and he laid it on top of the plain ice.

These three actions were completely simultaneous and took not more than two minutes, and Charles went out of the kitchen with his ice-creams in a lordly dish.

I went back to my scullery and I'm *not* a bit ashamed to say that I cried for the sheer beauty of it. I wanted to *make* such beauty, I wanted to be in it and share it and belong to it —not for the eating of it, just for the doing of it—and standing back and surveying the wonder of having created it.

When it was all over, we had supper—oh, everything, and masses of it.

Then, about twelve o'clock, Barbara and I got down and scrubbed the floor.

It's funny, you didn't get tired until it was all over—excitement kept you up—so that it wasn't until we got between the sheets that I even knew I'd been working practically non-stop for three days.

It was certainly nice to turn over for a half-hour in the morning and know that our floor was scrubbed.

THIRTY-TWO

I should have stayed with Chef for another two years. It wouldn't have done me any harm if I'd stayed with Chef for another *ten* years, I would certainly have saved myself a lot of pain and sorrow.

But in a fit of childish temper one day, because of a silly quarrel with Barbara over the scrubbing of the kitchen floor, I gave my notice.

And I wasn't going back to the scullery either. I went to a well-known agency and they gave me about ten jobs to go and see. I wanted a kitchenmaid-with-scullerymaid job, and very soon I found one that I liked.

The cook was young and pleasant, and she was quite satisfied with the training I'd had. We would be going to Staffordshire, to Hoar Cross Hall, home of the Meynell family, and we had a shooting lodge in Lincolnshire, and, of course, London in the season. I would get every Thursday afternoon and evening off, and, of course, Sundays alternately.

In the usual way I came by taxi and, by this time, I was growing nearly quite callous about taxis. I suppose it cost me about two and sixpence from the bottom of Regent Street to Grosvenor Crescent in those days, but I quite cheerfully made out my list of "expenses", and put "taxi five shillings". It seemed to be the recognised thing to do.

I was taken up to my bedroom—still I had to share—and I was longing for the day when I would have my own bedroom and a bedside lamp.

Up the usual five flights of stairs to the top, but this house had a back staircase right to the nursery floor, so that there was no danger of being "caught".

I don't know what people used to pay to rent these houses for the London season—so correct, so necessary, so expensive, and so silly. But I'll bet it was a pretty penny. They were all, any one I was ever in, in a bad state of repair, and the owners did nothing to them, because they knew that the flock of sheep which was Society would take them for the few weeks in the year which were so important, for any money.

And the front looked good; the drawing-room and dining-rooms were always lovely, so that that was all that mattered. It was all the visitors ever saw. What the kitchen premises were like—whether they were fit for human habitation or not, whether they could reasonably be expected to cope with the work which would be demanded of them—none of it mattered.

I had the experience, some years ago (in 1946), of working for the Ministry of Education in a house close to Eaton Square near the one in which I had worked twenty years before, and identical in every way. I cannot describe the feeling, a kind of ghostly shiver as I walked in the front door and up to my office, which had once been the drawing-room. There was still the remains of the white fireplace, one or two white doors, tall and wide, and ornate ceilings.

It was a physical pain in my heart—*not*, I must hasten to add, a nostalgic pain—to go down to the basement where we kept rows and rows of files.

Here was the servants' hall, here was the butler's pantry, this dark little room was either the butler's room or the cook's.

And this, this dark dungeon, with the long dresser and this great ugly stove, and the now rickety wooden table, worm-eaten, had been the kitchen where I, and others like me, had quite literally sweated away an existence that was accepted as "that station in life——".

If any of the girls came down with me to look for a file, I tried to say, "Look, people used to work down here—this was the kitchen; look, this was the scullery," they used to look at me as though I had two heads and one eye, then say with a shiver, "God! What a dump! There's ghosts here, or something." They just didn't believe me.

Yes, there were ghosts, and I was one of them.

Enough of the glimpse into the future—we, in those days, had no reason to suppose it wouldn't always be like this.

Our scullerymaid was a good girl, and I was now in the position of being able to teach her—this was very encouraging to me.

And she tried to help me, too, one day. I had a trifle ready for dinner and I was just finishing it off with piped cream. It was a dream—it was for a special dinner—and I had everything ready. Mrs. Morton was upstairs and wouldn't be down till about six.

I used up all the cream and stood back proudly surveying

my handiwork. Young Molly came and breathed delight. It was lovely, she said.

I put small pieces of cherry over it, and then said, putting my head on one side, "Yes, it wants a bit of green on it."

I went away and did one or two odd jobs while I looked for the angelica. When I came back, Molly was standing guard over the trifle, her face shining with pride and achievement. Scattered over my trifle was a big handful of chopped parsley!

"Oh, God!" I screamed. "What the devil——"

Molly's face puckered up in astonished dismay—she had no idea she had done wrong.

I wished I could find words to tell her all I was thinking. I did manage a bit, but she soon realised that she had done a terrible thing, and she was frightened, as I used to be frightened.

Somehow, I got all the top piping of cream off, and then went raking about looking for cream—there just wasn't any —so I took the cream and the parsley, and in a few minutes had put it through a hair sieve, so that the parsley was caught on the sieve, and the cream came through.

I couldn't beat it any more, it would have turned to butter, so I had to spread it on my trifle, and fork it here and there— put my cherries and angelica on it. It wasn't nice, and Mrs. Morton said:

"I thought you could have made a better job of it than that, Jenny. I don't know that I can trust you to do another one."

I blushed and stuttered and made some lame excuse. But I didn't tell on Molly.

We went to London the following summer, and I was to get a holiday!

When we finished in London I was going home for a fortnight, and I'd get a pound a week board wages as well as my month's wages.

The fare from London to Glasgow was just over three pounds, and I had soon saved that up. Somehow, when it came to a time when I needed money it was there!

Sometimes!

I made another attempt while I was home to get on the stage.

A company came to our local theatre. A musical company. The manager of the theatre used to go to a lot of the dances that I went to when I used to be at home, and he said he would introduce me to the manager of the company.

My friend—I couldn't really call him a friend, just an acquaintance and a good bit older than I—told me to come one afternoon about three o'clock. The theatre was deserted except for the manager of the company.

I had brought some songs to sing. I was nearly twenty-one —it was the summer of 1927. I was very nice, and my voice was still very sweet, at twenty-one.

The manager of the company didn't want to hear me sing. He took me down to the dressing-rooms—he wanted to see how I looked stripped.

Again that fear of people got me. I was afraid to obey him, and I was afraid not to. In my mind there was a confused gabble—if this is how you get on to the stage, then I suppose I'd better do it.

I tried—I took my frock off.

But I'm no Marilyn Monroe, and, in any case, I couldn't go on. I knew my mother, and my father, would have died at the thought of such a thing, and so I mumbled something, tearfully, and then fought my way out. Of course, once he started fighting it was easy. I could deal with that.

What I couldn't deal with was the soft persuasiveness he started with, the "Oh-it's-all-right-I-have-to-see-how-you'd-look-in-costume" gag.

And, as I've told you, I was still very silly.

Well, I'd tried before—the Birmingham Rep.—they had wanted "experience". I began to see what they meant.

That put me right off, and it was many, many years before I would try again.

But, apart from that, which shocked me more than I can say, my holiday was wonderful. It was so lovely to be able to go out when I liked and come in when I liked, and to take Mother out on her day off.

It was quite pleasant to go back, too.

THIRTY-THREE

You must forgive me if I stress the point about my capabilities, because it is so important in view of what came later.

I think the best word I can use to describe myself at this time was "crisp". Intelligence, I think I may say, I've always had; the "grounding" I had assuredly got; a keen interest in learning had grown, and a new sense of responsibility was gradually, very gradually, replacing my erratic, harum-scarum, volatile nature.

I was by no means the perfect product yet. I wanted to be cool and efficient like Gladys, or Barbara, but I was a good help to Mrs. Morton, and she taught me a great many things.

I could not only *read* a menu now, I could *write* one, and I could prepare and finish off a good many of the dishes by myself. (And I don't mean eat them!) I still had a long way to go, but I felt I was at last finding my niche.

One day Lady Dorothy Meynell sent for me to her boudoir.

Timidly I knocked at the door, and a very charming voice said, "Come in."

I tiptoed in and faced, for the second time in my life, a real live Lady. She had married a Mr. Meynell.

She was very tall and dignified and kind. Her voice was level and warm.

She said, "Good morning, Jenny."

I said quietly, "Good morning, m'lady."

"Jenny, I have just asked Mrs. Morton how you've been getting on. She tells me you are a little erratic at times, but you are learning very quickly and doing quite a lot of the dining-room cooking."

"Thank you, m'lady. I try to please Mrs. Morton."

She nodded.

"Mr. Meynell wants to take a small shoot, about eight guns, to our shooting-box in Lincolnshire, near Gainsborough, and we hoped you would be able to do it for them —it would be about three weeks. You would have a woman in from the village, and you will have only the eight men, the butler and housekeeper, a married couple, and yourself. Would you like to do that?"

I was *thrilled*.

"Oh—oh yes, m'lady! I would love it."

She smiled. I was so terribly enthusiastic!

"Very well, Jenny, we will make all the arrangements."

And she indicated that the interview was over.

I murmured, "Thank you, m'lady," and went out quietly.

Once outside I danced down the back stairs, tore along the corridor, and exploded into the kitchen!

THIRTY-FOUR

We went in the Rolls-Royce, eighty miles across the country to Lincolnshire, in the crisp October air.

I sat in front with the chauffeur, and there were three gentlemen inside the car.

We arrived eventually, and I found that the "shooting-box" was a fair-sized house, standing right beside the village green.

The butler and his wife, the housemaid-housekeeper, welcomed me and showed me to my room, a little slip of a room but very nice and cosy, and it was just on the first floor, where all the other bedrooms were.

A little old lady came in from the village to wash up and do vegetables and scrubbing for me, and I put all I had learned to very good use.

The main purpose of the shoot was wild duck shooting. There was other game too, but ducks were the principal sport. I grew accustomed to the different kinds, teal and mallard, and I knew I must serve orange salad with them.

Ducks, of course, are early risers. Shooting had to start about 4.30 to 5 a.m. That meant breakfast at 4 a.m. That meant I must be in the kitchen just after 3 a.m.

But it was fun, and I enjoyed every minute of it.

The eight gentlemen seemed quite pleased with my efforts, and I got a pound from Mr. Meynell when he was told it was my twenty-first birthday on the 30th October 1927.

Of course, I had to do the staff cooking as well, but we had our meals, the four of us, in the tiny sitting-room, the butler at the head of the table and I at the foot. For I had, for course, the status of cook-housekeeper here.

One night I thought I'd give them hot cheese souffle as a savoury.

I had not made one before but I had watched them being made and I knew how.

I prepared it very carefully, but I was really stumped when it came to cooking it. I had never really taken much notice of the timing—all I knew was that "they" were supposed to wait for a souffle!

So I consulted a little cookery book, the first and almost the last I ever did consult, except for ideas. The book said, "Cook in a hot oven for 2 minutes". Whether it was a misprint or whether the author just didn't know any better (and I am inclined to the latter), I don't know, but I gave my souffle two minutes, as per instructions.

Well, of course, it hadn't even begun to cook when I sent it in!

But that was the only failure I had.

It was late April when we went back to Staffordshire to meet the new cook—a temporary cook who would do the London season, and come back with us to start the shooting season in August.

THIRTY-FIVE

The new cook, Mrs. Callan, was in the kitchen when we arrived back. I went in and said, "Good afternoon. I'm Jenny."

"Oh, you are, are you? You're the one who's such a big one now—you've done a couple of little shoots? Well, we'll soon get you off your high horse, my girl."

I thought she was joking, and that kind of aggressive fun is not unknown to Scottish people.

But she wasn't. I laughed, and her face turned an ugly red, and her mouth tightened.

"Get upstairs and get changed. You'll have no time to laugh when you start work."

So I went upstairs, and all my new-found confidence was gone. I didn't know what was waiting for me, and no warning bell rang in my mind when I went downstairs again in my clean little mauve and white-striped cotton dress, my apron, and light stockings.

I went into the kitchen and went straight to the fire, but she was there, just behind the screen.

Not a minute was lost. She turned on me and snarled.

"What do you mean by coming into the kitchen half-dressed? Who gave you permission to take off your cap? And where's your black stockings?"

I tried to stammer.

"But we never wear our caps in the afternoon and light stockings are much easier on my feet..."

"Get upstairs and get dressed properly. You're not coming in *my* kitchen half-dressed. Shameless hussy!"

"Her" kitchen!

Shameless hussy!

I went out, slowly and listlessly, and dragged myself back upstairs to the room I shared with the scullerymaid and the fourth housemaid.

We had a new scullerymaid I noticed. A young sixteen-year-old, bright, rosy-cheeked girl, bubbling over with vitality and fun. When I looked at her I felt a hundred years older.

The fourth housemaid was washing herself, stripped to the waist, her open Bible beside her on the washstand. She was a religious fanatic and never moved without her Bible. She annoyed me. I was in no mood for religion just then.

I got into my morning dress and apron and cap and black stockings, and went slowly downstairs.

I set the table and got a tray ready for Mrs. Callan's tea, and told Margaret to take it in to her.

I had my own tea, and prepared for the evening. There was no menu, and I didn't know what was for dinner. All I could do was set the table and keep the fire up.

Eventually she came in to start work, about six-thirty, and soon what was to be the familiar nagging and persecution began. If I had done a thing, I shouldn't have done it. If I hadn't done it, I should have.

If I wanted to use up something that I knew wouldn't go back to the dining-room, I was told she wasn't there to cook for the staff. If I didn't use something, I was told I was wasteful and extravagant and couldn't think. She found a perfect ally in the butler, who joined in the fiendish game of baiting me.

She was a tall, fair-skinned, and fair-haired woman, who had probably once been beautiful. She still had lovely clear skin and good teeth. Her only cure for anything the matter with you, from a headache to a broken neck, was "a dose of salts". No matter what anybody had, her only answer was a growl, "You want a dose of salts".

But her cooking!

Only to Chef would I give her second. It was superlative. My potato straws had to be twice as thin, my Brunoise so small you couldn't see it; anything to be sieved had to be sieved twice.

The stuff she used during her four months' temporary stay would have kept my family for ten years.

Only the best of everything was good enough for her, and her own palate was exceptionally fine.

THIRTY-SIX

Young Margaret, our rosy-cheeked scullerymaid, used to run with her big cabbage pot and potato pot into the kitchen. Used to run with her dishes, run here and there, with the sheer joy of living. My pans had to be pushed aside to let Margaret get her pans on.

I knew my stove—I knew its vagaries and its oddities.

If I heard the oven door being shut when I was down the bottom larder, which was level with the back door and twice the length of the kitchen away, I could tell from the sound of it whether my fire needed making up. I knew the fire, and it knew me.

But Mrs. Callan wouldn't let me make up the fire. It didn't suit her at that minute—perhaps she had a cake in—and it was useless to tell her I knew how to make a fire up with a cake in the oven. I tried once, when she told me something, and I said, "Yes, I know".

She turned on me like a fury.

"Oh, you know, do you? Then I won't have to show you anything. You'll be teaching me next."

On her first morning there, after I'd cleared down the breakfasts, I brought up a piece off the side of bacon to cut it for next morning's breakfast. It really was the best time to do it, and it was a comforting thought that the breakfast was ready for the morning, anyway.

"What do you think you're doing?"

"Cutting my bacon for breakfast—I always do it at this time."

"Well, you don't now. You'll do it when I say so, not before, and not after. And anyway, how do you know I want to give them streaky bacon? Maybe they'd like the back for a change. Bring me the side of bacon."

"The whole—side?"

"Yes—the whole—side," she mocked.

I looked at her, almost defying her, but obedience was deeply rooted in my character. I turned and walked down to the larder. I struggled with the hook where the side of bacon hung and, after a lot of struggling and heaving, I got it on my shoulder, and staggered up to the kitchen with it and dropped it across the table, and stood up.

My back ached.

She looked at the side of bacon, it weighed about sixty pounds.

"What are you cutting now?"

"A bit of the streaky off the other side."

"We'll use it up, and then use the back, and then when I want this again you can bring it back. Take it away now."

I moved over to lift it, but Margaret was passing, and she said in her bright and boisterous way: "I'll help you with that, Jenny."

I looked at Mrs. Callan, then at the pig, then at Margaret, but she turned away and didn't say anything. So Margaret and I staggered down to the larder with the side of bacon and let it lie there.

The next time the farmer came in she asked him to cut it up.

Asked him, did I say? Ordered him. Because she was the same, or nearly so, with everybody, and both indoors and out she was universally detested.

Now, it will be said, "Why didn't you leave?"

I will explain that.

First of all, I had been very lucky. With Mrs. Preston, Chef, Gladys and Barbara, and Mrs. Morton. I had had to work, and work hard, but they had been reasonable, if strict and just, and usually kind. I treated Mrs. Preston shamefully sometimes, but I never meant to. I was just trying to be big— I wasn't so big after all.

But the usual kind of cooks one met and heard about *were of the Mrs. Callan stamp*. But they were supposed to be the best cooks and the best teachers. They, in their turn, had been trained with the whip and wanted to take it out of the poor devils who had to work for them. They thought it proved their superiority and efficiency, and that it was the only way they would get obedience.

Just as your pukka sahib says the only way to make the coloured boy understand you is to flog your words into him with a whip. They "like it that way".

It was the old tale of someone "dres't in a little brief authority".

Even as late as 1945 I met a chef who believed you couldn't be popular *and* efficient. I need hardly say I worked with him for just two weeks. And leaving wasn't so easy.

It wasn't just a case of giving a week's notice, going home in the evenings and week-ends to Mum and Dad, and going to another office next week.

I *lived* here. All my belongings were here, right in the heart of Staffordshire.

My mother was in service in a village seven miles from home. My sister was in the mill. My father was in Australia.

I would have to give a month's notice and then take a job on chance, without an interview, and God knows where I'd land.

Then I knew she was temporary and so it couldn't go on for ever.

But, more than that, was the damage done to my impressionable mind. Intensely truthful myself, I never doubted anything anyone told me, and when she constantly told me that I was no good, to her or anybody else, I could only believe her. Perhaps I hadn't been such a success as Mrs. Morton had told me? Perhaps I wasn't such a capable kitchenmaid as I had thought? Perhaps everybody was laughing at me, perhaps I'd been getting swollen-headed?

And there was another reason—I always sent some money home.

My grandmother and grandfather had come to live with us at home when a flood came rushing down the hill and buried their basement kitchen knee-deep in mud, just a few months before Grandpa died.

They looked after my sister, and kept themselves going,

but Grandpa was just beginning to get ill, and it all helped to make him worse.

Then there was only Grandma, with her little widow's pension, and my aunt, who had never married, and who went out cleaning every day, from eight till five, for two and six-pence a day—beating heavy carpets, polishing, scrubbing, cleaning windows; later it went up to five shillings a day, but she never got any more than that.

My sister's pay was about eighteen shillings a week by this time, but she grew fast, too, and needed new clothes, and she had a healthy appetite. And she liked dancing, and she was the baby—no, she wasn't spoiled, because she was the best sister in the world, but the home needed so much that her little pittance didn't go far.

And I was getting so much: lovely food, as much as I could eat, and seeing the whole of the countryside and getting it all free.

So I stayed, to be sure of helping my home.

And, after all that, to tell you the truth, I never even thought of it!

And still another reason—only very intangible as yet and half-formed. I wouldn't let her beat me, and, in the end, she didn't.

Besides, I am telling things as they were, not as one would have liked them to be.

THIRTY-SEVEN

We went to London, to Princes Gate.

If life in the country had been a nightmare, then my life in London was Dante's *Inferno*.

We were allowed out till ten on our half day, but if there should be a dinner party or tea party on that day, even at the last minute, it meant that we couldn't have that day—not even if you'd made arrangements.

My cousin Sheila was a cook by this time, and worked in a place in Addison Road, Kensington. She was there for a good many years while I dodged about, or was pushed around, just as you wish, from pillar to post.

But if I were even five minutes late, Mrs. Callan almost

met me with a rolling pin, and once I was twenty minutes late.

Perhaps she was concerned about my welfare, I don't know.

I used to visit my cousin. Everybody used to visit my cousin. She was like that, then.

I've seen fourteen of us sit down to supper, to a cold leg of lamb and salad and chips, trifles and jellies, or an orange souffle and biscuits and cheese—all in the servants' hall—boys and girls. The parlourmaid and housemaid were sisters, Glasgow girls, and they both married policemen. But one could drop in there any time.

The elderly Duchess, if she knew, didn't seem to mind the inflated household bills.

When Jessie, the parlourmaid, left to get married they got a temporary one in, and she was soon running an affair with the nephew of the Duchess. I used to wonder, innocently, why she made up her face to go to bed at night, when most people take off their make-up.

But I had to be back at ten, or I got such abuse. I used to wonder where she found the words to say.

Margaret cut a finger and, instead of healing, it turned septic. As usual, the only sympathy she got was, "You want a dose of salts."

She went to the doctor and, of course, his orders were that she mustn't put her hands in water.

It is easy to know who did the washing-up.

Yes. Me.

Margaret made the most of it, for a time, because just as one finger got better, another one started, and before another week was out, she had eight fingers, all septic, and bandaged.

Such a condition would not be tolerated now, of course, but Margaret kept on working—at dry jobs. Sweeping, and putting away dishes, and making up the fire. But the washing-up had to be done, and it was soon evident that I knew how to do it.

Then came the climax, as it was bound to come.

But I must first tell you about our first footman, John.

He was about twenty-four, tall and dark and handsome, in a Charles Boyer kind of way. He always went to the dances with us and he danced a lot with me. And then he started keeping beside me as we rode home on our bikes about two o'clock in the morning. And one night, I don't mind admitting it, I nearly fell to John's persuasiveness. I hadn't yet, but he hadn't given up trying, and we were very good friends.

I think he was the only one outside the kitchen who really saw what that woman was doing to me.

One evening in the country John came to the slide as usual with his silver dishes for the dinner. He passed some joke about the dishes, or the dinner, and I laughed. It was not even the tiniest breath of a dirty joke—I never listen to them or tell them—I can't be bothered, I think they're just silly. It was just a silly remark about the dinner.

Mrs. Callan shouted across the kitchen: "That's enough of that! I won't have any of your filthy talk here—you've got other things to do besides listen to smutty jokes from the footmen."

John started to defend himself, but she came over and slammed the slide shut in his face, and gave me some more of her tongue to be going on with. I was too cowed to answer.

Any self-defence could be called insolence, and would have been in my reference.

Well, we come to the days and nights of the big dinner-dance in July 1928.

THIRTY-EIGHT

It was to be on a Monday evening. What the occasion was, I can't remember, for Miss Daphne had been presented before this, but it was a sufficiently important occasion to warrant preparations being begun on the previous Friday.

When Margaret took up Mrs. Callan's tea on the Friday morning (a changed Margaret now, who no longer ran, full of the joy of living) she came back down and reported that "she was up and dressed and in a fiendish temper". That was nothing new, but it didn't always start so early.

This "she" throughout is, of course, Mrs. Callan.

I was naturally the first to feel the blast. She had come down in the lift and had seen the third housemaid going up with the secretary's breakfast, a dish of cold ham and a boiled egg. The tray was all right, the boiled egg had a little cosy on it, the ham was beautifully sliced and on a neat little dish, but the tray had to come down again—I hadn't put a bit of parsley on the ham.

So that was the start.

But I tried to please her. I was so painfully conscious of all I should have done that I felt sure it must be all my fault.

A hamper of fruit and vegetables arrived from the country, among them baskets of strawberries, to be kept till Monday. No fridge, only a big ice-box, and we couldn't keep ice over Sunday in a London summer.

That was only one of the things.

Stock for soup, iced consommé! Stock for aspic jelly, and all their trimming.

Chickens to cook; quails to be stuffed and put in aspic—quails at six shillings each.

It was just at this time my sister was put off work, my father came home and insisted on my mother leaving her job—he made such a scene that she had to, and he had no money and no job—and my sister got six shillings a week from the Labour Exchange, to keep herself and my mother.

To say I was sick at heart is too mild. The price of that tiny bird, for one person—and even then it wasn't ready to serve, but had a lot more still to be done to it—to keep a grown woman and a growing girl.

There was nothing I could do. I ate all the food I was given and enjoyed it. It didn't even choke me—it should have done.

All I could do was send some money home as soon as I got paid on the first of the month. This, at any rate, I *never* missed.

But the week-end wore on in a welter of heat, and food, and finding a cool larder, and trying desperately to make the strawberries last over till Monday. Trying to please Mrs. Callan and finding that everything I did was wrong.

She gave me a loin of lamb and told me to bone it and roll it. I had done this many times, I knew how to do it. But she started to tell me and grumbled that she had to waste time showing me. Then she told me to roast it, then nagged me all the time it was in the oven.

"Did you baste it? When did you baste it? Are you sure you basted it? I don't believe you basted it . . ." and so on, interminably.

At last came Monday, and we were all in the kitchen by five o'clock in the morning. It was one of those days in

117

London that start off hot in the early morning, even when the morning mist is rising.

By eleven o'clock we were in full cry. We had a pastry-cook in, to make cakes and biscuits and brandy snaps, and she was a very nice person. I kept them all supplied with tea, and Margaret mooned about looking important because she couldn't do any washing-up.

I got my staff meals done, and gradually the heat was beginning to tell on me. Not the heat from the stove, but the heat from the sun, as it struck on the window of the basement kitchen, although it was really a big airy kitchen, but it was one of those days of humid heat.

Things were going fairly well.

Mrs. Callan's sister came in to help, also another woman, and a chef. And again I had to clear up after them.

The work would never have worried me, I had been too well "grounded" for that. But I was being slowly but surely pushed into the scullery, while Margaret took my place in the kitchen.

About eleven o'clock I was told to make a lot of mint sauce, and I got the mint ready and put it on a board. My own place and board were taken, and I had to find a corner of the small table where we had our meals, and it was low.

I put my chopping knife on the mint and made a few chops.

"Jenny."

"Yes?"

"Yes, what?"

"Yes, Mrs. Callan."

"Get me some butter."

Down went my chopper and I fetched the butter.

Back to my board, pick up the chopper, a few strokes.

"Jenny."

"Yes, Mrs. Callan."

"Get me some more eggs."

At four o'clock I got the last of that mint sauce off my board, and that was my only contribution to that party.

"Get me sugar."

"Wash this saucepan."

"Make some tea."

"What about the staff lunch? Or do you expect me to do it?"

With five of them to look after I was not in any condition

118

to be capable of doing anything else. And yet with Chef, or Mrs. Morton, I would have been. I *was*.

It was about tea-time when I was longing to sit down with a cup of tea, that she brought me a basket of mushrooms— about four pounds, I believe.

She said, "Peel these mushrooms and chop them up."

Now those were her actual words.

If I have occasionally tidied up a speech in this chronicle it is only because it is not always possible to remember a complete conversation, but the main gist of it is there, and mostly it is verbatim.

But that speech, "Peel these mushrooms and chop them up," is burned into my brain.

They were lovely big mushrooms, and if she had been Mrs. Morton I could have said, "Isn't it a shame to cut these up, they're so lovely."

But I couldn't. I wasn't allowed to think. She was paid to think—I was paid to work. And I had not even seen the dinner menu or the dance-supper menu.

So I peeled the mushrooms and I chopped them up. All of them.

She swooped on me when I told her they were ready.

I couldn't hear her words, because I was saying over and over again, "You said peel them and chop them up—you said peel them and chop them up—you said…"

But she just went on screaming—she had meant chop up the peel and stalks.

I know now that I must have been hysterical, but there was no time there for hysterics or nerves. You had to get on with it.

I shall never know what she did with the mushrooms.

Some little time later she sent me to do something else, and gave the order in her parade-ground manner. Suddenly, surprising myself more than anybody else, I snapped back, "I'm not your little dog!"

For a moment there was silence. Then she spoke again and her voice was quiet and icy cold. She told me to do something else, but her face and her eyes said plainly, "You'll be sorry for that, my girl."

When it came to dishing-up time, I was only fit for the scullery.

You must remember I'd had three months of this concentrated treatment and she had now got me, if not on the verge of insanity, at least on the verge of insensibility.

So it was only a little more persecution when she sent me in to wash up, and took Margaret in to help her dish up.

Washing up never held any terrors for me, and I went down the one step into the scullery and started. The wild chaos went on in the kitchen, and I never saw a bit of that truly wonderful dinner and supper being dished and sent up.

She was like that—wildly chaotic. If her Ladyship said, "I'm giving a small lunch party," she nearly went overboard. But if her Ladyship said, "There will be four (or six) to lunch," it was all right. The word "party" seemed to do things to her brain.

I went into the kitchen with some clean dishes about twelve o'clock and found Margaret putting the finishing touches to setting a table at the other side of the kitchen, with a white cloth, table napkins, flowers, glasses, and silver from the pantry. It was set for six. Herself, her sister and her friend, and the other chef. The pastry-cook, and last, but not least, Mrs. Callan's husband!

I couldn't help looking at it in sheer astonishment.

Then, on the stove, I saw silver dishes keeping hot with what was left of the dinner, and set on the table were more silver dishes, with what they seemed to be able to spare from the dance-supper—cold salmon in aspic, chicken chaud-froid, noisettes of lamb, and even some of the little quails. There was a bottle of champagne and another bottle which I think was some kind of red wine, and there were dishes of fruit and petits fours and cheese straws—there was everything—and I felt sick right down to the bottom of my stomach.

She saw me look at the table, and she just yapped at me.

"There's some cold meat in the larder if you want some supper."

"Thanks. All I want is a cup of tea." Then I called out quite loudly:

"Margaret, do you want some supper?"

"No." Then her face lit up a bit. "But I'd like some ice-cream."

"Bring a saucer and I'll get you some."

I never asked if I could—the ice-creams were ready to be dished up when they were wanted, and it was just when I went out to get some for Margaret that the butler came into the kitchen and said, "We'll have the ice-cream now."

She couldn't leave me alone to dish up my ice-cream. She

had to come and see to it herself. I don't know if she ever did get any good out of her posh supper.

But physical strength had gone with my mental strength, and I tugged at the tops of the cans in vain. She came out, shouting and storming, to the little back yard in the open air and pushed me aside. Her rotten temper accomplished what my puny tugging had not been able to do, and she got the tops off.

John came out to get the ice-cream, and she was still yelling at me. John just raised his eyebrows and made a face at me. I tried to smile. Fortunately she didn't see that, or there is no telling what construction she would have put on it.

John went away with his two dishes, the strawberry ice and the vanilla ice, and Mrs. Callan went back to her supper.

Margaret and I had some tea and ice-cream. I couldn't have touched any of the lovely food if it had been offered to me, but it wasn't. And if I'd wanted it very badly I could have got it.

By now, it was after one o'clock in the morning, but none of us was tired. In the first place, it was not an emotion which had been encouraged, and nerves or excitement always kept us up until it was all over. So when I'd cleared the scullery I got a bucket and scrubber and soap, and got ready to scrub the kitchen floor.

By this time I was so demented I didn't care about anything.

So I banged about, making as much noise as I could (and I'd been taught to work quietly, and I *do* work quietly). I scrubbed one side of the kitchen while the cooks were eating at the other side. She was as mad as hell, but there was nothing she could do about it.

Just where the kitchen went down one step into the scullery, in the corner, stood the inevitable donkey boiler. It had a brass tap at one side, but whether this was a safety tap or what it was, I don't know. I have a horror of anything mechanical, and I don't know a nut from a bolt. I had been told not to touch that tap, and that was good enough for me. I didn't touch it.

But as I dumped my bucket in exaggerated effort to make more noise, the handle accidentally hit the tap, and turned it on. Believe me, I was too scared of anything like that to do it purposely, as I was later accused of doing. I will not "protest too much", simply repeat that the handle of my bucket, wielded wildly and clumsily, turned it on accidentally.

With a sudden alert awareness of danger of some kind, I dived at the tap and tried to turn it off. It turned all right, but the water didn't stop.

I must have called out in panic, and now I frantically turned the tap this way and that way, but the water gushed merrily on. The scullery floor was about an inch deep in water, and soon the water would be up to the level of the step if it wasn't stopped.

Mrs. Callan started up from her supper and streaked across the kitchen.

"What the devil have you been doing now, you silly bitch? Turn that tap off, of all the helpless fools—I'll do it, out of my way——"

Suddenly the whole tap came away in her hand, and a gush of water shot up to the ceiling; she had to jump quickly out of the way.

Now the water had filled the scullery floor and was seeping over the kitchen floor.

She went out and called to the butler, and he came running in.

I stood there, mutely conscious that somehow I had done something wrong, but I couldn't tell what it was.

The butler took one look at the damage, at the water still spouting. It had gushed hot for a while but now it was cold. He said, "I'll have to turn off the main tap, but I don't know where the hell it is".

John came in and went to the tap, and held his hand over it. That was all right while it was cold, but it started to get hot again and he had to let go. He reminded me forcibly of the story of the little Dutch boy who put his finger in the dyke to stop the water coming in, and I started to giggle, and from giggling to near crying. But there wasn't time for the relief of tears.

John let go, and almost at once the water stopped. The butler had apparently found the main cock.

John went out, back to his pantry. Mrs. Callan came back to me, and her voice and her face and her eyes were venomous.

"Get upstairs to bed for heaven's sake—get out of my sight."

From somewhere in my fuddled mind I got the courage and found words to say, "I'll be very glad to".

I turned to walk away. The floor was slippery—she gave me a push, my heels went from under me, and I went down

122

heavily on my right elbow, and lay flat on my back on the wet floor.

That's all I remember—till afterwards.

THIRTY-NINE

I can only tell you what happened after that from the versions I got from several different people, and they were all the same.

She may have been frightened, I don't know, but it seems she called to Margaret to fetch the butler. Margaret ran in panic and told John I had fainted. John tore into the kitchen and saw me lying there, picked me up, and yelled at Margaret to bring a chair outside. He carried me out and sat me on the chair near the slush of melted ice and the empty ice-cream buckets.

Mrs. Callan followed him out, with one or two of the supper party—but her husband, having had his supper, had gone. He was a valet to Lord———.

She looked at me, and then said in the same venomous tone she'd told me to get to bed:

"She's shamming—throw a bucket of water over her!"

John turned on her.

"You—stinking bastard! You ought to be in jail for what you've done to this girl," and much more to the same effect.

Knowing John, I can imagine his adjectives.

Then he turned to Margaret.

"Go and ask Mr. Alford for some brandy, and hurry!"

Margaret scuttled off.

John stood beside me and held one hand—he didn't notice that my right arm hung limp at my side. I believe he opened out on Mrs. Callan quite a bit more, and he had no mercy on her.

So I came back to reality with my teeth chattering, moaning in fear, and with my nails digging deep into John's hand, and I couldn't move my right arm. In a little while he put his arm round my shoulder and gave me some of the brandy.

I remember the stinging taste of the brandy, and it made me sit up and look round me.

Mrs. Callan was standing in the doorway, and now she *was* frightened. Her voice was cold and impersonal, but it was not a venomous yell.

Margaret held me on one side, and John the other—he was very gentle and kind. I went up in the lift to the nursery floor.

Nanny was still awake, and Margaret led me into her nursery.

"Jenny's hurt her arm. She's not well," said Margaret. She was very frightened.

They helped me take my apron and dress off, and then Nanny felt all over my arm. Then she bandaged it tightly from shoulder to wrist.

It wasn't broken, and even now I don't know what happened to it. Something in the nerve or muscles, I don't know, but sometimes, perhaps not for years, and then within a few days, for no reason at all, it will go quite limp and I can't even pick up a handerkerchief. The muscle goes, seemingly, into little knots, the whole arm feels hot, and the hand and fingers go a purple-black and get quite swollen. Sometimes it lasts for hours, sometimes only a few minutes, but while it lasts there is just nothing I can do about it.

I suppose it's just one of those things.

I dragged myself to the bedroom I shared with Margaret. She helped me into my nightdress and then went back downstairs. But she was sent up again to go to bed.

For a few minutes I had the bedroom to myself.

I stood at the wide open window and I felt completely detached and empty. I wondered if I were dead.

I couldn't cry. I thought I'd never cry again.

My arm was painful, but it was nothing to the pain in my mind, and the hurt is still there as I write. I was an utter failure. I was sure of it now. I'd never make a success of anything. I was no use, even to myself.

Stars twinkled in the velvety blue of the sky, but a faint light was gradually putting out the twinkle. I stood and looked at the sky, and out of all my misery and fear and pain, I said, to nobody at all, "I don't care. Some day I'll be a famous actress, and I'll have dinner with a duchess—if it takes me twenty years!"

And I went to bed and slept, comforted by my foolish vow.

Well, the twenty years have gone—and more—nearer thirty years. I have *not* become a famous actress, although I have made some professional appearances.

And I have *not* had dinner with a duchess, although that's something that doesn't matter two hoots to me now.

There's only one duchess who could arouse in me the slightest sparkle of interest and I don't think for one minute I'll ever have dinner with her! Nothing like that matters now, anyway.

FORTY

At seven o'clock next morning I was down in the kitchen. Margaret had helped me to dress and I had to move very slowly. My arm was still helpless, but not so painful.

I got a shock when I looked at myself in the cracked swinging mirror on the chest of drawers, propped up with wedges of newspaper.

My face was grey and my eyes were glazed. I think that's the only way I can describe them. They were big and staring and glazed. I was quite sure I was mad.

When I went into the kitchen the fire was burning, the floor was scrubbed and spotless, the tables all scrubbed, all the food cleared away, and a steaming cup of tea was poured out.

I was grateful for that, for I was as weak as a kitten. I hadn't an ounce of strength, and I was moving very slowly. But I had to shake it off and work it off. There was no time to be slow.

When Mrs. Callan came down she just said, "Good morning."

I said, "Good morning, Mrs. Callan. What shall I do for breakfast?"

Not a word was said then, or ever, about the previous night. I never saw a doctor, or had any kind of attention whatever, except for the bandage Nanny put on.

Work went on. I got gradually better.

It was no use telling anybody about it—even my cousins would have thought I was silly to complain. They couldn't believe it was really as bad as it was for me, because they had met almost the same kind of tyranny; but they were not cursed with a sensitive mind nor such a weak body.

And if I may quote Walter de la Mare: "It is foolish, because disabling, to feel."

We soon went back to the country, and I was glad. It was peaceful there, and I thought that perhaps I might soon get a little holiday and go home.

FORTY-ONE

In the routine of breakfasts and dinners and lunches—life was really one long meal—she wasn't quite as bad, at least she was sometimes even civil.

But the change in Margaret was appalling.

She was bent up like an old woman—she shuffled along, and she was quite breathless with the least exertion. She could do her own work now though, which made things a little easier for me, but I certainly didn't know what was wrong with her.

Mrs. Callan broke out again one day, over something quite trivial, and not over the thing that I would have expected her to pounce on me about!

She never showed me anything. I learned in spite of her, not because of her.

The only thing she insisted on was tasting everything. Nothing must go up without being tasted—except a joint, or a whole fish, or fillets of fish. But any mixture—sauce, a gravy, or the water the potates were boiling in—everything had to be tasted, and tasted intelligently and analysed. She brought my palate up to a peak of perfection that it had not had before or has had since.

But if she were doing anything special she sent me down to the larder for something so that I wouldn't see it.

And one day she made me carry a hundredweight sack of flour on my back from the larder to the flour box in the kitchen. The grocery delivery man, a new man, had put it there without knowing where it should go.

One Sunday she thought she had got me beat.

She said suddenly, "Have we got a salamander?"

126

I said, "Yes, in the corner here."

"Get it hot."

So I did. I made the fire up, and when it was red in front, I put the salamander to get hot.

And then she went off to church.

Having recovered a little of my natural vivacity, and my arm not troubling me for some time, I must see what's been going on.

I went to the little table and there was a round souffle dish filled with something that looked yellow, under a glittering brown top of—what? I poked my finger on it to see, and it shot down on one side and splashed some sweet custard into my face! I hurriedly picked it up—it was a complete circle of browned sugar, about an eighth of an inch thick, and transparent.

Now I was in a mess. Some of the custard had been spilled, but I knew the name of the dish—it was Creme Brulée —and I saw some egg whites standing in a bowl on the table, and she had sent me to the larder for a lot of cream this morning. So putting two and two together, I got three eggs, used the yolks and some cream, and made a little creamy custard. Whether I did it in right quantities or not, according to a book, I wouldn't know. I never used, or saw any of my cooks, or Chef, using a book. It's sufficient for me that I was able to replace that Creme Brulee almost as I had found it. I poured my creme custard into the dish and it was almost the same texture. Then I started on the salamander. I sprinkled sugar thick on the top, and held the red-hot salamander over it. Then I repeated the process, all about four times.

It was practically new.

She made no comment on it at all.

And that's how I learned to make Creme Brulee. As I learned a great many things.

But she blew up one morning about something else. And as I went down to the larder to escape her tongue, a thought suddenly hit me, as it had never done before. I had been too intimidated.

I could *leave*.

Of course I could!

Who would stop me?

I would even go and ask Chef if he could give me a job, or know someone who could. But I need not endure this slavery any more than another month.

I went out of the kitchen and along the passage to the housekeeper's room. This was the holy of holies, and we were not normally allowed in here.

But I went in and gave my notice.

"Are you sure you wouldn't like to leave this till, say, the day after to-morrow, Jenny?"

I said sulkily, "What difference will that make, I've had enough. I can't stand any more. Anyway, what about the day after to-morrow?"

She looked out of the window.

"Her Ladyship has been able to get a permanent cook. She arrives the day after to-morrow."

I was thunderstruck.

I knew Mrs. Callan was temporary, but I had never dreamt that my deliverance would come so soon—and so suddenly.

I could only breathe: "To-morrow! To-morrow will be Mrs. Callan's last day, then?"

She nodded.

"So—if you would care to think it over, and come and see me again; and if you insist, I shall be very sorry, but I must accept it."

So I promised to wait until to-morrow, or the day after, when the new cook came.

"But I warn you," I said (*I* said to the *housekeeper*!), "if she's anything like this one, I'm going, I've had more than anybody would have taken."

She put her hand on my shoulder and said, in a very gentle tone, and she was not a gentle woman:

"We all know, Jenny, what has been happening, and be sure her Ladyship will be told, but we hope you will stay. Now go back, and this has been confidential."

For the rest of that morning I was quite immune to her black looks or her peremptory orders. It was a busy morning, for we were to have visitors.

Visitors for one night. For dinner, breakfast, and lunch next day.

I don't know who they were, but they were a lady and gentleman, a valet and lady's maid, a grown-up daughter, and a very young child. Young enough to have a nanny. That meant three extra in the dining-room, two extra in the steward's room, an extra nanny, and an extra child. All on different sorts of food

It was just a case of keeping on and on, and it was no unusual thing. What was unusual, however, was when Margaret whispered to me delightedly, "I've got the night off!"

"You've what?"

"I've got the night off—afternoon and evening."

And when she'd finished about four o'clock, off she went, very smug and superior, to spend the evening in the housemaid's sitting-room, by special invitation!

I can't blame her. She was young and should have had more of her life to enjoy—but she didn't.

I suppose it is in human nature to crow over a more unfortunate creature, but I knew the fault lay with Mrs. Callan—for it was only blind, unreasoning spite that made her give Margaret that night off. It was her final throw against me.

Every hand was needed that night. The extra vegetables alone took me the whole early evening after tea at four-thirty, and then there was an ice-pail to set and turn, and you couldn't leave it once you'd started it.

There was the fire to keep up, game chips to cut and fry, bread sauce, breadcrumbs, gravy, grouse, fish to prepare, probably cheese to prepare for something savoury—I forget now what was the savoury, but I know it would involve something for me to do—and Melba sauce for the ice.

When I had done the vegetables, I started to set the ice-pail, from the ice-pail to the fire, set the table, cut the chips, make a cup of tea, and, at six o'clock, Mrs. Callan came in to start work.

Then it became evident that not only was she doing an extra special dinner, she was intending to prepare the next day's lunch, the first course of Gnocchi, and the sweet, as well as the basis and the pastry for steak pie.

It was quite impossible to get to the washing-up during the evening. I was so rushed, and as it was also quite impossible to be in two places at once, I said to her, "Which do you want me to do, stay here and fry the chips, or turn the ice-pail?"

She knew something would have to be done, so she very grudgingly told me to go and fetch Margaret to turn the ice-pail.

Margaret was lying on the settee in the housemaid's sitting-room, reading a cheap novelette and smoking a cigarette.

"Margaret, Mrs. Callan says you're to come and do the ice-cream."

Margaret looked up and tried to be insolent, but she only succeeded in being silly.

"It's my night off."

"Don't be so cheeky," I said. "Her Ladyship wouldn't think much of anybody having a night off *to-night*. Come on and get that ice-pail turned."

Beggar on horseback?

No.

Just temper—wild unreasoning anger at the dreadful injustice. It just wasn't fair, and they all knew it. And if it had been possible for me to do all the jobs needed that night, you may be sure Mrs. Callan would not have given me any relief. But the ice had to be done, and it couldn't be done too early —there was not an unlimited supply of ice.

So Margaret came down and did the ice, as far as just turning it till it was stiff. I still had to "pack" it.

The meals went out. I worked quickly and furiously, but I wouldn't give her the slightest chance to tell me about anything; quite suddenly, in the stress of necessity, I found my skill again, and found something else too—an inward knowledge that I *had* learned some things in spite of her, not because of her, and a cold dignity that carried me without faltering through that night.

When I sent in the staff supper at nine o'clock, that was the last.

Mrs. Callan said she didn't want any supper—she had packing to do, and she was going to bed early. She said good-night and I said good-night, and she went out.

Always, before this, she had at least cleared her board and taken some things out to the scullery. Or even left them on the end of the dresser, but this night her board was littered, deliberately.

The stove had saucepans on it, the table was full, all the dressers were full—the food had come back from the dining-room, steward's room, and nursery—silver dishes had to be emptied, ice-pail emptied—everything was left, as well as every bit of washing-up since six o'clock.

It was just another day, as far as the kitchen was concerned, but without the hands to cope with the work.

I stood and looked at the wreckage and walked out to the scullery to survey that.

Take the worst of any third-rate boarding-house or eating dump you've ever seen, multiply it a hundred per cent., and it may give you some idea of the chaos.

I made a cup of tea, but I didn't want anything to eat, and I didn't sit down—that would have been fatal. I just took my cap off.

Systematically and calmly—too calmly, as I know now—I started first on the kitchen. It was, as I have told you, a long kitchen, and it was a long passage to the larders. How many times I walked up and down to those larders, I don't know, but I skipped nothing. Everything was done properly, and then when I'd cleared everything away, I got a bucket of water and scrubbed my boards, and washed down the tables, and swept the floor.

It was now about eleven-fifteen. I was ready to start the scullery, and I thanked God for my "grounding".

Gradually, I produced order out of the chaos, and I even felt mildly content. I think I started singing softly to myself. I cleared the pans and kitchen utensils away, and started on the plates and china bowls and things. I was enjoying myself, in a quiet calm little way. I had loads of hot water, plenty of soft soap and soda, lots of tea towels, and complete isolation, and it was eleven-thirty at night and I didn't care if it snowed. I wasn't tired, although I had now been on my feet for seventeen hours.

I knew I'd be tired when I'd finished, but I had a glorious day to look forward to, so I wouldn't mind that.

A step in the passage, the scullery door flung wide open—my enemy, the butler.

He looked at me and barked, "What the bloody hell are *you* doing?"

And I turned on him and gave him question for question. I had had quite enough of the whip.

"What the bloody hell do you think?" I barked back.

He looked startled for a minute, then he looked feebly round the scullery, said, "Oh," and then, "H'm. Well, put the lights out when you've finished, Jenny."

He shut the door, and then opened it again, put his head in, and growled, "Good-night," and banged the door shut!

I nearly fainted!

I put the last spoon away. I rinsed out all the tea towels and put them all over the clothes horse. I swept the scullery floor, and walked round surveying my domain.

131

Everything spotless.

A joy to come down to in the morning.

I looked at the kitchen clock—it was exactly 12.41 a.m.

I went along the outside passage to go upstairs, and my mood of devil-may-care was still with me.

"I know! I'll have a bath! I don't care what time it is, I don't care if I wake anybody up—I'm going to have a bath!"

I said these things to myself as I felt my way along the passage, for, in spite of his orders to put the lights out, the butler had put them out himself.

We had lately had a new bathroom put in downstairs, just opposite the housekeeper's sitting-room. I felt my way up to the third floor where our rooms were, got my dressing-gown and towel, and went downstairs again.

I put on the bathroom light and, as I did so, the house-keeper came out of her room.

"Jenny! What are you doing at this time of night?"

"Just finished work. I'm having a bath."

"Just finished work? What do you mean?"

"Just what I say. I've just finished clearing the washing-up."

She looked quite bewildered.

"But where was Margaret?"

"She had the night off."

"The night off? With all these people in the house?"

"Yes."

Her voice was quieter when she spoke again.

"Margaret didn't go out, did she?"

"No."

"Where did she go?"

"When I went to fetch her to do the ice-cream, she was in there." I pointed to the housemaids' sitting-room.

"I see."

Then, "Go and have your bath, Jenny."

"Will you just remember that if the next one is anything like this one, I'm going?"

She knew I didn't mean baths!

"It will be all right, Jenny. I'll see her Ladyship in the morning. Good-night, Jenny."

"Good-night, Mrs. Latham."

Still with that feeling of calm detachment, as though I were looking on at somebody else, I had my bath, and went up to bed and slept.

The morning was perfectly usual, quiet and orderly, but one could feel the tension and excitement in the air. Almost, Mrs. Callan confused me again, almost, her repetitive and contradictory orders had me worried.

When I had lit my fire (for she had stopped Margaret doing it when she first came) I scrubbed the floor in the usual way, and prepared the breakfasts.

There was not a great deal to do, because of her extensive preparations the night before. The Gnocchi was quite ready; I grated the Parmesan cheese immediately after breakfast and brought the cream to her to finish it.

Just after eleven o'clock, she put down her tea towel, which we always wore over our apron strings, and said:

"I'm going now to get dressed."

And she went out.

I felt a wave of relief and a return of responsibility. Margaret came in, not the running Margaret of four months ago, but a pale, thin scarecrow—I seemed to notice it for the first time. Her fingers had never really healed, she kept getting them septic; as fast as one got better, another would start, although she had not had all of them bad since that first time in London, and it was quite impossible to keep her hands permanently out of water, so she didn't really get much chance to get well.

She had only seen a doctor once, and the only advice or sympathy she got from Mrs. Callan was her constantly reiterated, "You want a dose of salts."

The chauffeur, Charlie, looked in.

"Where's Mrs. Callan? The car's ready."

"She went up to get dressed. Oh——"

She just came in.

She went to the stove, looked over everything critically, said, "You'll manage the lunch, I suppose."

I said, "Yes, thank you."

"You ought to, I've done it all."

She came over to me—Margaret was standing behind me, a little to my left—I was on Mrs. Callan's side of the table, facing towards the stove as she came round the screen.

She put her hand out and smiled. She was, as I have said, a very lovely woman. She wore a green costume of some kind and a little hat. She looked very fair and good, and nice, especially when she smiled.

My hand went out instinctively to meet hers, then, to my

133

horror and disgust, she bent forward—and kissed me on the left cheek!—and said, "Good-bye, Jenny."

I would have been considerably less astonished if she had struck me, and, I think, less sick.

She went to Margaret and did the same to her, and Margaret started to howl, and fled to the scullery.

I put one hand on the table to steady myself, my legs were like two sticks of boiled macaroni; I felt my cheek and rubbed it hard. I couldn't move. The foul treachery of that Judas kiss was like a stain—it seemed I could never wash it off.

Only the sound of something on the stove made me move —the call of duty dragged me back from the ugly depths of that last insult.

I heard the car pull away from the front door.

The day became a little more normal, although it still seemed to have that hard brightness about it that I associate with nervous crisis and tension.

John came to ask what silver dishes I wanted.

I told him calmly and a little severely. He did not linger or pass any joke with me. He just said, "What dishes do you want, Jenny?"

I liked people to use my name, and John did then, tenderly and kindly.

The car that took Mrs. Callan away was to bring the new cook back.

She would arrive just before one o'clock.

Mrs. Latham came down to the kitchen.

Even she must have felt the air in here. She only said quietly:

"Are you all right for lunch, Jenny? Shall I send Millie down to help?"

"No, thank you, Mrs. Latham. Mrs. Callan did most of it yesterday. I shall be all right."

She nodded.

"I've had a talk with her Ladyship."

And she looked at me.

"Her Ladyship hopes you will stay, Jenny."

I couldn't speak properly. The tones of kindness after months of brutality were almost too much.

I managed to mumble, very ungraciously, that it would depend on "this next one".

Mrs. Latham said, "She should be here soon. I'll get back to the front hall."

I got the staff lunch in without any incident, and made sure the other lunch was all right.

Then I heard footsteps, and voices, passing the slide—the kitchen door opened and Mrs. Latham came in, followed by a young woman, about twenty-six I thought, dressed very simply in a navy blue coat and skirt, and white blouse, and some kind of a hat.

Mrs. Latham led her forward, and I went to meet her.

"Jenny, this is Mrs. Garston—this is Jenny."

She shook hands, and she smiled. Her face was plain, but her eyes were nice and friendly, and she spoke.

"I'm very pleased to meet you," she said.

I just gaped, and gasped: "Goodness! Are you Scottish?"

"Yes," she smiled.

"Oh! Thank God for that!"

Then, of course, I apologised for being rude, but she was very nice about it.

"Are you managing the lunch or shall I come and help you?" she asked.

"I can manage, but I'll show you if you like."

"I'm sure Jenny will manage. I'll take you upstairs, Mrs. Garston," said Mrs. Latham.

She went away. I sent the lunch in. I took her lunch from the dining-room lunch, and set a neat little tray. I sent Margaret into her sitting-room with it. I cleared away the lunches, scrubbed the boards and tables, swept the floor, and made up the fire.

FORTY-TWO

I got home for the New Year, always a good time to be home, and I was able to help a little; things in the town were still bad, and the long queues at the Labour Exchanges made my heart ache—when I remembered the luxury I had just come from. Made my heart ache and my blood boil. But what could *I* do? Just one—what I could do was to make sure *my* mother and my little home were looked after, and that I did.

When I went back I felt in a few weeks that I was rest-less—I wanted to move; I could never stay in a rut. I had to be always searching for something better.

So after consultation with Mrs. Garston and Mrs. Latham, I gave notice.

We both felt I was capable of taking a head kitchenmaid's place. That is, where there were four in the kitchen, and I would have two girls under me—the second kitchenmaid and the scullerymaid.

So I wrote to a well-known agency, and by return of post I had a thick envelope full of papers—jobs all over the country.

We also looked in a well-known daily paper, and I asked Mrs. Garston one day. "What do they mean by 'lady' cook?"

" 'Lady' cook! It means somebody who can make you a wonderful souffle, or a marvellous vol-au-vent, but they couldn't skin a rabbit or wash a saucepan clean, nor show anybody else how to do it. 'Lady' cook! Don't you worry about them, and their 'Schools of Cookery'."

Neither she nor I knew what a menace and positive danger these "lady cooks" and their "Schools of Cookery", and their "certificates", were going to be to our livelihood in the days to come. It was something new—cooking, considered "low", was even then making its first tentative advances to the "upper classes", and soon the secrets of the great chefs were to be put up in packets and tins—just add hot water.

And we, who learned it from the bottom, were to be ruth-lessly flung aside in favour of a bright young thing with yards of certificates and a college background, and not a clue about *real* life in the kitchen.

But *then*, we foolishly dismissed them as of no account.

I eventually settled on a job in Portman Square, and some place in the country. I don't know where it was, because I never got there.

I was determined about London, because I had a wild idea, and I was going to carry it out—and *nothing* was going to stop me.

Foolish Jean!

I was to get £52 a year—a whole pound a week! And I made up my mind that I would go and get my voice trained! As head kitchenmaid, I would also have more freedom, for I would not be restricted about coming in at night.

I had no idea how to set about it, but one day I saw an

advertisement in the front page of the *Times* that "Madam So-and-so takes pupils in singing, to train for concert, opera, or musical comedy". *That* was what I wanted.

So I rang up the number given in the paper, and was invited over for an audition. It was in a corner house in a quiet square off Holland Park Avenue. The teacher was a big fat German woman, and she seemed very pleased when I sang my little piece in a wee sweet trembly voice. She said I was very good and had all the makings of a musical comedy star.

I believed her! I always believed people—it's been my biggest curse.

And, of course, I wanted to believe her.

I think she wanted five and sixpence a lesson, to be paid monthly; I can't remember, I know there was something about five shillings in it, and there was a pound in it, and it couldn't have been a guinea a lesson a week because that was all I earned.

Well, I was very excited and very thrilled—at last I was on the way to success!

I told my cousin when I went there to tea after my lesson. She thought I was daft and said so.

"But you know I've got a good voice, Sheila, and I don't want to be in service all my life."

"I know you've got one of the best voices in Scotland, but you're in service, and that will stop you getting *anywhere*. So buy a new hat with your money—it will do you more good."

But I didn't, naturally, take her advice.

I hadn't thought at all about practising. It hadn't occurred to me that I would have to do some scales every day and keep my voice and throat supple.

I could hum a little in my bedroom, but that wasn't enough. For the first time I had my own bedroom, and it was a wonderful feeling.

And I had not reckoned with the difficulty of *regular* time off. It was no new thing to be told on the morning of my day for a lesson that there would be a dinner party that night.

I must admit that in the few lessons I did manage to get, Madame Something-or-other, I forget now, did bring out the quality and timbre of my voice; she showed me how to let it come out, instead of singing inside me, and showed me how to breathe properly.

I began to have dreams.

I was slim and light and well-proportioned. I was quite attractive looking, and while I could not do speciality stage dancing I could move well, and I would soon have picked up or been taught enough to go into musical comedy.

Every year, when the lilac blooms, I can recall vividly walking through from Holland Park Avenue into Addison Road—maybe I took the bus part of the way, I don't know —I walked on air, after one of my lessons. I wanted to go straight away on to the stage!

The lilac was blooming, life was good. I was young and I was sure I would this time get my chance.

I was not a success as a head kitchenmaid. Let me admit that at once. Perhaps I could have been; I knew a lot more now and nothing was really a mystery to me. But not only was I expected to be a good head kitchenmaid, I was expected to be a thought reader as well.

For instance, on the menu there would appear the words, "Pouding au Chocolat". Now there are many different kinds of chocolate pudding: there is the sponge mixture, of butter, sugar, flour, and eggs; and there is another, with breadcrumbs and whites of egg, and many others.

The cook, Mrs. Skinner, got quite annoyed when I asked her what she wanted for her "Pouding au Chocolat".

She might have been another Mrs. Callan, only not in such a brutal way.

She was a little wizened creature, with large hands crippled by rheumatism—she flapped them as she walked along.

She never appeared for breakfasts, and only looked in the kitchen to give me the menu book, without a word. When she thought it was time for her to put on her "Pouding au Chocolat", say about twelve, she would come in and expect to find it all ready to be mixed. Of course it wasn't. Then I had to rush and do breadcrumbs—and she went away and came back—then rush with whipped whites of egg (and, remember, there were no mixing machines yet).

So that she made me look and feel incompetent and inexperienced. And I had had my fill of *that* feeling.

I struggled on uncomfortably for another month, until my third pay day, the 1st August. I had, of course, given her the expenses for my journey, plus taxi fare from Euston, plus extras that I now had no compunction in putting on.

Then I was summoned to the steward's room, where Mrs. Skinner sat at a desk.

She gave me my pay and then she said—but I knew what was coming:

"I feel that you want a little more experience before you take on the responsibilities of a head kitchenmaid, and I am sorry, but I shall have to make a change. I am giving you one month's wages and one month's board wages, and I hope you will settle down and put your mind on your work...."

I would have taken that, as it was meant, if she had left it at that. But she went on:

"I don't approve of what I've heard about—taking singing lessons" (if she had said taking drugs she couldn't have put more disgust in it)—"and you would be wise to think no more about it. Stick to your cooking and get more experience. You want to be a good servant: the other way is very—well—not very nice. Good-bye."

"That station in life!..."

So there I was, high and dry again.

I will not deny that I felt bitter.

Just because I could never be content with my station in life. God had given me a voice, but wouldn't let me use it.

My agency sent me a telegram in response to my letter, asking me to go to a remote country house on one of the islands off the west coast; I would be met at Fort William.

I arrived at Fort William well on into the afternoon of the next day, and I took a car to the point where they had told me to get the ferry across.

It took me to a pier, where I was met by a car, and driven along a road by the side of a loch for about a mile, then in a small driveway and to the back door and the kitchen.

The cook met me and gushed at me. I thought she was nice. The scullerymaid was a dour, elderly village girl, without much imagination, but quite a good worker.

It was a fairly large house, and quite a reasonably nice kitchen, rather reminiscent of a farm kitchen.

I had a room to myself up a small staircase in the back quarters.

The same routine of life-being-one-long-meal began.

We had glorious weather all during August and September, and the sunlight sparkling on the blue waters of the loch brought some balm to my weary soul. I was content to just sit and look at the water when we could get an afternoon's walk.

The people we were with were very nice; they were not titled, but they were wealthy and able to indulge in their sport to their hearts' content.

The cook, Mrs. Taylor, and I got on quite well together—although her cooking was not up to the standard I'd been used to. She wouldn't let me make real glaze, for instance, she bought gravy browning and made that do. In lots of ways she was slip-shod, and, I began to see, actually dirty.

The trouble really began when I had saved up some dripping for her to sell to the village women. This was always the cook's "perks", and she got sixpence a pound for it. The scullerymaid got rabbit skins, the cook got dripping, and the poor old kitchenmaid got nothing!

She said to me one day, "Would you like to send some dripping home to your mother?"

I thought that would be very nice, and said, "Yes, thank you, I would."

So she gave me about two pounds, and I got a tin and sent it home.

A few days later she said, "I think I'll send some dripping home."

So I helped her to wrap it up, and just before I closed the parcel she brought something else wrapped in greaseproof paper. She gave me what she thought was a sly wink, but was really a leer.

"Just a bit of butter—they won't miss it."

Of course they wouldn't, when she bought the stores!

I'm convinced now that she must have been mad or very, very ill.

She started throwing things about, and she was rude to the butler and everybody else, but terribly charming to the lady.

I had to leave the kitchen when the lady came in in the mornings, but there was no nonsense about the kitchen being cleared, so long as it was tidy.

It never was tidy for long, because Mrs. Taylor could make a bigger mess faster than anyone I've ever seen.

Whatever job she was doing, she was all over the kitchen with it, rather like a college-trained assistant cook I had, whom I met later.

In a few weeks she had got her parcels home to a fine art.

Letters from her husband, and her sister-in-law, were really only long shopping lists.

"We need tea, butter, sugar, bacon, lentils . . ." an endless list.

And it was I who parcelled them up for her and carried the heavy parcels a mile to the village post office. She made sure of keeping me quiet by giving me a little ham, or half a pound of butter occasionally, and salved both our consciences by saying that it could well be spared—they had plenty and she was sure my mother could do with it. She was so right, but my mother soon put a stop to it.

She just wouldn't let me send any more—she said I wasn't to take it. She knew it wasn't honestly come by.

So when I refused her next offer Mrs. Taylor began to turn nasty. She threatened all kinds of things about my reference, what she would say about me to the lady, and I was only too well aware of the fact that the upper servants had the upper hand all the time. For the poor devil of a kitchenmaid, or under-housemaid, couldn't get to the lady at all; and if she had managed to penetrate to the presence she would have been soundly reprimanded and sent downstairs as being hysterical or, bluntly, off her head.

So I continued to send her parcles but I didn't take any more for myself.

The climax came one day in the middle of October, just about two weeks before we were due to leave. She started the Mrs. Callan game of deliberately confusing orders, saying one thing and then swearing blind she had said something else.

We'd had quite a busy day—I'd helped Dora, the scullery-maid, with the game, and shown her how to cut the vegetables for a braised brisket of beef. I had the beef cooking, I had the braised vegetables ready.

Fred, the footman, came to ask about dishes, and I told him what I wanted.

Mrs. Taylor chimed in, "And a silver dish for the brisket."

"I'll put the brisket in a china dish for carving, surely, Mrs. Taylor."

"Don't you tell me what to do! I want a silver dish for the brisket, and you won't get it unless I do."

I shrugged and told Fred, "Never mind, Fred, it will be all right."

She raved about the cheek of butlers and footmen, and also of kitchenmaids, and generally lost her head. I can remember the kitchen was littered—no amount of clearing up seemed to keep it clear for two minutes together. The space on the table that I'd been taught to use for dishing up was already littered with stores which had come in that afternoon and she wouldn't let me put away.

Then that day I had also spent about an hour doing up two big parcels for her. She was having a field day, knowing there was only two more weeks to go. It was with something like despair that I looked round the kitchen when it came to dishing-up time.

She had muddled Dora, too, and I had to go and find spoons for dishing up, and wash them.

With an effort I sent the soup in, in its silver tureen.

I don't remember what the fish was, but I know there was a cold game pie and its trimmings—it was all ready.

It came to the time to send in the braised brisket.

My braised vegetables were ready, small button onions, carrots scooped out into balls the same size as the onions, turnip the same, some peas and cubes of celery, and small mushrooms. I took the brisket out and had it pressed sufficiently to send it in, and had my hot glaze ready to pour over it.

She snatched the china dish out of my hand, and Fred came in for the meat course.

"Get me a silver dish," she snapped.

"Mr. Stamford says no," said Fred.

"I don't give a b—— what Mr. Stamford says. I'm not spoiling the look of my dinner on a china dish."

Fred looked at me, I looked at him.

He shrugged his shoulders and walked out.

Mr. Stamford came in to the kitchen, furious and steely.

"Mrs. Taylor, I have a dinner party waiting for this course. Will you send it in at once, please?"

"When you give me a silver dish," she snapped.

Mr. Stamford made an impatient gesture.

"Mrs. Taylor, you know perfectly well I cannot carve beef on a silver dish, my knife would scratch the silver."

"I don't care about your bloody carving or your scratches —I won't give you that meat till you give me a silver dish."

The butler turned to me.

"Jenny, give me the meat course, please, I'll take the responsibility."

At that Mrs. Taylor screamed, "She's not touching that meat! Nor you nor anybody else till I get a silver dish!"

Mr. Stamford lost his already sorely tried temper—he came round to the stove, on the other side from me, so that I was between the stove and Mrs. Taylor, who was now quite literally out of her senses with rage.

Before he reached the stove she bent down and picked up the small bucket which was standing at a corner behind the stove with ashes in it, from making up the fire earlier. There was not a lot and they were not hot now, but there was enough to make a mess.

She picked it up and stood it straight up over Mr. Stamford's head!

The ashes cascaded all over him—over his white evening shirt and tail suit.

He shouted and swore at her and made after her as she ran screaming from the kitchen.

Fred came in.

"How about that joint, Jenny?"

"Yes. Dora! Your vegetables, please."

In two minutes we had the meat course in, and Fred and I carried on the dinner right through.

That whole interlude had taken twenty minutes. The party in the dining-room had joked about it, said they should have engaged an orchestra to play to them while they waited!

It seems Nanny went to Mrs. Taylor and gave her a sedative and put her to bed.

I'm sure she was a sick woman—perhaps some private trouble, I don't know. But right to the end she tried to say the delay had been because I didn't have the vegetables ready!

The ashes on Mr. Stamford's suit were a witness to the falsity of that statement.

She was sent away next morning, and I didn't see her at all. She didn't come down to breakfast, and she was taken out by the front door.

The lady sent for me to the drawing-room and asked me if I thought I could manage for the next two weeks. I said I thought I could.

And I did.

Somehow I'm at my best in an emergency! When things are going too well, I get lulled into a sense of false security and then find I've made some awful mistake. But when things really begin popping, then it's a challenge to my ego, and I come out fighting! *Always* fighting.

So the two weeks passed uneventfully; I got my wages, a

143

pound extra, and my fare home. I already had my return fare to London.

Which I thought was very nice.

FORTY-THREE

I stayed at home over that Christmas and New Year, and I had enough money to give them all a good time. I made a Christmas pudding and bought a chicken, and crackers, and presents, and brought a little of the English Christmas to our little home.

I picked up the threads of my old dancing days and wished passionately that I could stay at home.

But I had made a discovery.

I had grown up.

Growing up is not a slow process. It is a sudden realisation. One day you will see children playing in the street—you may be eighteen or twenty, thirty or forty, according to your heart, and you will discover that you don't want to play, that you are grown up, without having the least idea how you got there.

That was how it happened to me.

I had time to sit back and look at what life was doing to me.

I was twenty-three.

I had the beginnings of some skill in what I had been assured was an "art". But not enough skill to shake the world by any display of it.

On the other hand, I was tall, fairly attractive, intelligent, educated, and with the gift of a pure sweet voice which lifted in song as easily as I breathed, and as naturally. All the longings of my soul lay in just wanting to sing.

I don't think I consciously made any sort of vow or anything, I just grew up, and decided to make another attempt, somehow, sometime. Meantime, London was the place. There was absolutely nothing at home. Things were getting bad in the town, although not so bad as they were to become, and for the moment it was all right for us. We could live fairly comfortably—I even had a bottle of port for our Christmas dinner! My mother was working as a laundrymaid in a house in a village about seven miles away and she was well and strong and happy. My sister was still in the mill, although a great many of the girls had been sacked, and she was not sure from week to week when it would be her turn.

It seemed the only thing to do—to go back to London. I couldn't stay to live on my mother's three pounds a month or my sister's twenty-five shillings a week. When my few pounds were gone, except for my fare back to London, I had to go.

Ours was not the only family broken up by economic disaster in those years.

This has been said before. Now I had seen it. Grandma got her pension of ten shillings a week. Auntie, who was, and is, an institution, went out cleaning other people's houses for two and sixpence a day—beating heavy carpets outside in cold winter winds, cleaning big kitchen ranges, polishing floors and furniture, cleaning windows, sometimes very high up, outside and inside. It was many years before she got five shillings a day for her work, and she worked from eight o'clock till five. She always got a good meal though, and she got personal recommendations all through those working years. So that when she came home at nights she was dead tired; my sister dashed home from the mill, nineteen and full of life, and living only for dancing, with no thought for the morrow.

You will remember how my father came home from Australia, starving and in rags. He always managed to have his money stolen somehow. He did when he reached London from Australia, crossing from the docks to Euston Station.

It must have been about this time that I felt the first beginnings of that load of responsibility for the family—that I, not my father, was the true head of the family. He was such a broken reed, and yet I loved him—my sister didn't.

As I said, I think I felt this first stirring then, and I realised that the job, or the career, which had been thrust upon me, was at least sure.

As Mrs. Preston had told me, "It's a good trade when you can get to the top—you can command your own figure then."

She had no reason to believe that it would not always be so. She could not foresee the changing social conditions, or the menace of "lady cooks".

So, going about the little home in the attic, to which we had moved, I pondered on a friendly cook's words to me.

"Why don't you go on your own, take a cook's place when you get back to London?"

"Do you think I could?" I asked her.

"I don't really see why not. You've had an excellent grounding—you know as much of the basic groundwork of cooking as you'll ever know; all you want is some more polish, and I think you're clever enough to pick that up yourself. Anyway, try a small place, with a kitchenmaid, to knock off the rough edges. If you can't manage it, let me know—I'll do what I can for you. But I think you'll be all right when you know that *you* are responsible. You seem to thrive on responsibility!"

"I like to be trusted."

She nodded. "I know."

So, flushed with my success of two weeks in charge (by accident!) on that shooting party, I wrote to my agency, and asked for a job as a cook-housekeeper in London.

As usual, I got a choice of several, and I chose for better or for worse a house in Portland Place, with a Mrs. Leonard, and wrote that I would come for an interview on a certain date.

It was with a sad heart and a trembling hand, and fear of the future, that I said good-bye to my mother and sister at Glasgow Central Station one night in early April in 1930.

Desperately I went over all I did know.

Vegetables and sauces, all the right kinds for the right things; cakes and scones and biscuits; fish, all kinds; meat, especially mutton and lamb, of which I knew every bone in the animal's body. Braising and stewing and roasting and grilling; and for sweets, all the ordinary milk puddings, fruits, jellies, compotes, and macedoines; all pastries, cold and hot souffles, ice-creams, and I could do a little sugar work. Not a lot, and I never have been able to make a speciality of sugar work, but enough for an ordinary household.

At this point I quite freely admit that I did need a little more polish—the kind of polish and finesse that I could only get from a chef or a chef-trained cook.

But to tell the truth, I was fed up being ordered about by bad-tempered cooks, and I was quite sure I knew as much as Mrs. Taylor, and would *not* insist on a silver dish for a joint which had to be carved.

I certainly knew better than that.

Well, now I was on my own.

FORTY-FOUR

I took a taxi from the station, leaving my luggage there, and arrived at Portland Place and rang the front door bell.

The butler let me in, and then washed his hands of me.

The footman appeared, and led me up to the drawing-room.

Mrs. Leonard came to meet me, and held her hand out, and smiled. She was French, slim and dark, and very charming, but she could also be a termagant, as I found out later.

"Good morning, Mrs. Rennie."

"Good morning, madam," I said, feeling a thrill at the promotion to the courtesy title of "Mrs".

It was always a source of annoyance to us, cooks and housekeepers, when we read in books, or heard in plays, anybody calling their cook "Cook", or alluding to her as "cook".

Even the so-called "best" authors did it, when we knew that no lady ever called us by anything but "Mrs. . . ." with our surname. However, since no one would ever print any objection we raised—and I wrote many a letter to the press —we dismissed it as showing how very much authors did *not* know about the people they were trying to portray.

Although Mrs. Leonard already had details of my experience, she asked questions all over again.

Could I do this? Could I make that? Did I know this or that sauce? Was I a hard worker and an early riser?

(Foolishly, I had thought my days for early rising were gone!)

And my age? Twenty-six. (I think that must be the only instance of a woman putting her age *up*!)

At last the catechism was finished, and she came to the all-important question of wages.

"And you are asking——?"

"Sixty pounds a year," I replied somewhat timidly. After all it was my first attempt, and I wasn't awfully sure of myself.

She beamed, although she tried not to show it. Her previous cook had had eighty-four pounds a year. So that was a direct saving on her household allowance, which could go to her dress allowance, and would ensure at least *one* new hat a year.

She shook hands again, and said that would be quite agreeable, and rang for the butler, and then introduced us.

I went to the station to fetch my luggage—another taxi—more "expenses".

When I came back the butler first conducted me down to my kitchen, a usual basement kitchen, quite large, but dingy grey, not a clean shining red. No fireplace, only two large gas stoves. The scullery was just a continuation of the kitchen, and was down a step. It was dim and creepy, and not in the least clean or tidy.

I was then taken up to my bedroom, a big airy room in the attic, directly over the front door. The house was on a corner, and the front door was actually not in Portland Place but in the street which led off it, and the Swedish Embassy was directly opposite.

I unpacked enough to see me through dinner, and went downstairs.

I found my young kitchenmaid, who had been missing when I looked in earlier, standing at the sink washing greasy roasting tins in filthy-looking water. She looked fed up and discouraged, as well she might. I set to, and pleasantly tried to help her, and show her how to wash up properly. For some reason, she seemed to resent it. And I wondered if I was doing the wrong thing. Where Katie was concerned, I certainly was.

She was a very pretty Irish girl, about seventeen. She had never been in a big kitchen before, and it is indeed questionable if she had ever learned to wash her own neck. I will not be misunderstood—there are dirty people in all races, including my own, but it just happened that Katie was Irish, and dirty.

Katie was only with me for about six weeks. She was very little help, because she had no idea what to do. You remember I said how no surgeon was ever better served than a cook or chef with a skilled staff?

What happened now?

I knew what I needed to keep my cooking up to the standard I knew—I never learned any other.

And I got nothing in the way of help from Katie. Very often I had to set to and wash a pan myself, digging it out of greasy water, or even taking it off the shelf and having to wash it. Never a basin of rough vegetables—she just didn't know what I meant, and I didn't like to be hard on her, and she played on that.

For those six weeks I rushed madly about, desperately hanging on to the job, instead of throwing it up and going back to see Chef. I had started on my own and I was determined to see it through.

Desperately I tried to please everybody and ended by pleasing nobody.

The staff consisted of the butler and a footman, head housemaid, second housemaid, cook-housekeeper and kitchenmaid, chauffeur and lady's maid.

The butler was a small stout man, typically manservant, but he was a sneaking, sly, underhand rascal, and I found him out later. He went to Mrs. Leonard with everything, and she listened to him. The footman was a tall dark-haired, dark-complexioned boy, with deep, large hypnotic eyes—whose sole ambition in life was to be an evangelist. He even tried to convert me! He wasn't a bad sort of boy, though. The chauffeur, Johnny, was just a handsome young mechanic, whose soul was inside the bonnet of his car.

Coming home from a visit to my cousin one night, I met Johnny at Oxford Circus: he was going home too. We walked slowly up Portland Place together, and the butler told Mrs. Leonard that I was keeping company with the chauffeur!

The head housemaid—oh, why are most head housemaids sour and vinegary, and bad-tempered slave-drivers? All the ones I met were.

The second housemaid, poor little devil, didn't have a soul to call her own, on or off duty. She had to obey old Annie in everything. She had a terrible life.

That, and the hard training I had had, was what made me more lenient than I should have been with Katie.

The lady's maid was new; she came a few days after I did, and she stipulated her terms before she came. These included the right to use the front door, instead of the basement door which we lesser mortals had to use, and a whole day off a week, instead of our humble half-day per week (perhaps) and every other Sunday.

She was a very charming girl, with exaggerated ideas of her own importance—her superiority to the common domestic servant was constantly stressed. And then she married the chauffeur! And I believe they were very happy—I hope they still are.

My life and work were a desperate battle that inevitably dragged on my nervous system, never very strong in any case.

I did all the cooking and baking, preparing all my own tins and weighing up everything; most of the clearing up from the kitchen, and the tables to scrub too. Katie did manage to do the washing up and the floors, but it was heartbreaking to see her, slittering about in dirty water, leaving the bucket with water in it, soap and scrubber and cloth too—dirty streaks on the floor, pans and roasting tins shoved in corners out of sight.

And I had not yet learned to command. At least, I had never had to command anybody who didn't know their job. I tried to treat Katie kindly and show her the right way, but I didn't learn for many years afterwards that that was a mistake. And Katie didn't want to learn anyway.

FORTY-FIVE

There was still a different procedure here with the menu book from all the others.

Mrs. Leonard rang the bell for the butler, who came for me, and conducted me to the drawing-room.

Then there would come the comments on the previous day's menu.

"The soup was excellent—*mais un peu de sel, n'est ce pas?* The fish"—"yes"—she would wave her arms, "it was, about good. The chicken—no, no, not at all good. The ice, but yes—very, very excellent, ah, yes, you improve—you learned the 'Wiener Schnitzel' as I showed you..."

Sometimes something was quite, quite *impossible* (in French), sometimes it was too, too exquisite. One never knew how to please her, and I was so anxious to please, and every word of criticism spurred me on to greater efforts and greater demands on my unconsciously diminishing strength.

At the end of the first month I took up the tradesmen's books, with a list of their totals, my own and Katie's salary, and my own "expenses".

These were, of course, my taxis and luggage and porters—although I had already legitimately had these from the temporary job I was in.

Oh, well, it was what everybody else did. I hadn't liked it at first, but I am reminded of a little verse I read somewhere about an asterisk:

> "... at first the little asterisk
>   Would blush a rosy red,
> But soaked with sin, it soon rushed in,
>   Where angels feared to tread."

And I went the way of all the others.

The tradesmen's books were always the signal for a nightmare interview.

I was sent for, to the drawing-room, where she would meet me, the books in her hand, which I had given her the previous day.

Sometimes she would hold an inquest on them, too: "Why do we need all this bacon? And when did we have loin of lamb?" "You had that as noisettes, Madame." "Oh. Sausages—what do we do with all the sausages?" "Sunday morning staff breakfast, usually."

"But it is too much! One sausage is enough."

"One sausage for a man's breakfast, madam?"

A shrug—"They can fill up on bread and butter."

"Yes, and then you're going to grumble about the bread and butter bills."

In the end I got the cheque, all the books, and my wages and the kitchenmaid's wages.

The grocer would change the cheque for me, and I'd go off in the afternoon to pay the tradesmen. I don't know how to describe my astonishment when the girl in the greengrocer's gave me £2 10s.

I said, "What's this for?"

"Commission, dearie. Haven't you had any before?"

"Good gracious no. This is my first cook's place."

"It's nothing like it used to be. The head staff of big houses used to be able to give the accounts to the tradesmen who would give them the most commission. This has been lying for about three months. You can have it every month if you like, but it makes a little more if you leave it. Are you settled in? Do you think you'll be happy?"

"Oh yes, it's all right. She's doing a bit of entertaining."

"That's good—you look after us, dear, and we'll look after you."

So I straightaway gave them another order, of the very best fruit and vegetables, but *nothing* I didn't need.

FORTY-SIX

April and May passed more or less pleasantly. At least I could please myself when I came in at nights, if I went out. And now that I could stay out late, I didn't want to. I visited my cousin a great deal. We were always very good friends, until the years separated us. She was very good to me.

I went a lot to the pictures, but I didn't go to dances very much, and although I was practically next door to the Queen's Hall, the world of music was an unknown territory to me.

I had heard snatches of music from the drawing-room in the house in Staffordshire, but always when I felt I'd like to stand and listen it was either switched off, if it was the new "wireless", or someone stopped playing when the gong rang for dinner. I knew that somewhere there must be music, real music, not the popular songs I heard, but I knew vaguely the names of Chopin, Beethoven, Mozart, Brahms—but it was 1941 before I heard my first recital, and that was Lamond, at what was almost his last recital. A new world was opened up for me.

But in 1930 the Queen's Hall was beyond my level of appreciation. I did remember, though, that Mrs. Preston had taken me somewhere to hear Kreisler, and it must have been the Queen's Hall. And I think I heard Melba sing at a big hall, but neither of these two events impressed themselves on my memory, mainly because at that time the whole of one's being was concentrated on getting back in time to start work for dinner or else get back before ten o'clock at night.

And while the violin was played by the world's finest virtuoso, it did not satisfy me. I discovered, when I heard Lamond, what was the music that satisfied me. And Melba? Well, let's admit it, I was envious.

The early summer drew on, and I used to see the girls in

offices leaving their work at five-thirty, walking happily along with tennis rackets and that free-now-to-do-as-I-like air. The whole world seemed to revolve especially for girls in offices. every story book featured the girls in an office, every article by "Beauty Experts" and others, in weekly and monthly magazines, told them how to be beautiful—how to get and keep their man—how to get rid of their "tiredness" after a "hard day at the office".

Although how they could be tired, after sitting on their backsides all day, or else walking about carrying nothing heavier than a bit of paper, or two letters, was beyond me.

How I envied you, but I don't think I envied you your bun-and-glass-of-milk lunch.

But the staff were beginning to get the upper hand of me, and I couldn't get back my authority. I had done too much for them—I made biscuits and cakes, dainty and different, for their tea; gave them coffee for breakfast, and the best marmalade: fought for decent food for them, as an instance, the "one sausage for breakfast" that I had been commanded. So they knew my weakness, and they made full use of it.

A cook they could actually bully!

You see, I didn't really know whether I was any good or not: I took all Mrs. Leonard's criticisms as a warning that I wasn't any good. And I *had* to be better.

But, she learned one thing, I know it now. She learned very early that I was a far superior cook to the one she had before. It is not my intention, and indeed I have tried not, to give the impression that I alone was perfect and all else was wrong. But it would not serve the cause of truth to say I am not a good cook—I am. For that I have to thank my Chef, Mrs. Preston, Mrs. Morton, and even the wicked Mrs. Callan.

I took pains, and is not genius an infinite capacity for taking pains?

As usual, sometimes I got my half-day in the week, sometimes she just forgot I should want any time off and ran a series of cocktail, lunch, tea, and dinner parties. Of course I could have another day, no question about that; but wouldn't it have been nice to be able to say to a friend, "I shall come to tea with you on Thursday, and then we'll go to a theatre?"

So my social life was practically *non est*.

(You remember? "You are not allowed a private life, or a soul, in service.")

Some days, of course, they went out to meals, then it was fairly easy.

And Mrs. Leonard was very kind in many ways. My mother got her holiday from work, and I hit on the idea of having her in London for a week. I had enough money, and so had my mother, and my sister was working again.

So I told Mrs. Leonard I was sending for my mother and was taking a room for her at a hotel as near as possible.

To my great surprise, Mrs. Leonard offered to put a room available for my mother just opposite mine on the top floor. There were plenty of rooms on the top—the house was big enough to keep several more servants than were actually there.

I went to Euston and brought Mother back in a taxi.

I shall never forget her face as she looked out of my window on to Portland Place and saw the cars and taxis all lined up in the centre of the road.

"Oh my! Jist look at a' thae motors!"

I took her out for a walk in the soft summer night, along the London streets as they used to be—elegant and dignified, not garish and brash.

She loved the shops and the people—she saw some ladies and gentlemen in evening dress, and she'd never seen *that* before.

During the days she was quite happy to wander about alone, and she found her way to Westminster, and Buckingham Palace, and Hyde Park, and without any trouble at all she saw the King and Queen, and the Prince of Wales, and Princess Mary!

She *was* so thrilled!

Surprisingly, too, young Katie took advice from my mother that she didn't take from me! My mother loved washing and washing-up, and she used to jolly young Katie along, and help her; and Katie adored her. Although that's not surprising, everyone who ever knew her adored her.

But Katie would take a cup of tea up to her in the mornings much more willingly than she would bring mine!

That lovable streak of inconsistency which is the Irish.

Well, my mother had a very lovely holiday, and she went home tired but happy for a wee while.

Katie mysteriously disappeared.

So did a fountain-pen belonging to the footman, a brooch

of mine, and a purse of old Annie's, and various other odds and ends that no one had really thought about.

Then, in about two days, Katie came back.

Now, all that happened during this time was somehow, and for some reason, kept from my innocent ears. All I can do is set down the facts as I knew them.

Katie came back, limping, in a taxi. The taxi went away.

Katie had sprained her ankle, and she was going away.

I wasn't taken into anybody's confidence, but somebody helped Katie to get some little bits of luggage together, and then she was taken to the front door.

And a woman came for her. To this day I do not know whether that woman was a procuress or a probation officer.

But when I went upstairs I went along to Katie's room. The head housemaid, the lady's maid, and the footman were there.

"Oh! My brooch!" I cried.

It was pinned into the underside of the mattress.

"My purse," said Annie grimly, holding it out. "Empty!"

"My fountain-pen," said Robert, the footman, showing me the pen.

I looked round the big bare room.

Inside the little cupboard which should have held shoes, were tins of polish, tins of Vim, floor cloths, soap, dusters, and one or two small handbrushes.

In the drawers—but it is too shameful to dwell on—let us just say that clean(?) garments and dirty garments were mixed in stinking confusion, with filthy stockings, one of my nightdresses. We burnt the lot.

And that's all I know about Katie.

FORTY-SEVEN

Sometimes I got a woman in for rough work, but it seemed it was impossible to get a kitchenmaid.

So I went on alone, day after weary day, working to make sure I would get a good reference, and feeling, of all things, that Mrs. Leonard might not be able to get a cook at this time of the year, so I couldn't leave her. Imagining, foolish girl, that I was indispensable.

Then—"I want a very special menu. I am giving a very important dinner and dance—there will be . . . about . . . twenty for dinner—and about a hundred and twenty for the dance. You will let me have a menu? And we will plan it together. You will need help? Yes? Oh, yes—I suppose so."

"My cousin is a cook, she will help me."

"Ah! Good! And so you will manage, with Mrs. Brown to wash up? Yes? Good."

So thus was a dinner for a princess arranged.

The lovely Princess Ingrid of Sweden was to be presented to Their Majesties King George V and Queen Mary, and Mrs. Leonard was giving a dinner and dance in her honour. A small, select group of intimate friends would dine, then the Princess would go to the Palace, and come back to dance in our drawing-room for a short time—then she would finish the evening and early morning dancing at the Swedish Embassy opposite.

Everything I ever learned went into that dinner and dance supper!

Mrs. Leonard's favourite soup—a good consomme, into which was whisked very finely sifted potato and fresh chopped watercress, but it had to be my best consomme. I forget the fish, for the dinner, but I know it was salmon in aspic for the supper. My cousin Sheila, bless her heart, came and did all the fish for me—I didn't have to touch it.

I expect it would be noisettes of lamb for the dinner, for I had chicken chaud-froid, and mousse of ham for the supper. There had to be two ice-creams—a good vanilla ice and a cream of rice, iced. The plain ice-cream I made with two dozen yolks of eggs. With so many things to see to, the first lot I made curdled, because I couldn't stand and stir it with a wooden spoon all the time, so I had to make it again, and throw the first lot out. With the addition of a quart of double cream, whipped, and a flavouring given by a vanilla pod and castor sugar, it was a dream of an ice, although I say so myself.

The cream of rice, too, was delicious.

God knows how I fed the staff that day, but they would insist on their meals on time and in order. They wouldn't even consider a kind of supper of some chicken chaud-froid that hadn't been quite the right shape, or salmon in aspic, which may not have been just the right dimensions. Oh no, they had to have their cold beef and bubble and squeak at nine o'clock—but that doesn't mean to say that they wouldn't eat the left-overs or the ice-cream.

There had to be, also, a large rich fruit cake to cut at. Several dozen shortbread biscuits, lemon curd tarts, and sponge cake fingers, iced. A slab of sponge cake made—and made by hand, not put in an electric beater—then, not iced all over and then cut up, but cut up into dainty fingers, and each one iced all over separately. Pink and white icing, with no decorations whatever to hide any imperfections. There must not *be* imperfections. Each finger must be just about two inches long, and not more than one inch wide, and the pink must be a pale, dainty pink, and the white a gleaming satin white.

There would be two large bowls of macedoine of fruit, with maraschino. A trifle, of course, and even the humble jelly, but the jelly must be orange and, of course, it must be made with fresh oranges and lemons, and sugar and gelatine, and whites of egg.

Mrs. Morton came to help me, and stayed a little while on the day of the dinner, but she could only stay a short time, and go back to do her own dinner.

Sheila did my fish, and helped me clear up, storming at me most of the time for being mad enough to do this.

"You know you're not very strong, you should have told her you needed more help—gimme that board, I'll scrub it."

In all this you must remember, we had no "Fridge". Just the old-fashioned ice-box, with blocks and blocks of ice out in the backyard in the coolest place we could find—and finding a cool place in London in June——!

I had two big larders, and fortunately both of them were very cool; cool enough to keep my chickens in, and near enough through a passage to the footmen's and chauffeur's rooms!

I saw the tail end of Robert's shoes disappear into his room in a hurry, about nine o'clock, and my larder door was open.

I went quietly along, and there they were, sitting on Robert's bed, devouring a whole cold chicken between them! There was nothing I could do, and I had plenty anyway.

I can only ask you, humbly, to believe that I did all this. How, I cannot now explain, but it is a fact that I did it.

Three days' work before it, and I had been well schooled in basic preparations—no skilled help, just a succession of women in to wash up, and culminating in the day of the dinner itself. The staff still to be fed, and still grumbling.

Mrs. Leonard sent her lady's maid down to see if she could be of some help. She was sure she could do some little job for me.

She squeezed two lemons, and then went off, waving her fingers fastidiously in the air. She didn't want to get her hands dirty.

After it had all gone up, about one o'clock in the morning, I went up to the top floor with three saucers of ice-cream for the lady's maid and the two housemaids.

They took me down to the nursery floor, from which I could see right down on to the front hall, and also the wide, spiral marble staircase leading to the balcony of the first floor. Spread in the semi-circle made by the curve of the stairs, was the table laden with the colourful supper, on silver dishes, on a white cloth, and I see no reason why I should not be proud of such a display. It reminded me of that first dance supper I had seen six years before—when I had first ventured downstairs without my cap.

I turned and went through the door on to the back staircase and went slowly down. Just before I reached the first floor, a gentleman in evening dress came out from the front hall, and then I saw that the butler was just outside the door.

The gentleman said something to the butler and gave him a pound note. I thought nothing of it. Tips never came my way, except for that first and only one of ten shillings. I never had another all my life.

But I heard the butler say in the pantry later, "Not a bloody cent from any of the b——s. Mouldy, stingy lot!"

I opened my mouth to speak, and then thought better of it. He would only have denied it and made more trouble for me. I saw Johnny, the chauffeur, get something when he opened a car door for a departing guest. Whether Robert got anything or not, I don't know, but they all assured me solemnly that none of them got a penny.

Gradually the guests drifted over to the Swedish Embassy, and the food began to come down.

About 2 a.m. we were told by the butler that the drawing-room was empty, if we'd like to come up and see the house opposite.

The blaze of light from the drawing-room opposite lit up the street, and the sound of music made my feet tap.

We could see them dancing, and someone pointed out the Princess to me. She wore white—I think it was a lacy kind of dress, and she had a red rose on it, or in her dark hair, I can't remember. She looked radiant and happy, and as though she could go on dancing right through till the *next* morning. I think she was only seventeen then.

I went back down to the gloom of the kitchen.

The empty, or near empty, dishes began to come down, but by four o'clock everything was put away, and I was helping in the pantry, with the glasses, wiping them and polishing them. There were hundreds, all shapes and sizes.

I hadn't really eaten a meal since six o'clock the previous morning. Tit-bits and tastes, from ice-cream to lobster and chicken sauce, and back to consomme, all day long, but I had not had a *meal*. I wasn't hungry, and I had had lots of ice-cream.

When we had cleared up a lot of the glasses, I went outside to the area door—I seemed to be all alone in the whole world. Even the dance music in the Embassy was hushed.

Dawn was just coming—a pink glow over the grey chimneys was all I could see.

It occurred to me at that moment to wonder what advice the elegant ladies of the magazines would give me now. I don't know whether I looked tired—I hadn't looked at myself for twenty-two hours—I certainly didn't feel tired, but I must have been tired. But to the ladies of the magazines I didn't really exist, except as a species, not as an individual.

I went back to the pantry.

The butler handed me a tumbler, an ordinary half-pint tumbler filled with a golden yellow liquid.

"Here, drink this, Mrs. Rennie. It will do you good."

"What is it?"

"Just some lemonade with a drop of brandy in it. Go on, drink it up."

So I did.

It was delicious.

I didn't know that he and the footman had been systematically emptying every glass of practically every known drink under the sun into that tumbler all evening. It was everything, from gin to vodka and back.

I floated on a rosy cloud up to the attic—I don't remember my feet touching the stairs at all. I dived into my room— you remember it overlooked the front door and therefore overlooked the drawing-room opposite. I wanted to see the Princess again.

I shoved my head out of the window, but I didn't know till I heard the shower of glass that the window was shut!

At some point during the day the sash-cord had broken and the window came down. I, not expecting a shut window, and being quite beautifully drunk anyway, just concluded that all I had to do was look out of the window and I'd see the Princess.

Mercifully, an ambassadorial car was just moving away from the front door—the shower of glass fell mostly on the roof, and some on the pavement, but nobody was hurt.

I just drew my head in again, dropped my overall and underclothes on the floor, and lay down in my bed, with only the sheet over me.

I woke at seven—feeling as fresh as a daisy!

Everyone was very late that morning, and Mr. and Mrs. Leonard went out, visiting, I suppose, for the day. She was very pleased with the dinner and supper, except that she thought the cream of rice was a little too sweet.

It's still a puzzle to me how anybody could taste anything, with all those different drinks.

However, she could never admit that the whole thing was a masterpiece of achievement by one pair of hands—unless you count the fish dishes out—as I didn't do them.

But she told me, very sincerely and very graciously, that I was especially commended by the then Bishop of London for a ham mousse that looked like a ham mousse, and tasted of —ham!

I was sufficiently repaid.

FORTY-EIGHT

Then there was Ascot.

Scenes upstairs about her new dress—tears and wild quarrelling in French—Mr. Leonard didn't like the dress, and refused to go with her if she wore it. Finally she was so upset that her lady's maid had to go with her, so then we saw the remarkable sight of our Miss Mason in the full glory of an Ascot dress and hat! Her own, of course: she had made the dress, and it was a wonderful creation. They all went off at last in the car—Johnny trying to look casual with Miss Mason sitting beside him! The huge picnic basket at the back, filled with good things that I had made. Nothing so simple as a cold chicken and salad—lobster patties and chicken patties, rolled bread and butter spread with creamed ham, lemon curd tarts, cake, cheese biscuits, home-made water biscuits, and the big lunch cake.

They were going to the Royal Enclosure for the races, and taking a party—then they would "rough it" with a picnic in the car.

I began to feel tired as the summer days went on and the heat intensified. The standard must never drop, and to keep it up called for long hours of standing and constant watch on ovens and stoves, on the huge stock-pot—although there were no coppers, and most of the pots and pans were of a distinctly inferior material, making work even more difficult.

Then came a morning when the last bit of strength in my weary body was gone. I went in to breakfast, and just sat blankly at the foot of the table, and couldn't even pass the cups of tea.

Kind hands led me to the basket chair beside the fireplace; weakly I tried to insist that I must see to the coffee—the coffee-pot was already burned dry—they made me sit still. Miss Mason was furious. She said she was going up to tell Mrs. Leonard that I was ill through overwork. When she came down, she said that Mrs. Leonard was most concerned, that she had repeated two or three times: "And she has become so ill in *my* service?"

Miss Mason told her that I had indeed become so ill in her service.

"Then she must have the day off. We will have something cold and help ourselves—tell her a cold lobster mayonnaise, with, of course, *consomme en gelee* to begin, a veal cutlet done in butter and cream, and a very nice salad—she knows how I like it—a cream of rice, and a macedoine of fruit—and if she will leave it cold, we will help ourselves."

They went out to lunch, but the staff wanted lunch and supper left for them.

Mrs. Leonard's idea of a "cold supper and we'll help ourselves" took me till four o'clock to prepare. I had to order a lobster, and a large veal steak, and fresh fruit, and I could only move very slowly, and I had no help.

Fortunately I had consomme—it was easy to put it in the silver soup tureen in the ice-box; but the rest of the simple cold supper had to be done, somehow.

At four o'clock everything was prepared and left in the cold larder.

By this time I was beyond all feeling—either tiredness or anything else. I was a blank automaton. I found myself upstairs and automatically went straight to the bathroom, for I had long ago graduated from the luxury of "having *a* bath" once a week to the necessity of "having *my* bath" daily.

I dressed in a little new summer frock and made my way to my cousin in Addison Road. I reached there about six o'clock, and I sat in the garden, not speaking or reading or anything, till nine o'clock, when she called me for supper.

As usual, there was a crowd in, and I brightened up a little with the company and the supper.

I didn't leave till after half-past ten, and I took the bus all the way back in the cool of the summer evening.

I looked in at the kitchen when I got back.

A simple cold supper and we'll help ourselves?

Every square inch of the table and dressers was littered with dishes and plates, and bread and butter, coffee-pot, staff dishes—everything was just dumped and left. It was nobody's job, but it would have to be mine. I put all the food away and washed up.

I had been thinking, coming along on a 73 bus, that perhaps I should leave and go home. But I thought, principally, that Mrs. Leonard might find it difficult to get a cook, and I knew she liked my cooking. I knew it was good. I thought, also, that it was too late now for a shoot, either in the Highlands of Scotland or any of the shires, so that it meant again that I would have to consider a small place—even smaller, and perhaps worse, than Mrs. Leonard. But my principal reason was, as I said, that I had the stupidity to think myself indispensable.

When I saw the mess in the kitchen I was not so sure that I cared very much whether she could do without me or not.

Although I was a good cook, I was definitely a failure in other ways. I couldn't control staff—if you could call young Katie and an occasional charwoman "staff". But I was certainly not good at being in authority. That I had to learn, too, the hard way. So I made up my mind to wait till the 1st October and give my notice.

What I didn't know, and nobody told me, although they all knew via the maid and the butler, was that Mrs. Leonard went out that day—the day of the simple cold supper—and got herself a cook!

When I went to the drawing-room the next morning she told me that she thought I wasn't really strong enough for this work and I should try something else—she waved her arms vaguely—so she felt that she was wrong to keep me when it was obviously too much for me, and she didn't really eat a great deal herself—but she thought I needed more authority: "I need a cook who can—ascertain herself...."

I knew she meant "assert" herself, but she just lost her English for a few minutes, in the extremity of her feelings, and I couldn't assert myself—I was too frightened.

I was to go the next day. I was paid up to the end of the month (which was in about two weeks' time) and board wages for two weeks, and that was that.

FORTY-NINE

I packed my trunk and sent it off in advance, and sent a telegram to my mother to meet me at Glasgow.

I looked ruefully at the new dress and coat, hat and shoes that I had bought, at a total cost of £8 10s., just a few weeks ago. I would have liked the £8 10s. now.

I made the journey to Glasgow and I saw my mother. She looked at me, but she actually didn't know me. I had to go right over and speak to her, and she nearly fainted.

I was as skinny as a rake. I was down to just over seven stone, and I could do nothing but shed floods of tears. She took me home. There wasn't anything wrong with me that a good rest, the wonderful air of my home, and the love we had in abundance wouldn't put right. My sister was out of work, but Mother was still working, and they managed, without undue hardship, to help me get well. We had moved to a district in the centre of the town, to an attic, with the wide view of the whole of the Clyde, from Dumbarton Rock, nearly to Dunoon, on a clear day.

I was young and resilient, and I was an important person at home—I have been very much loved. So I was well enough in a few weeks to start work again.

This time I decided to stay in town—I could get a job with one of the West End families, and I would be able to get home and see my mother oftener.

Besides, there was another reason!

I met Bill; we danced together and fell in love.

He was tall and fair and handsome and clean-looking.

And I thought this would last for ever.

I met him on 13th November 1930, on a wet Sunday night, and I loved him till November 1945.

He told me he would never marry and I thought I could make him change his mind—but it was all on my side.

I know now I was too glad to be with him, too easily attainable, too openly and sincerely devoted, and I frightened him by being so fiercely possessive. Well, I've told you I never was wise and clever—I've always been foolish and honest.

Poets and writers have told of first love with abler pens than mine. There is something about our first love that stays, an inward memory that never loses it sweetness. Although the years and circumstances change our ideals and our hearts, nothing can destroy or take away the magic moments of our first real love, even in the deeper contentment of shared joys and sorrows.

FIFTY

I got the job I had planned as cook, with a kitchenmaid, in the West End. There was a butler, parlourmaid, two housemaids, myself, and a kitchenmaid. The butler had been with the family for about forty years, the head housemaid for about five, the under-housemaid about the same. The parlourmaid was new, and my kitchenmaid and I were new.

I found I had to clear the kitchen, as I had first seen it done in Yorkshire, for the lady of the house, Mrs. Caird, to come down in the morning. Sometimes she came at ten, sometimes just after breakfast, sometimes not till eleven. She wasn't a bit pleased when she found I had some work on the table and some pans on the stove when she came one morning at eleven. Fresh scones had to be made every morning, and dished on a folded napkin in a silver dish to go up for breakfast. The butler told me that fresh scones had been going up to the dining-room every morning for forty years, and never seen one eaten yet.

So one morning I warmed up the scones from the previous day—they were lovely scones, and well kept. They were crisp, but soft to eat, and well-risen, and they went up hot. There was none eaten, but Mrs. Caird said she preferred fresh scones for breakfast.

I was, of course, free to go out when I liked, after dinner, and I had one afternoon and evening a week, and the usual alternate Sunday afternoons and evenings. It was much easier here, as there was no entertaining. In fact it was quite dull, and I couldn't do any really nice cooking at all. They liked good plain Scots fare!

One morning as I did the kitchen fire (oh, yes, that was my job; when I was scullerymaid it was my job, when I was kitchenmaid it was my job, now I was cook, it was still my job!) I heard a loud clatter—something fell in from the chimney, and the fire wouldn't light!

There *was* a to-do!

Such a thing had never happened before, it must, of course, be my fault. The chimney got mended, and life went on its unruffled way. Such things should not be allowed to interfere with the comfort of the Cairds. There was a fixed routine—fixed by God—for the class to which Mrs. Caird belonged, and another fixed routine for the common people —also fixed by God.

Part of Mrs. Caird's routine was a systematic walk, every morning, armed with sheets of fresh tissue-paper, round the front hall, staircase, and public rooms which the housemaids had left spotless and polished and dustless at five minutes to nine. As soon as she'd finished breakfast, she would get her box of tissue paper out and, with a fresh sheet, she would "dust" every surface she could find. She made not the slightest scrap of difference to the bannisters, or the tables, unless it was to make scratches on them.

She must have been a god-send to the paper manufacturers.

With memories of how my cousin Sheila had entertained her friends, I asked one or two friends in for supper occasionally. My old friend whom I used to dance with, one of the two who fought about me, and another boy I knew, with my sister and one or two other friends.

It was unheard of—"*FOLLOWERS!*"

So, after two or three times, when the butler turned nasty with me, it eventually came to madam's ears, and she was most icily indignant about it.

"Men" in her house!

Well, I shouldn't have done it, but I could see no harm in it. The supper was modest, and usually it was made up shepherds' pie, or something equally economical. But I did it—and I was wrong. So one day Mrs. Caird informed me that she thought she would have to make a change.

"I wanted, really, an older cook. There was not one when I engaged you, but they seem to be getting more plentiful now."

As if they were a crop that had its season for blooming!

She also told me, and this was six weeks after I had been there, and I had made cakes and scones and biscuits, and even some bread, to keep my hand in, that she had had my reference from Mrs. Leonard, and Mrs. Leonard couldn't say whether I was a good baker or not, as I had never made any cakes for her!

Shades of pink and white fingers, and rich lunch cake, for the Princess's dinner!

That blow fell just before Christmas, but in two days I was in another job, just across the road. A smaller house—I was gradually coming down in the social scale!—and only three servants!

And I was back to the front-door steps again!

But what a lady!

She was small, and timid, and sweet—she reminded me of nobody so much as my own mother, and in all my experience I never met a kinder or more considerate woman to work for: it was a pleasure and an honour to serve her.

I went to her just before Christmas 1930, and early in the year we three servants—housemaid, parlourmaid, and cook—went down with 'flu, all at the same time.

Mrs. Lane was an angel.

She looked after all three of us; she and her two daughters kept the house going, and the cooking done, as well as bringing little tempting dishes for us upstairs. I must have been a nuisance to everybody, for I started having nightmares in which a big black bear would hop out of my wardrobe and I would wake screaming. These nightmares didn't last long, though.

As soon as we could, we got downstairs, and we all felt so grateful to Mrs. Lane for her kindness. But she only said she was glad we were better—she was so good.

Later, in the early summer, the family all went to America, so we were all out of jobs. The other two girls were from the Highlands and I think they went back there. But Mrs. Lane gave me a personal recommendation to another lady—this time with only two servants! But I thought I'd better take it, as I'd been recommended.

But I was in my home town, I could see my mother, and also the boy I was so madly in love with. And I did.

I had very good time off—and with the young parlour-maid who had been at Mrs. Caird's, we met for picnics and rambles among the hills and glens in the summer sunshine, and parties when it came to winter.

Meanwhile, still dormant, but not dead, was my dream—the only real dream—of singing. And, strangely enough, it was the fishmonger's delivery boy who gave me courage again.

It was a gay, bright July morning—I cleared the kitchen from the breakfast things and flung the back door open, as I cleared out the little larder just by the back door.

I started to sing, timidly at first, then, as nobody stopped me, I gained in volume and clarity. I danced across to the kitchen and saw the fish boy standing there with a parcel of fish in his hand. He was a young English lad.

I stopped and gaped at him.

Cheekily, but with tremendous assurance, he said: "Coo! Working in a kitchen with a voice like that?"

Cheeky youngster! I suppose he was no more than four-teen.

"How long have you been there?" I demanded.

He grinned.

"Long enough to enjoy your singing. Why don't you go on the stage?"

I flicked my dishcloth at him and he went away, whistling the song I'd been singing.

But he gave me an idea and the courage to carry it out—I

still *had* the voice, it seemed—fish boys are notoriously critical!

So I made the second of my four attempts.

I wrote to the gentleman who had been our head music teacher in high school, and I recalled to his memory that I had been considered the best singer in the choir of that time, and also that I had sung a solo—a verse of a song with three girls singing the other three verses—at the breaking-up concert in the year I had left. The song we sang was "Maiden of Morven", and I can see myself now, knowing it was my last day at school, singing with a broken heart:

> "... *Blunt my spear and slack my bow,*
> *Like an empty ghost I go.*
> *Death the only hope I know—*
> *Maiden of Morven*"

And I was indeed an empty ghost on that night!

He replied that he remembered me perfectly and he would be delighted to teach me to sing.

So I went to him, and he did do my voice a great deal of good, but things were getting bad in the town, and it seemed awful for me to put my hard-earned money on what might after all be *only* a dream.

I kept on, and then Mr. Fraser said he would like to enter me for the county Musical Festival, to be held in February. So he did.

I practised as much as I could: I couldn't much in the kitchen, because the people would have objected, and it wasn't easy at home—only a little attic, with two rooms and kitchen, and the two rooms with no heating in them, but I did try.

I improved my cooking, too, and Mrs. Eldon told me she had never had such cooking.

On my Sunday nights off they had a "cold supper and helped themselves". I remembered that from London.

They helped themselves all right, and left things where they were. So the dining-room had to be cleared, and all the things washed-up when the other maid and I came in on a Sunday night.

She gave a few parties, but nothing like I had been used to.

It was a static job, and I am the *least* static of persons. The sort of job which would have suited an elderly woman who only wanted to be sure of a roof over her head for her later years.

168

I was not an elderly woman, and the last thought was a roof over my head.

I was still young, and erratic and flighty, and, even if I *was* very much in love, still a good girl. The rest came later.

But the job was a job—in this town and age of no jobs—and I was well and gloriously happy. I was in love—really in love this time—this was no affair of dancing and motor-bikes, and kissing in the servants' hall, and I was singing again.

What more could I ask?

But even that, it seemed, was too much to ask of Fate.

On a Sunday evening in January I was at home. I went with my mother to put her on her bus for the place she worked in, and I said, as we walked down the road, "I've got a wee sore throat when I swallow——"

"Take a hot lemon when you go in, and if it's not all right in the morning come home and get the doctor."

I took the hot lemon before I went to bed, after I'd done all the washing-up, and in the morning I couldn't even speak. I couldn't raise my head from my pillow. I knocked on the wall when I heard Maisie, the house-parlourmaid, in the kitchen, looking for her morning tea.

She was horrified.

I was a ghastly grey and my throat and face was all swollen.

The doctor came—I was really determined to have something this time, no single illness would do for me, I must hog the lot.

'Flu, tonsilitis, and quinsey throat.

Three weeks before the Festival.

If I could have cried I would have done, but I couldn't cry.

As soon as I could be moved, Mrs. Eldon sent me home in her car, and the very next day, she sent me a letter with my insurance card and a month's wages—she "didn't think I was strong enough for this work, and if I was going to concentrate on singing my work would suffer...."

Hasn't all this happened before?

Yes, of course it has, and it happened again, too.

Other people get ill, and go off and get well, and come back to work. I take ill, or try to use my spare time to make myself a niche that I want to be in, and I get the sack. I have often wondered why, and I have never found out, but it went on happening.

It would be lovely if I could tell you that in spite of all these set-backs I went ahead and won a gold medal at the Festival. Well, I didn't.

It's true, the worst of my attack was soon over, and as soon as I could croak at all I went back to Mr. Fraser. He told me to take it easy till the week before the Festival; when he heard me then he was dubious about my strength, but he said my voice was very sweet and clear. It was very weak, but then so was I, and singing needs the strength of a lion, which I've never had.

I went to the Festival, and sang the two songs "Braw, Braw Lads" and "The Gallant Weaver".

The adjudicator said, as he awarded me fourth place:

". . . this very excellent competitor makes us all feel it is a joy to listen to her. Her words are perfectly clear, and her top notes are a delight. I could wish her lower voice a little steadier and her breathing wants a great deal more attention. I'm sure her teacher will see to that. But I would like her to smile a little when she is singing of the boy she says she loves —*I* thought she was going to cry!—still perhaps when she *is* in love she will give us that smile which tells it in a song. But for these things I have mentioned, I might have been able to give her better marks, but I'm sure she has a great future, if she works hard—it is a very lovely voice..."

May I beg your indulgence—these were not the *exact* words, and I didn't even hear all of them. But I heard the beginning, and the end, and I heard the bit about being in love.

So I had a great future, had I?

FIFTY-ONE

By this time life had resolved itself into a desperate necessity just to be in work, anywhere, any kind. I didn't want to leave home, but it looked as though I would have to.

I took various posts, I tried many things.

A well-known Scottish weekly magazine put out a competition for a summer love-story.

I wrote one and sent it off and thought no more about it.

To my astonishment, in about three weeks' time, I had a

letter from the editor to the effect that the story had not been considered up to the standard of a prize in the competition, but he was keeping it for publication at ordinary rates!

Well, it must have suited the editor's mentality, for it was a stupid hotch-potch of outworn cliches and stock situations, and the inevitable happy ending—it was silly mush, and I'm not surprised that the readers didn't demand more of the same kind!

But I got a cheque for four guineas.

It was not long before I was back in London, having taken a post as cook in a house in Seymour Street.

I was in Lyons at Marble Arch one evening having supper. A very dark, handsome young man sat down at my table and said hadn't we met before somewhere? I said I couldn't remember him. He appeared to be racking his brains for something—remember, I had never met this "line" before, *nor* the "husband-whose-wife-doesn't-understand him" line either—and I thought he was quite genuine in his belief that he had seen me before.

You see, although my life had been hard up to now, it had been very sheltered from the storms and stresses of the outside world.

So I was very polite, but I tried to be kind.

Then he said he thought he'd seen me in a musical show. I brightened at that, "Oh no, I'm not in anything like that, but I want to be, so much. You see, I can sing, and——"

"But of course you should be! You have the looks, and the figure, and you have beautiful eyes. Tell me, what are you doing now?"

My eagerness went.

"I'm—I'm working—for—a lady."

"Oh! Secretary? Lady's maid?"

"No—I'm a cook."

"Good heavens! You should be starring in a West End show! Can you meet me to-morrow night! I could take you to a friend of mine who runs a show."

"I couldn't be here before half-past nine."

"That will do beautifully. I'll meet you here to-morrow night at nine-thirty, and you'll soon be in the West End! Don't forget."

As if I could!

I finished my coffee in a dream—it never dawned on me to wonder why he had rushed away without even finishing his coffee, or why he couldn't have taken me to his friend that night, or any of the hundred and one other things that were so self-evident.

Soppy idiot! I just believed him.

I went down to the ladies' toilet, and thoughtfully powdered my nose. If I was going to be in a show soon, and I was quite sure I was, I would have to get a little flat—I believed that was what all the West End stars did.

Oh, yes, I was a star already!

I was certainly willing to work hard, but I was convinced it wouldn't be long until I was at the top.

I didn't hurry—there was now no restrictions on my in-comings—and I made my way out.

Just at the door, in among the crush of people, I saw him: he had his back to me, and he was talking to another man.

I made my way to him, as I reached the door he was just saying, obviously carrying on his conversation, without knowing that I was there, ". . . yes—some bloody skivvy with ideas!"

I stood rooted, and his friend saw me, without, of course, knowing that I was the skivvy under discussion.

I walked right past them, and was followed by a burst of horrible laughter that hurt, and brought tears to my eyes. So I went home and shed them.

FIFTY-TWO

Searching for work, for I had decided to leave Seymour Street, I read the evening paper, and I can see now the advertise-ment that changed my way of life, for a short time anyway.

I read: "Attractive dance hostesses required for select West End Night Club. No experience required", and it gave a telephone number in the West End.

It seemed to be the answer to my prayers.

"No experience." "Attractive." "Dance Hostess."

I certainly had no experience—I was not beautiful, but I *was* attractive, and I *could* dance!

In trembling anticipation I phoned the number given. I was told to come along straight away to an address in Shaftesbury Avenue.

I went.

I found the place, downstairs under a shop. There were some tables round a tiny floor; there were one or two men standing about, and then there came forward to speak to me a little man, who was obviously Indian. He was, as I found later, a kind, cultured, and altogether likeable little man. He told me that they paid no salary, but that the girls were paid for dancing with the customers, and some of them made £10, £20, and even £30 a week!

Well, of course, *I* didn't know any better.

To me, the glamour of the words "night club" was still very real. I didn't know the tawdry side of it.

And the way I took my fate in my hands on that plunge amazes me now!

For plunge I did.

"Whatever you do—do it with a will——"

I was due to leave my present post at the end of the week, and to start in the night club on Monday night. My hours were to be from 10 p.m. till 4 a.m., and all I would have to do was to wear evening dresses and be nice to the guests, and dance. When I asked if any theatrical people ever came in there, I was told, grandly, that of course the best people came there. So I was sure now that this would be my Chance.

On the day, I took a taxi round to Mount Royal. I'd always wanted to stay there, and now I *knew* I could afford it!

I sent some money home, rather more than usual, and I had a few pounds saved; I thought I might not make more than five pounds for the first week, but I would certainly make more as the time went on.

So I went into it—wide-eyed, eager, and innocent.

Let me explain that word "innocent".

By this time I was neither virginal nor innocent—I was desperately in love, and I thought of all kinds of things to make him want to marry me. All the wrong way, of course, but I still didn't know that:

But innocent in this—that I had not the faintest idea what went on in a night club, or out of it, for that matter.

Intensely truthful myself, I could never believe that people were not telling me the truth, and being honest was a terrible handicap.

Well, I had a very nice and very glamorous week-end in London; and on Monday I went to look for "digs". This was something entirely new to me, and already I was revelling in my new-found freedom.

I wandered up Shaftesbury Avenue, and I turned into a street on the right-hand side—Neal Street. The actual building is gone now, but there was a street door, with a stone passage inside. I was admitted by a blowsy-looking female who said, "Of course she had a lovely room, dearie." I said I was going to work in a night club, and would be going out at night till the morning, would that be all right?

Yes, yes, that would be all right—here is the room.

On the left of the passage—a bare linoleum with a rag of carpet beside the iron bed; a washstand with some broken crockery on it; a chair, and a fireplace, and a cupboard.

And a key for the door.

That was a mercy.

It would be ten shillings a week rent.

I paid her two weeks in advance and went and brought my luggage, *all* my luggage—a trunk and two suitcases, filled with lovely clothes, and my white overalls and working shoes.

The room was passably clean, and the bed linen, although not fresh from the laundry, was at least unused.

But nothing mattered, except one glorious fact, I was Out of Service!

And I was Free!

There was only one snag—there was no bathroom, and I was used to my daily bath; but that was a small discomfort when I thought of what the near future would bring. But it was hard even to do without hot water.

However that, too, I took in my stride. Nothing could go wrong now.

I went to bed in the afternoon and had a sleep. About two doors away was a little café, and I called in there when I had dressed, for a cup of tea and a little meal.

The café proprietor looked at me in some surprise, but he made no comment then.

Then I passed the time in resting and reading, and even in some unpacking!

I dressed slowly and carefully, in my good black and white evening dress (I had bought it at a lady's "Wardrobe" shop, and it had belonged to a very famous stage star). It was a lovely dress, and even up to 1945 it was still wearable. I made it into a summer house-coat, and dyed it red, and it's still alive! It was really lovely, and I paid twenty-six shillings for

174

it. I think Evelyn Laye must have paid about sixty guineas for it—but I'll bet she didn't get as much pleasure out of it as I did! Every time I see or hear of Evelyn, I think of that lovely dress.

I had, too, a cheap, imitation grey squirrel coat that I thought was the last word in elegance. It really looked quite nice, although I knew it was not the right kind of thing to wear over the model gown. But there, it was the best I had, and it *looked* nice.

So off I went—to my very first night club!

I walked down Shaftesbury Avenue in my silver shoes (the kind I'd promised myself I would have when I saw the Duchess wearing them).

I got to the club and went downstairs.

The place was a blaze of light now, and I could see the wall decorations—there seemed to be a lot of nude females in the paintings, but I wasn't altogether sure if I approved of such blatant obscenities.

I met the "girls".

Rosie, a big dark-haired handsome girl. Mary, red-haired and hard-looking—I didn't like her very much. And Pat, who sold cigarettes, and wore long black stockings, and a wee frilly skirt that just covered her bottom, and a very low cut blouse. They were all heavily made-up, and I must have looked a country bumpkin!

For a good many nights I just sat, longing to dance; I saw the floor show and the band, and I saw how everybody sat up and looked hopeful when the doorman bawled at us, "Customers!"

But I was still entranced with it all.

I made no money at all the first week.

I asked Rosie when I would get paid for the dancing I'd been doing. I hadn't enjoyed it, because the men who danced with me were mostly drunk, and one or two put their hands on my bare back and tried to get round under my dress.

But *still* I couldn't see...

I couldn't make men buy drinks for me, and I wasn't at all a success.

I persuaded the band to let me sing one evening.

Fancy singing "The Bonnie Banks o' Loch Lomond" to a bunch of morons at three o'clock in the morning!

That's what I did.

And I was nervous and had stage fright, and the band

weren't interested anyway. I was just a dull, uninteresting female who—what was it?—"...a skivvy with ideas...."

I was there three weeks, and I made the total sum of twelve shillings and sixpence—and that was, legitimately, for dancing. But I had to ask for that, and I just *couldn't* bring myself to ask a man for money. Not even although it was in the job.

We also got a good breakfast, of two or three eggs, sausages, tomatoes, and chips.

I'd got quite friendly with the café proprietor in my street. He was very kind, and he tried to help me all he could.

I don't think he ever slept. He would be there when I came back about four or five in the morning, and I went in for a cup of tea. I loved the London streets at that time in the morning—they were so clean and empty and romantic.

One morning I was having my cup of tea as usual, and a little cripple man came in and looked at me, in evening dress.

"Good morning," he said.

"Good morning," I said.

"In show business?"

"No—night club."

"Do you want to be on the stage?"

"Oh yes!" Soft mark! Jean, will you never learn?

"What can you do? Sing?"

"Yes."

"Dance?"

"No—just ballroom dancing."

He nodded.

"I've got a lot of connections," and that was quite true, too. That little man was notorious around theatre-land—all who know the theatre will know who I mean. He died very recently.

"I've got my flat just over here, come and let me hear you sing."

"At this time in the morning?"

He shrugged. "I sleep most of the day, like you——"

"But people—won't it disturb them?"

"I don't think so, come with me."

Well, believe it or not, I went up some dark and evil-smelling stairs, and into a foul-looking room. I was petrified —but not for long.

He wasted no time on preliminaries.

I scream very well indeed.

"You so-and-so little fiend," he yelled at me, "how the hell *do* you think you're going to get into the theatre world?"

But I got away safely.

If the way in was via his filthy bed, I'd stay out.

I was afraid to go near my café again in case he'd be there, but just the next morning a very queer thing happened that changed my life again.

I'd been living in my little hovel of a room for nearly three weeks and I had had no trouble at all. My money was nearly done, but I had paid my rent.

Only, one night there was a knock at my door. I opened it, and there stood a great tall handsome black boy! He had a cheerful grin and he raised his hat and asked me if I'd like him to come in for the evening!

Hurriedly, I shook my head and shut the door, with him still trying to persuade me that he'd be very good to me—he had lots of money—he showed me a roll of notes.

I was terrified in case the landlady would come.

But I had no more trouble, and he always grinned at me when he saw me. I think if I had been forced to choose, I would have chosen that boy in preference to the man who so glibly promised me "a chance". He did look *clean*.

But that was the only episode in the actual lodgings.

The morning after that fight up in the bedroom, I came back as usual about four-thirty and looked fearfully in the café!

My would-be "benefactor" wasn't there, but seated there was a tall, fair-haired young man, big and broad-shouldered, with a look of the sea about him. He was wearing a seaman's roll-necked jersey and sea boots.

He saw me and I saw him, and he said, "Hello".

And I took another plunge—no, I didn't fall in love—that was already arranged, but I was attracted, so attracted that, like the little asterisk again, I rushed in.

Like the heroine in silly stories in magazines, I blurted out:

"Oh! Will you help me?"

He looked astonished, but he said, "I will if I can."

I wasn't sure about his accent, but I found out afterwards it was Australian.

Then I told him about the little man, and the café proprietor, bless him, backed me up.

". . . so, you see, if you could be in here to-night I could come in just before I go to the club and pretend you're my cousin, or my brother, or something. Then he wouldn't annoy me any more."

"He was in last night, looking for her," said the café man.

"There, you see!" I said.

But it worked, just as I planned, and just as the story books put it.

Fred and I became very good friends, not lovers, as he would have liked, although we did later take rooms in the same house and have midnight picnics of cold chicken.

But I was saved for a wee while anyway.

Then came the Thursday night of my third week at the club.

My money was getting really low and I couldn't tell anybody, because I had raised such high hopes when I came into this life, and for the first time in my life I didn't send any money home.

My father was unemployed, like so many, and my sister, who only got a very small wage, was not always able to send a great deal, perhaps ten or fifteen shillings a month.

In addition, my father had attempted to walk with the thousands of men who hunger-marched on London the previous year. But he always suffered very badly from varicose veins in his legs, so he was unable to go very far. But the miles he did walk made him unfit for work, and as he hadn't enough stamps he didn't get any sick benefit. He never troubled to keep up union subscriptions, although many times he said he needed a lump sum to clear his union card, but it all went on drink. So it was then that my mother was driven to the Parish Relief; and I didn't know—she took the hurt and cruel savagery herself, and went on with the struggle.

But I just didn't have any money to send—the dreams of ten to thirty pounds a week were just dreams. Through it all, the little Indian proprietor of the night club treated us all in the same urbane, gentlemanly way, but it didn't give me any money.

During that third week the only meal I had was the huge breakfast we got about 4 a.m., and it was really good. One night one of the customers danced with me, bought a bottle of champagne, gave me five shillings, and made an appointment to meet me for lunch the next day. My only interest in the proceedings was the thought of lunch next day.

178

He didn't turn up.

On the Thursday night business was quiet and, even to me, the tawdriness was showing through.

The long night passed, and cured me for ever of night clubs. About three o'clock a well-dressed, rather stout little man went up the steps to go out. I hadn't even noticed him.

Half-way up the stairs he beckoned Rosie. Rosie went up, and they whispered together. Then she came down to me, to the table where the four of us were sitting.

With a jerk of her head she said, "He wants you, Jean."

"Me?"

"Yes, go on. Don't keep him waiting."

Wondering what was going to happen, I went up to meet him on the stairs.

He said very bluntly, "I'll take you home for a pound."

I looked at him in blank astonishment.

"I haven't got a pound," I said.

I wasn't being clever—I really thought he meant that he wanted a pound from me.

I told you I was quite ignorant of the whole set-up.

"Don't be so bloody insolent. I've only got a pound in change, and I'm not going to give you a cheque. Come on. I'll get a taxi—where do you live?"

I was in a shuddering state of fear. I have always feared a man's anger, and my remark, made in all sincerity and innocence, had made him very angry. He was quite purple with temper.

But I kept my ground, although the shock of knowing that he wanted my body for a pound was awful.

"You're mistaken. I don't do that sort of thing."

He sneered.

"You're not trying to tell me you're a virgin?"

"I'm not trying to tell you anything, except that I don't do that kind of thing—on principle."

"Principle!" he sneered again. "Talking about principle—*you*—in a place like this! Come on—don't be so bloody silly."

He grabbed my arm, but I pulled myself away, and left him standing there.

Then we heard the door bang as I reached the table again, white and shaking.

Rosie said, "What did he want, Jean?"

I said in a very wee voice, with the thought of unutterable things in my mind.

"He said he'd take me home for a pound."

Rosie said, "What did you say?"

"I said 'No' of course."

Rosie slapped me on the back.

"That's right, girl, never go under a fiver, we don't!"

If I was astonished before, I was absolutely speechless now.

"B-b-but—but, Rosie!" I stuttered, "I've never done anything like that in my life!"

"You mean you're a virgin?"

That was twice in one evening I'd been asked that.

I shook my head. "No ... but—I—don't ..."

Rosie looked serious.

"Now listen, girl. I knew you were different the minute you stepped in here—and it's no good you telling *me* you're not a virgin. I know a good girl when I see one. What clubs have you been in before?"

"I've never been in one, and I'm not an awfully good girl ... I ..."

"This is the first night club you've been in?"

I nodded.

"How old are you?"

"Twenty-nine."

"All right, if you want to put ten years on, but I don't believe you're a day over nineteen. I think you're some Society dame finding out how the poor working girl lives."

"I'm not! I'm not! I *am* twenty-nine, and I've never been in a night club——"

"What *have* you been working at?" said Rosie, with the obvious air of "*Now* I've caught her!"

I had to summon some courage to own up to what I had been doing—I don't think I could have taken another "bloody skivvy"—"I'm a cook," I blurted out.

The three girls looked at me in sheer amazement, and, more, a look of respect.

Rosie managed to speak—in a voice totally different to the one she'd been using.

"Do you—mean—you can—actually COOK?"

"Yes."

"You mean—you can get money—for cooking?"

"Yes."

"Real money? In your hand?" She made a gesture with her right hand on to the palm of her left, as though putting money in it.

"Yes."

"How much can you get?"

"Thirty-five shillings or two pounds a week."

There was a gasp.

Rosie took a deep breath.

"You mean you can actually get two pounds a week—every Friday, two pounds in your hand—for cooking—without—all this." And she waved round the room in a fateful gesture of despair.

"Yes, I can."

"Christ Almighty!" she breathed.

"When can you get a job?"

"To-morrow."

Rosie called a waiter over and ordered four whiskies.

They arrived in a moment, and Rosie pushed one over to me.

"Drink that—I don't know about you, but I need it. Now listen, kid——" She looked at me very seriously, and there was a kind and even affectionate look on her face, and in her eyes. It was very real. "Get out of here, and if I see you in one of these dumps ever again, I'll turn you up and spank you. Whatever you've done, and however old you are—although I can't believe you're twenty-nine—get out, get a clean job. Christ! What I wouldn't give to get a *clean* job." The girls drank their whisky, and seemed to be backing up Rosie. "So you get the hell out of here—and stay out! I knew you weren't one of us. Now come and have your breakfast, and promise me you'll get a job to-morrow?"

I promised, but I was very near to tears.

Thank you, Rosie, for giving me a new perspective, and pride in my knowledge.

We ate our breakfasts, and I said good-bye to the girls. I've never forgotten them—or that night.

FIFTY-THREE

Since that awful summer of 1935, let it be recorded a little to my credit that never again, till she died in 1949, did my mother know real hardship or suffer hunger. However much I hurt her, and only God and I know how much that was, I tried to make it up to her in material things. What the hurts of all the years did to her soul, I can only guess at. Nothing could alleviate the attacks on the clean, guileless mind. From my own adult life that had known many a sleepless night, eventually relieved on doctor's orders, by drugs, I can know that she must have lain many, many nights wondering what she had done to deserve yet one more blow.

It is not with any smug self-complacency that I say I was able to give her some ease and comfort in her later life. I was never able to take her away, for instance, from the attic we lived in and put her in a lovely house by the sea, with a garden, which was her proper setting. I was not able to help the poor mind when it finally went back to its happy, carefree childhood, and at a crisis in my life—did not even know me, her first-born.

But I am thankful, in a humble way, that I was at least able to buy her a good new bed, to see that she had coal for the winter, to have an electrician put a point in her bedroom, and give her an electric fire there, so that she was always warm.

And I am thankful, too, that during the next few months, she never knew the depths to which I nearly sank, but couldn't quite.

For two years I did temporary work. Then I fell ill.

I think I was really not quite recovered, and I was also still very weak, but my money was going down, and I had to get a job, and as it was 1937, and there was to be a Coronation, although not the one we had hoped for, I wanted to stay in London.

So when I felt able to walk, I went back to my agency.

As I was going in I bumped into a young man coming out. As we apologised to each other, I suddenly said in astonishment:

182

"John!" as he said "Jean!"

John, the footman who had come to my help when Mrs. Callan wanted to throw a bucket of water over me.

We went and had a cup of tea in Lyons, and he told me he was going to join the Navy in a few months, and he was taking his last job as a butler.

"I'm sick of that sort of life—I'm sick of being at their beck and call—there will be none of it left one day, soon. Anyway, I'm for a man's life."

He took my address, and I said I'd be moving in to a new job soon. He looked at me rather anxiously.

"Have you been ill?"

"Yes, I've had 'flu. Had it three years running. I don't know what's the matter with me."

"You've worked too hard. Look here, why don't you come down to mother for a week-end? It's lovely down there at Epping Forest."

"I'd love to, John, but I can't. I must get a job. I have to look after Mother. But maybe I will, soon."

"Jean—" he hesitated—"you—you haven't got married, or engaged, or anything?"

"No, John, not married *or* engaged, but——"

"But there is somebody?"

"Yes, John, there is somebody."

"Are you going to marry him?"

"No."

"Why not?"

"He doesn't want to marry me."

John looked at me, then he just said, rather under his breath, "The bloody fool!"

John was going to a job in the country for a few months, then he was going to the Navy.

We parted with a warm, friendly handshake, and I went to my interview with Dame Una Pope-Hennessy.

I saw her in the drawing-room, and she told me they had to be in town for three months, and her cook in Yorkshire was too old to travel, so she only wanted a temporary cook. She was willing to pay me thirty-five shillings a week, and I didn't ask any questions. I didn't care—it was a job, and I knew that whatever happened I would give my best, *all* the time, and would probably regret it, and vow never to do it again.

Besides, by this time I didn't think there was anything else that *could* happen to me!

What she didn't tell me, when she told me about the family, was that there was a Nanny.

There were no young children now, and this Nanny had attained her objective of making herself indispensable, so that she fancied herself as a housekeeper, and only wanted a bunch of keys to complete the illusion. She had been with the family nearly forty years—quite a lifetime, and quite long enough to have gained the confidence of the family.

There were a parlourmaid, a housemaid; one had been there ten years, the other eight. So I was quite a baby! And didn't they make me feel it!

The first morning I got there, Nanny presented herself efficiently right into my kitchen and announced that we always take eight pints of milk in the morning, and I will order the meat for you, and I know the greengrocer very well —and——"

"Thank you, Nanny. I *think* I'll manage the ordering myself. I've been doing it for nearly ten years now."

Well that was an open declaration.

I cooked, and washed-up, and scrubbed and cleaned, and got no thanks at all. And I worried—I really did worry—because I began to be afraid, perhaps I wasn't such a good cook after all? I know now it was only because I had been ill and was now in an actively hostile atmosphere, which thrust me back into myself, so that the happiness I found in giving was all thrown back at me.

The whole thing was they didn't want me.

When my cousin saw them when she came to tea one day, she said, "No wonder they don't want you, Jean—jealous old hens!"

"Jealous? Of me? For God's sake, why?"

"Just look at yourself, and look at them—if you're not quite daft, you'll see."

"Oh! *You're* the daft one! I'm nothing. My God! After thirteen years, where am I? No money, no prospects but years and years of this—and what about my voice? For I *have* a voice. You know I have——"

"Yes, I know you have. But those old hens are jealous of you because you look young and fresh, and your life's beginning——"

"*Beginning?*"

"Yes, your luck will turn some day, but even if it doesn't, remember singers are ten-a-penny—a good cook's worth her weight in gold. Don't you let this lot worry you."

Well, nobody has ever weighed me in gold, and I do know that singers, or even alleged singers, get more in an hour than I got in a month.

Ah, well!

It transpired, too, that the lady was a famous authoress. So, when she was in a fairly human mood one day I ventured timidly to inform her that I also wrote—fiction, short stories—in my spare time.

Yes, in spite of all I'd had, the rebuffs and slights, I still stuck out my neck for more.

She looked at some of my stuff, and she was most gracious about it. She said, of course, that it wanted developing—I certainly had a small gift, but in this particular story—she couldn't *see* the heroine—I wasn't very good at descriptions.

Fair enough. It was a reasonable criticism, and at least she did not laugh at me or throw the papers back in my face. Oh no—she was preparing a much more subtle revenge for my having seen through her Nanny.

Oh—Nanny.

"Nanny wants her supper early. Nanny's going out."

"Nanny wants her supper late. Nanny's having a friend to supper."

But only when the family was out, or away for a few days.

Well, I had several letters from John, who was going into the Navy, and soon he was asking me in his letters to marry him before he joined up.

I told him I couldn't, but I gave him the date I was leaving, and he wrote back and said he would come and collect me and take me down to his mother for the week-end.

I was writing one night in the sitting-room, and went to bed about eleven o'clock. I left cold suppers, as usual, and went straight to sleep as soon as I hit the pillow. I was awakened by a noise which sounded like the area gate. I thought of burglars, and I jumped to the window.

A huddle of people—I could see only indistinctly in the half darkness—then two figures left the huddle, two male figures in the unmistakable garb of the Royal Navy, and walked smartly across the road and up the street. I watched them for a few minutes until they disappeared.

I heard the back door shut, and went back to my bed. I hit the foot of the bed with my toe and swore, so I do assure you that I was not dreaming. There was a bruise on my toe for several days after that.

I switched on my light and looked at the clock—it said one-thirty. While I was up, I thought I might as well go to the bathroom, so I went out on the landing. The landing light was on and the two girls were just coming up, looking very guilty, carrying their shoes.

I just said "Good-night," and went on into the bathroom and back to bed.

When I got down in the morning I expected the usual slitter of dishes and cutlery and everything left. There wasn't so much as a teaspoon lying anywhere, the cloth was folded in the drawer, and even the left-over bread had been put away.

I said nothing at all about the incident. They could do as they liked with their free time and their lives (but when I invited John in to tea I was the one who was told I mustn't have "men" in the house). I wasn't interested in them. I think I can safely say that this was the only place I had ever been in where I had not one friend, and one must live through an experience like that to know what it's like. It's bad enough if one doesn't care, or doesn't feel anything, but I liked being friendly, and I still felt things deeply.

However, my time was soon up, and the day came when I was to meet John. I was really looking forward to a week-end in the country, and I left the future to take care of itself.

I was up early, and left the lunch and dinner all prepared, and now that they knew there would be no one to cook for them and clear up after them they tried to be nice. And they goggled when they saw John! He was even handsomer than he'd been ten years ago—I don't know why he hadn't married, he was now about thirty-three.

But I left the house gladly, and we took a taxi to Charing Cross, where I left my luggage. We reached the little cottage in time for lunch; it was a heavenly little place, near a railway, but not too near to be spoilt. The garden was a picture and now, in late April, it was glowing with daffodils, and some tulips were just showing. There were rose trees and strawberry beds, and a profusion of everything—peaceful and lovely.

The old people were nice—kind and friendly—and I was almost tempted to take John's offer and marry him! But I was stubbornly, foolishly in love, and I just couldn't.

I had a lovely, quiet, restful week-end; I just ate and slept, and walked a little with John, and went to church on Sunday morning. It was Tuesday morning when I came back to London, just the first week in May. London was exciting, all decorated for the Coronation, and I thought I'd take a job in Town, so that I could be here for the Great Day.

I had enough money, and I sent a few pounds home, and left myself with only about two pounds, but I didn't worry about that. I would be in a job in the morning.

I went to my registry office and said I'd like a job in Town —I didn't mind what it was, so long as it was in Town.

I thought she looked at me rather coldly. Then she said, "I'm afraid we haven't any jobs, Miss Rennie."

"Oh, well, I'm not worried for a day or two. I'll have a wee holiday. I'll look in again."

"I don't think we'll have anything suitable."

And now I realised she was serious.

Cold and cutting and callous.

"But—surely—there's lots of people in Town—the season's just beginning——"

"I'm afraid we won't be able to keep you on our books. Miss Rennie."

I just looked at her—speechless.

"Mrs. Pope-Hennessy does not give you a very good reference."

"But that's ridiculous, she always liked my cooking."

"She says your cooking is excellent, but——"

"But what?" I said quietly.

"Well—she tells us that you've been wasting time scribbling when you should have been working, and you've had men in the house" (she said the word "men" as though she'd heard of these animals but had never seen one). "And also" (she thought she'd better get it over all at once) "you've just been and spent the week-end with a man."

Of course, the correct servile attitude to that would have been to fall on my knees, wring my hands, and throw myself on the mercy of this all-powerful female and promise never to be a wicked girl again. That's what they would have liked.

I'm afraid I did none of these things.

The blood of my ancestors boiled over, against every one of these unjust and untrue accusations.

"The dirty rotten bitch!" I said. "I'll show her whether she can take away a girl's character or not. You can keep your jobs."

I had been on that registry's books for just over two years now, maybe more, I forget. They had found me dependable and co-operative. I went wherever they sent me, and carried out the contract, and *always* I had been well recommended. The fact alone that they could send me a telegram and know that I would go was surely enough.

But money cracked the whip—and they jumped.

I went round to the house, it was only a few steps away. I went up the steps to the front door and rang the bell. The parlourmaid opened it, and smiled—a treacherous leer that looked guilty.

"Oh, hello, Jean! It's nice to see you———"

"I want to speak to Mrs. Pope-Hennessy." I stepped past her into the hall, and she led me into the library.

"I'll—I'll see if she's in," the girl faltered.

"Aye, she's in all right! I've just seen her at the drawing-room window."

She scuttled out.

In a few minutes Madam came in, very haughty and Victorian-mistress.

I opened fire at once.

"What do you mean by telling the registry office that I had men in the house? Or that I wasted time scribbling?"

"I am not prepared to discuss the matter———"

"Well, I am! There *were* men in this house, till half-past one in the morning, but they weren't my friends. And you know perfectly well I did my writing when my work was done—you're not the only one who can write."

"I'm not prepared to discuss it. I'd much rather listen to my older servants who have been with me for years than to someone who comes into the house and makes trouble."

"Makes trouble? Who's made trouble for me? How am I to get another job? You've taken my character away. How am I to get my living?"

She shrugged, "I'll write a reference for you—you will wait here."

She went out of the room, and in a few minutes she came back, and handed me a folded piece of expensive notepaper.

Written on it were these words, burned into my brain.

May 1937.

To Whom it may Concern

Miss Rennie has been my cook for two months. She is a very good cook, and leaves of her own accord.

Una Pope-Hennessy

Damning with faint praise indeed.

I read the note, and something died, and something else was born inside me.

Storming at her was no good. I only made myself ill, and nothing could hurt her. I must regain what I had lost of my dignity and pride.

I tore the note across and across, and dropped it gently at her feet, turned round, and walked out. The parlourmaid was in the hall, obviously having been listening. I let her open the door for me, and walked out, my head high, but my eyes blinded and my heart sore, and it was no doubt a grand gesture, but utterly futile for me, and it didn't touch her at all. She forgot me as soon as the door shut.

All these many years I had heard of the power of "reference"—now I saw it in action, and I knew real Fear.

No matter where I went the people I went to would always insist on a reference from my last place, and I couldn't say I had been on holiday, or sick, for a couple of months.

I went back to the other registry office I used to deal with, and while they were rather kinder, the girl at the desk obviously didn't believe me, and said they would want to tell any prospective employer my previous place, and if my reference wasn't very good—well—she didn't finish.

I came out and wandered for a while in the park. I cannot find words to describe how I got through that day. I was thrown entirely on my own resources, and although I'd been working hard and sometimes unhappily for years, I had never been so utterly destitute, for now I had no character, and I began to wonder if I *was* a bad girl after all? Or if it would be better to be a bad girl?

Coming fresh from that simple, clean, lovely cottage with the steadfast kindness of the old folks, and John—it was a cruel shock, and I wanted to cry. Maybe I did, as I wandered.

The only clear thing in my mind was that I must keep this

from my mother. To do that, I must let her have an address so that she would know I was all right, and she would write to me.

I couldn't go to my sister—she was in the country—and I didn't like to go to my cousins.

It didn't occur to me to go and see Chef, although he must have been in Town with the Coronation so near. It didn't even occur to me to ask for a job in Lyons. I was completely stunned and unable to think, but I knew I must fight my own battles.

Vaguely, I saw vans and cars passing, and I suddenly remembered, or thought rather, about my grocer. He had said to me once, "If you ever want a job, let me know—I know most of the big houses."

His place was near Chelsea, and I walked there. I went into the shop and asked to see him.

I waited, wondering, when the man went to tell him—was it just another of those things that would end by his saying, "What a pity you didn't see me a week ago! I had a lovely job, would have done you nicely!" That sort of thing has happened to me too.

But he had always seemed a kindly, polite man, and I had always "nursed" my tradesmen, so that I didn't feel I was asking too much now.

The man came down and said, "Will you come up, please, Miss Rennie?"

I went up, and into a beautifully furnished office, carpet covered, with light oak furniture, a big desk, one or two chairs, and an open cocktail cabinet.

Mr. Barry stood up and held his hand out.

"Well, Miss Rennie! How are you? I haven't seen you for a long time. Would you like a drink?"

I said yes I would—it seemed to be quite the thing these days, although I shuddered to think what my mother would say!

He poured me a sherry, and then said, as he took his own, "Now what can I do for you? You want to change your grocer?"

"No—I want a job."

You see—straight out! No finesse, this girl! No gentle leading up—no savoir faire! Just straight, blunt, and to the point.

He laughed.

190

"You mean that?"

"Yes." I told him what had happened. He shrugged it away.

"These people—not *real* people—not worth worrying about. How'd you like to be head kitchenmaid at Court-auld's?"

"Where is it?"

"In the country." (I forget where they lived.)

"I want to stay in Town till after the Coronation."

He nodded.

"Well, something else will turn up. Meanwhile, where are you going to stay? Got any plans?"

"No—I sort of thought I'd be in a job. I suppose—no, I couldn't afford a hotel——"

"You couldn't get into one anyway. Come with me. I know a nice place in Victoria. She's clean and respectable, she only takes ladies, and she won't allow men visitors," he smiled.

He was picking up his phone and asking for a number.

"Mrs. Allen? Mr. Barry here. Have you a room for a very nice young lady? Oh yes—very respectable. Oh, about two weeks. Yes, all right, I'll bring her round now. Yes—the usual charge I take it? Right."

"All right. There we are—you'll have a roof over your head anyway. It's just a pound a week. Would you like to come down to the country for the day on Sunday? I've just bought a cottage near Slough, and I'm doing painting and gardening. I'll pick you up about ten. Let's go now."

He drove me to one of the hundreds of streets in Victoria, and rang a bell at the front door of a grim-looking house.

A very plain, rather forbidding woman opened the door. Mr. Barry said, "Here is Miss Rennie, Mrs. Allen. I'm sure she'll be very comfortable. Now I'll wait here for you while you see your room, and I'll collect your luggage for you."

I went up with Mrs. Allen, and she showed me into a very clean, bare room, with a gas fire and a gas ring, and a meter. It was clean, nice, and I would be able to rest. She gave me two keys, one for the front door and one for my own room.

I parted with one of my precious pounds, and wondered when I'd get any more.

We collected my luggage and I went into my room and unpacked.

I was still numb and a wee bit frightened. It was going to be such a big battle to fight.

I didn't have the sense to buy any tea, or milk, for the morning—I'd always had plenty at my disposal, and I didn't realise I'd have to get my own.

I went to bed very early, a little bit hungry, because I hadn't remembered to have any supper.

But in the morning Mrs. Allen knocked at my door, and I told her to come in.

She did, carrying a cup of tea.

"Don't you lock your door?" she asked disapprovingly.

"No!" I said in surprise. "I've never locked a door in my life."

"Well you must lock it when you go out. I can't be responsible for your belongings. I've brought you a cup of tea this morning. I knew you wouldn't have time to get your own supplies in."

I thanked her very much, and assured her I would both lock the door and get supplies in. I did lock the door, but I didn't get any "supplies" in.

FIFTY-FOUR

The rest of the week hung heavily on my hands. I had nowhere to go, and I didn't even know about the National Gallery. I spent a lot of time in the shops, and now I just looked blankly at clothes and walked on, where I used to buy everything I could see, almost.

My Bill had gone back to Scotland, there was work there apparently—shipbuilding had taken a little turn, perhaps for the better—there was a big ship building at Clydebank.

At the end of the week I sent my mother ten shillings. Not for anything would I have let her know how down I was. I sat in my room in the evenings and read; I went to bed early; occasionally I would spend a precious one and threepence on the pictures, and I ate only very sparingly. I had two interviews, one in South Audley Street.

Perfect satisfaction until it came to my last place.

"I think I'd better be perfectly honest about that."

And that was the biggest mistake I ever made—being perfectly honest.

The tale sounded very lame, and in truth sordid, told.

The lady visibly froze.

"I see." Then a silence.

Then, "No. I'm afraid you wouldn't be suitable."

I flew up again (I wasn't, yet, too hungry to flare up).

"Why not? You'd think I'd been in prison!"

"Perhaps you have."

"I'd be a great deal better thought of if I had been!"

So that was the end of that.

Another interview wasn't quite so stormy, but—I was "unsuitable". I didn't argue this time, I just walked out.

On the Sunday Mr. Barry picked me up—I had my usual cup of hot water for breakfast, and it was a pouring wet day. We drove down to Slough and went to his cottage. There was no gas or anything laid on, and I think he was going to have one of the new slow-burning stoves.

He dumped some tins of paint and stuff, and we drove back to a pub and had an early lunch. I could have eaten the same again, but it was a delicious lunch. Then we came back and spent a busy, happy afternoon, painting a floor surround black, while Mr. Barry went out and did some digging in the garden.

We nibbled biscuits all afternoon and then went for tea.

The rain eased off a little bit and he showed me the garden, and explained to me what he was doing—it was very nice, but I wanted to get back to where I could eat!

Eating seemed to have assumed a most unusual importance. I had eaten so regularly, and so well, all these years, that you would have thought I could do without for a month. Unfortunately, the human body's not a reservoir.

We drove back to Town, and he drove me first to his own flat for a drink. We had a drink, and cheese biscuits, and a smoke. He was a bachelor and had a very cosy, in fact luxurious flat.

I have not, in this chronicle, at any time neglected to tell when I was faced with a man's suggestions, in whatever way they were offered, and you know I've had to fight my way out of several—no hundreds—of corners. You know also that I am no angel.

Neither was Mr. Barry.

But his suggestion was neither in the nature of a primitive

struggle nor a promise to get me on the stage—it was a frank suggestion, or a question, rather, if I'd care to move into the bedroom?

I said I'd rather not.

"Don't worry, it was just an idea, all the same to me. Have another drink."

We talked and laughed over the affairs of the day, we even laughed at Madam and her impertinent "reference", and he said something would be sure to turn up after the Coronation. Meantime—"How are you fixed for money?"

"Well, I'm all right, but if I pay my rent to-morrow I'll be pretty down."

He nodded.

"I thought so. Right, give this to Mrs. Allen in the morning and come and see me the day after Coronation. All right now? O.K., let's go. You don't want to be too late."

He took a pound note out of his wallet.

"Here you are—for Mrs. Allen. Now I'll put you in a taxi. Have a nice time on Coronation day, and come and see me the day after."

I tried not to take the note from him, but I was weak, I suppose, and I couldn't face having nowhere to sleep. So I could only take it and thank him. He was a kind and wise man, and I know you may feel that he was too good to be true. I can't help that—I did meet some kind people in my life: Rosie, for instance, and Chef, and others.

FIFTY-FIVE

I put my last shilling in the gas meter on Monday morning and found I had one little threepenny piece left. I treasured that little coin, and in fact, I have it yet.

The only thing to do was to stay near the Park—the crowds and the decorations were always a distraction, and helped to pass the time. Towards the end of the day I was conscious of not so much hunger as blinding headache. One missed one's constant cups of tea.

I suppose I slept through exhaustion, and I believe the French have a saying, "*Qui dort, dine.*" Whether it's true or not, it had to be, for me.

I had a letter from my mother, and she told me that a Scottish contingent of the army had left to form part of the lining of the Coronation route, and the boy who lived in the flat below had promised to look out for me. I took a long chance and went to Hyde Park. Among the tents I found the few who came from my own town. One or two I didn't know, but they brought me kind messages.

Two of the boys had never been to London and they were very anxious to see round. They had to stay in camp that day, that was the Tuesday, and the next day they were on duty all day, and they were to be taken to the Palladium at night after the procession. But the next day they would be free, and they would commandeer me to take them round.

I made arrangements to meet them at Hyde Park Corner at ten o'clock on the Thursday morning and went off, pretending I was fine and was heavily booked up. One of the boys had asked me if I wasn't working and I said casually, "Yes, but I've got a few days off." They accepted that.

The hours hung heavily and my legs got tired with walking.

I hadn't even a penny to go into a ladies' toilet, so when I did go to the toilets I had to go to the free ones.

Hunger had passed—now I felt sort of floating, and the ache in my legs gradually went.

In the early afternoon of Tuesday I was looking in Lyons Corner House at Marble Arch, just gazing at the food in the window. A voice beside me said, "Are you going anywhere?" I turned and saw a tremendously tall, well-built man, young and handsome, and I think he was Welsh. I said, "I was just wondering whether to have tea first then go to the pictures, or go to the pictures first and have a meal later on."

"I was just going in to the pictures. Are you just up for the Coronation?"

"No, just a holiday for a few days."

"I hope you don't mind me speaking to you, but I'm a stranger in town. Will you come in to the pictures with me, and we'll have tea when we come out?"

I would have preferred some tea first, but the promise of something definite in a few hours was at least hopeful.

I said, "All right," and we went in to the Odeon at Marble Arch.

He took two seats upstairs, and the place was comparatively empty.

He, too, wasted no time on preliminaries—first he took my hand, then my two hands in his one big fist, leaving his other hand free.

I must have made some kind of a scream of protest, although I wondered if I could stand this for the sake of a meal when the programme was over, but I knew I couldn't. I struggled, and then I bit his hand—he swore, and I jumped up and ran out.

I ran down the stairs and straight outside, and down into the station ladies' room. When I got my breath back, I ventured out and walked through the Park and home.

I flung myself on my bed and—what the hell's the good of weeping?

I was a complete and utter failure—no use to anybody. I was no use when I did my work conscientiously and faithfully, and I couldn't even be bad successfully. It was raining, and life couldn't have been more hopeless. I had two or three cups of hot water, and amused myself going over all my clothes—mending stockings, polishing my shoes for to-morrow, brushing my brown velvet tunic suit, and, at last, utterly exhausted, physically and emotionally, I went to bed.

My stomach seemed to have shrunk, and I no longer felt any sensation of wanting to eat. I drank my hot water and dressed very carefully next morning and set out to see my first Coronation. When I arrived in Hyde Park I had nothing in my purse and nothing in my stomach, but, oh, how elegant and successful I *appeared* to be!

The crowds gathered, and the hours passed quickly. I was standing on the Park side of the procession route, and behind me were the temporary toilets which are usually erected for a big day. I got chummy with two girls, very nice girls, and we were hopping up and down, trying to get a glimpse of where the procession would come.

Four young chaps saw us and gallantly offered to help us. One of them clambered up and stood on the planks that were laid across the shelters. Then, making a long arm, and with the boys below pushing on our behinds, he hauled us three girls up. I haven't the slightest doubt that the boys down below were just as interested in our underwear as in the procession which was just coming! I knew mine was nice anyway, so I didn't worry. I wasn't too hungry to lose all sense of personal fussiness or "Daily Dipping", as was the current advertising slogan.

Well, we had a glorious view of the procession.

We saw the gold coach, and the King and Queen, and we waved and shouted and cried, and laughed and rejoiced. Hunger, injustice, and intolerance all forgotten in the symbols of apparent justice, tolerance, and plenty.

When it was all over, the boys helped us down, and insisted on us all coming for a drink.

"For sure," said a voice in an Irish brogue you could cut with a knife, "we must drink the health of the King and Queen, bejabers!"

So four boys and we three girls went up to Edgware Road —we must have been in time before they closed, or maybe they had an extended licence, I don't know. All I remember is that all seven of us went into the first pub in Edgware Road and in a very short time I had consumed four double whiskies (and I think it was Irish whisky). Hardly the best treatment for an empty stomach!

But then the boys thought they'd like to have something to eat, and desperately, unashamedly, I stuck with them. We lost the two girls and one of the boys, and the three boys and I went boisterously round streets, and I vaguely noticed we were somewhere at the back of Oxford Street, near Selfridge's, and we went into a little cafe, where we had to go downstairs.

They ordered sausages and chips and eggs.

I wolfed mine greedily, and the talk and laughter flowed round me, and over me, and under me, and the whole place heaved, and I ran upstairs and outside—where I was disgustingly and revoltingly sick all over the pavement.

Like a drunken trollop, which I felt, I stood there, ill and helpless; the boys came up the stairs and sneered, and made vulgar remarks.

How could they know that it was not a sign of debauchery or over-indulgence? I couldn't tell them my last meal had been early on Sunday evening, and it was now about five o'clock on Wednesday. And if I had, they wouldn't have believed me. They left me reeling about and starting to cry. But I stopped that—I had to pull myself together—I couldn't give way to anything like the luxury of tears now. I was still drunk, but the sickness soon passed, or the worst of it did anyway.

FIFTY-SIX

Slowly, very slowly and wearily, I walked into the deserted and littered Park again.

Inside me, all I could think of was how much I wanted my mother, but how could I get to her? I knew that no matter what I had done, my mother's arms would comfort me, and her voice saying, "Wheesht noo! Wheesht noo!" would be sweeter music than angels singing. Angels are vague, my mother was substantial.

I found a seat and rested my shaking legs. I was wavering on my feet, just as though I was on the deck of a heaving ship; I was light, and light-headed, and I thought I was going to die. I wanted to—it would be so much better for everybody, for I was no use to anybody.

A man spoke to me, and I just jumped and ran, crying in desperation and fear.

No! I couldn't bear *that* again!

I reached Hyde Park Corner at last, and found that it was dark—the darkness seemed to have sneaked up on me—it was nearly nine o'clock and the King was to speak.

I heard him, standing in the rain at Hyde Park Corner, then I walked down Grosvenor Place, and home. I drank my usual hot water, and went to bed.

I had a nightmare—I forget what it was, but I woke up crying, and I was a little bit sick again—but I felt a little better, although very weak, in the morning. I drank my hot water, then had my bath, and dressed—different clothes, different everything, clean and nicely made up, good stockings, good comfortable shoes to walk about London—and I set off for Hyde Park Corner to meet Jack and Peter, and be their official guide to London!

Only Jack was there—apparently Peter was still under the weather from the night out at the Palladium.

Jack saluted and said, "Good morning, Jean."

I said, "Good morning, Jack."

Then he said, "Have you had breakfast?"

Jack, if you could only know what those words did to me! I said, "Oh, I very seldom eat breakfast."

Jack said, "Well, *I* eat breakfast. Come on!"

We went across to Lyons and, remembering the fiasco of the day before, I had a cup of tea, toast, and marmalade. Jack had a *breakfast*!

We took our time, and it was well after eleven o'clock when we set off on our sightseeing tour. We walked down Constitution Hill, and I showed him the Palace, then round to the Mall, and across Horse Guards Parade, and along to Wellington Barracks. Back to Westminster, and we stood and looked at Big Ben, and then down to the Bridge and the Embankment. By that time Jack thought it was about time we had a drink. So we went into a pub, and Jack thought I looked pale, and I'd better have a nice glass of port.

We talked of home and families and work, and the Coronation and world prospects, and the long, lean years, and— me.

I couldn't tell him everything, of course, just that I hadn't been very well—a bad attack of 'flu, and had lost my job. And I was just taking this week's holiday, but, laughingly, I'd have to take a job next week—I was broke!

"How are you fixed—for digs and that kind of thing?"

"Oh, I've got a lovely room. I'm all right, I'll be starting work next week."

Jack didn't say any more, but he was not easily deceived.

"What about some lunch? I'm hungry!" he said.

"Well, where would you like to go?"

"Wherever you say, you're the guide."

I didn't know how his pocket was, so I thought I'd better stick to Lyons—you could be sure of Lyons.

So we walked up Whitehall. I showed him Downing Street, and I was so proud of him when he saluted the Cenotaph.

We walked slowly up, and round Trafalgar Square into Leicester Square, and along to Lyons Corner House.

We had a wonderful lunch, with a glass of beer, and then we came out and found it was raining.

Jack had to be back in camp, and ready packed up, by six o'clock, and it was now after three.

We were both tired, so we slipped into a news reel cinema in Piccadilly for an hour: it was quite a well-deserved rest— Jack fell sound asleep!

The day would soon be over; when we came out we had time for a cup of tea, and then it was time to part.

I'd had a lovely day. It was so good to feel needed, to be doing something for somebody, and to be treated as a friend, an honoured friend, and not either a cheap pick-up or a drunken trollop.

(Both of those episodes had served me right. I'm not whining—I never whined in my life, but I couldn't have stood any more of *that*.)

We had to rush when we had finished tea—Jack had to be in camp. Recklessly, he called a taxi, and bundled me in and told the man Hyde Park Corner. Just from Piccadilly!

The rain had stopped, and Jack admired the flowers all along the windows in Piccadilly and at the green of the Green Park, and in no time at all we were at Hyde Park Corner.

There was no time for ceremony—Jack jumped out and paid the driver, set me down on the kerb, and with a big firm handshake, he said, "Good-bye, Jean. Best of luck, and thanks for giving me a grand day. Buy yourself a pair of stockings."

An extra shake, nearly breaking my hand in two, and he was striding across the road to the Park.

When I could open my hand I found a ten-shilling note in it. Dumbly, I looked at it, and then, out of habit, I turned and walked slowly down Grosvenor Place, and home. A tremendous surge of homesickness swept over me—not only longing for my mother, but for the sights and sounds of my own land, for the tongue of my own people, for the grandeur of the old grey town on the banks of the Clyde, in spite of its poverty.

I wouldn't refuse the small gift, given in true friendship, even if I could have done. Somehow, I would use it to get home.

I think I must have been quite numb by the time I got home because I don't remember getting there, or going to bed, or anything. But I woke up next morning to find Mrs. Allen bending over me, and a man, obviously a doctor.

It must have been the doctor who told me about a Scottish Benevolent Fund, and he thought they might help me. He gave me the address, and I went to see them. I had my ten shillings now, so I could take a bus and get a cup of tea. Mrs. Allen had brought me a cup of tea and bread and butter when the doctor had gone. He said there was nothing wrong with me that a good dinner and a sight of my mother wouldn't cure.

I saw a very supercilious young woman at the office, to whom I had to tell my story. She was inclined to be sarcastic, and when I told her about the registry office, and the lady, and the "men in the house", and scribbling, it sounded so fantastic, even to me, that I wasn't surprised she scarcely believed it. And I'm afraid I wasn't as humble as one is supposed to be when asking for benevolence; nor a bit penitent, having nothing to repent.

So she snapped at me once: "Don't talk to me like that!"

And I snapped back: "And don't you talk to *me* like that!"

That seemed to do the trick, for she knew she had no right to question my behaviour or morals as she had done. She was as nice as pie after that, went away, and came back in a few minutes with a railway ticket to Glasgow, and five shillings!

When I got home I found that mother had no money, rent had to be paid, and my father's job didn't last very long. I wasn't really strong enough for a job, and I was forced to recognise that.

"Do you think we should ask for Parish Relief, or Public Assistance, or whatever they call it, Mother?"

My mother went white, she doubled her hands into fists, and tensed visibly. Without a word she got up and walked into her bedroom. I followed her and found her sitting in a chair at the window——trying not to cry, but when I put my arm round her she did let go, and got some relief in her tears.

She told me what had happened a few years before when she had been driven to ask for help.

A woman came to visit her. I will spare you the nauseous details, but she didn't spare my mother.

"What was cooking in the pan?" "What about all this silver?" (my grandmother's silver-wedding presents) as she went from kitchen to room: "You've got a good chest of drawers here"; "You surely don't need two rugs on the floor"; and "You could sell that wedding ring, couldn't you?"

My mother, never belligerent, was too timid now to take a stand against this unholy lady. It took men to evolve the Means Test, but it took a woman to carry out the full horrors of it.

I have lost all respect for a System that can so degrade and intimidate honest working people, and I am amazed that my countrymen have not had more spunk than to let it happen again.

FIFTY-SEVEN

The weary hunt for work started again, the letter writing, nightly, and in detail all my experience, except the last place.

Then there came a letter from Edinburgh. It had looked like a decent job when I saw it in the paper and, for the first time, when I wrote for the job, I mentioned Chef's name and the Duke and Duchess I was with during my training with him.

I got a letter to go for an interview to a Ladies' Club in Edinburgh.

It was only when I got there and had my interview that I found out that my Chef, in collaboration with Chef Saulnier I have told you about, had written a book—a journal of cooking. It was recommendation enough for the secretary that I had been trained by one of the joint authors of this book.

So I got the job, as cook-housekeeper, at £110 a year, with a kitchen staff of six including myself and, of course, with waitresses and housemaids.

So the months passed happily, till the summer of 1938. There was talk of what we would do if war came. I said I would try to get into some kind of entertainment. That was ridiculed, of course, but I was better able to stand it now—I just let it go inside, where the protective wall was getting harder and stronger.

The head waitress said she would stay right where she was. She said there would be such a rush of girls to services and factories that a good waitress could more or less demand her own money. Which I thought was a very peculiar way of looking at war.

But the war didn't come, instead, a miniature war began to rumble through my kitchen staff. There were grumbles about time off, although I'd spent hours and hours on a rota that would give them more time off than they'd ever had. I took a Sunday night duty myself quite often, when it wasn't at all necessary and had not been the custom before. I saw that their meals were good and plentiful, and treated them as I would have liked to be treated, instead of with the whip.

I didn't know that it was just the new revolution having its birth-pangs. Work of other kinds was getting plentiful, giving them a false impression that war, and rumour of war, was a better state of affairs then peace. They knew of factory girls who finished at five-thirty, and twelve o'clock on Saturday, and had Sundays free, and had bigger wages than they had. And they were beginning to rebel, even if it was only a rumble as yet, and not even a united rumble, and a firm hand just then would have gained an ascendancy; but I didn't have that firm hand and my cursed gift for putting myself in the other fellow's place, for thinking that *I* must do something about it, made me feel that, whatever the grumble, it *must* be all my fault.

It was something new to me to sit down to lunch in the staff dining-room and be waited on, and, moreover, have an hour to have my lunch.

But I had for so many years had to eat running about, or else snatch a meal quickly—one day I ate my lunch in three minutes flat—that the time wasted in eating irked me. I couldn't sit still all the time. So that, after a time, especially when I began to hear grumbles, I was afraid—afraid that I wasn't doing enough, afraid that whatever I did was wrong, afraid of losing my job if I didn't do more.

I think I'd had reason for this fear. I *had* lost jobs, even when I knew I was giving conscientious devotion to duty, and I hadn't known why. So the fear was very real. All very well to say there were other jobs—what other jobs could I do —now?

So I gradually lost even my surface confidence, and used to eat my lunch quickly, and go back to the kitchen. Which meant that they thought I was spying on them, when all I wanted to do was help them, and put myself right in their estimation.

So, in exaggerated dignity, one day I resigned. Miss Forrest was deeply shocked and surprised—especially at my reason.

But she was far too sensible and efficient a woman and a secretary to attempt to make me change my mind. I think, basically, I had hoped for that. All through the years, I had heard tales of people having given their notice, ". . . and do you know, she just *begged* me to stay on. Nearly got down on her knees and *begged* me to stay. . . ."

I had had no reason to doubt these statements. *I* wouldn't

have said them if they hadn't been true. I know now that it is not a good thing to do, and I have at last realised that I shouldn't have believed all I heard.

I have also learned a profound truth—that nobody in this world is indispensable.

FIFTY-EIGHT

That was in May, when I left the Club.

More and more I regretted leaving the Club. One day I went to Miss Forrest, the secretary, and asked if I could keep my job. She was very nice about it, but she showed me that it wouldn't do. I was terribly disappointed and a little upset, but I saw she meant it.

She asked me if I'd like to go back down south. I said I wasn't keen on London, but she said it wasn't London, it was near a little country town in Surrey.

On the 1st February 1939 I went to be cook-housekeeper to the Lady Constance Combe, at a salary of £120 a year, with a kitchen staff of four included in an indoors staff of fifteen.

FIFTY-NINE

Of all the houses and castles I had been in, none had I seen as gloriously lovely as this grand mansion set on a little hill overlooking a silver stream and the wooded slopes of the Surrey countryside.

It was comparatively modern, but built on generous lines for the bride of sixty years ago—a duchess's daughter, who married a commoner—and it had grace and dignity, and beauty and love, in every corner of it.

The front door opened into a small hall, stone paved, with oaken chest and table, massive and shining, and a suit of armour in a corner. This entrance, through an archway, opened into a vast hall, as big as a concert hall, with a wide dark oak staircase on the left, the floor covered with priceless Indian carpets—a full-size concert grand piano in the far corner beside the tall french windows, which opened out on to the lawn.

This room, which served as a lounge, drawing-room, concert room, ballroom, was about eighty feet long and sixty feet wide, and its height was the whole height of the three-storey house, with a glass-domed roof. The walls panelled in oak, which was the same right through into the dining-room. Rich austerity was the note of the dining-room: red carpet, a massive oak table, and a wide Jacobean fireplace, with an open steel grate that could burn a four-foot log; the walls hung with pictures of the lady's forebears. Perhaps a few of the gentleman's, but the lady's were more predominant.

The dining-room was immediately on the left of this large hall, and the passage between that and the staircase led to the green baize door and the beyond—the other world.

Past the staircase, on the same side, was a billiard-room and library, and opposite was the drawing-room proper—all white and gilt. I never saw the drawing-room in all its glory when I was there, but I visited the place two years ago.

It was from the drawing-room terrace that one could see the slope leading down to the gardens, and the silver trout-stream, and the main road.

Up the main staircase, round to the right, Lady Constance had her suite of rooms. Her bedroom, her sitting-room, and bathroom, and a small boudoir. This landing had the balcony which looked down on the grandeur of the magnificent front hall. To the left was another suite of rooms and various spare rooms. I don't know if there was anything above that, I didn't see any other part of the house.

The whole effect was of space and grandeur and magnificence, and not the smallest whisper of vulgar or ostentatious riches made in trade.

Beauty of any kind touches me deeply—that house lives in my memory—as a beauty too deep for words to describe it properly.

I remember writing enthusiastically to my mother when I first went there and saw it, ". . . this *is* one of the Stately Homes of England".

So masterly had been the hands that built it that, although it was only about sixty years old, it gave the impression of centuries of ancestral inhabitants, but it had happiness, and care, and the strength of youth with the mellowed dignity of age.

SIXTY

The same masterly architecture that conceived the front of the house was carried through to the working quarters. Through the baize door, down a few steps on the left, the butler's pantry, with big windows and plenty of room. The passage made a right-angle turn, and on the left was my kitchen. A big lovely kitchen, like the one in the Border castle, or the London house of the Duke and Duchess.

The steward's room on the right, a smaller staircase with a little room at the foot of it, the housemaids' sitting-room. Round by this staircase, a continuation of the passage, leading to the big servants' hall, and a back door from there out to a courtyard, and opposite was the laundry.

The kitchen led into a big, airy scullery, with three sinks and lots of cupboard and table room.

Up the little staircase, white wood scrubbed, were three bedrooms—mine, the head kitchenmaid's, and the head laundrymaid's.

The indoor staff were myself, cook-housekeeper, a head kitchenmaid and second kitchenmaid, and scullerymaid. We also had a woman in once a week to do our bedrooms and odd jobs in kitchen and scullery. Four housemaids, a butler and two footmen, an odd man and hall boy; a lady's maid, two laundrymaids, and two nurses, a night nurse and a day nurse.

For the master of the house was an invalid, and he had constant care.

SIXTY-ONE

So in fourteen years I had come to full authority.

Once I had had a glimpse of the forbidden steward's room, now I was in it.

And it was now I was thankful for my hard training, and for my own high standards, for these people had known the patronage of kings and the ministrations of the world's greatest chefs.

The first morning the butler took me up to her ladyship's sitting-room and introduced me in the proper way as "Mrs. Rennie". She called me "Rennie".

She was then nearly eighty, and her last pleasure in life was gossiping—about her other servants, to me, and about me to her other servants.

She always received me in her little sitting-room, in a pink satin negligee and a lace-trimmed pink satin cap. She cared very little now for what she ate, she lived practically on a little dish of chicken cream and champagne, and her brandy every night. Her husband, Mr. Combe, ate very little, but we made it all as tempting as possible.

One was not, of course, allowed to sit in the Presence, and I have stood in her sitting-room for an hour and three-quarters sometimes. Some mornings she would dismiss me with hardly a word, and only a quick glance at the menu book.

She never forgot that she was a Lady, and the daughter of a Duchess.

And she bitterly resented the fact that now "the poor" could get medical treatment, and even an operation, quite free, for which she would have had to pay sixty to a hundred guineas.

She had decided views on miners: she thought it must be dreadful to be down a mine—she had never been down a coal-mine, but she had been in a diamond mine in South Africa; and she told me of how she had to crawl on her hands and knees, and how glad she was to get out in the sunlight again. She was not a bit concerned about the men who spent their days there to give her diamonds.

She talked to me endlessly about her early life, and her young married life, her tours round the world, her meetings with kings and queens, her housemaids' dusting and polishing, her husband's illness. But her bitterest attacks were kept for her husband's nurses—more particularly his day nurse.

All I could do was endure; what is a servant to do when her lady maligns another servant to her?

You couldn't disagree with the Lady Constance and, anyway, my mind was on what might be going on down in my kitchen. My head kitchenmaid was very good, but she liked me there to see to things, and I liked to be in my kitchen.

But the awful part of the whole thing was that *I* was accused of carrying tales to her Ladyship. How anybody

207

ever got a word in edgeways to carry any tales to her, I don't know. It was as much as I could do to get her to look at the menu and discuss it reasonably; and even if I had had time and opportunity, it was not one of my failings—carrying tales.

The whole truth of the matter was that she herself created bad feeling by her spiteful gossip, in which she was ably assisted by the nurse she so constantly vilified.

She was so intensely angry that her day was over, that there were signs that "Jack was as good as his master", that an era was already passing, and her impotence to stop it manifested itself in vituperative attacks on all who came within the orbit of her still considerable power. She was an infuriated Queen Canute, powerless to stem the inexorably rising tide.

SIXTY-TWO

I was always glad to get back to the sanity of my kitchen, where we four were perfectly happy.

Our young scullerymaid was a fresh country girl, very new and very young. She put on her cabbage one day and then, as the fire was low, she poked it clear and made it up. To our horror, we saw her take the poker, fresh from the inside of the hot fire, and quite cheerfully lift the lid of the cabbage pot and use the poker to push her cabbage all under the water and stir it round!

We all three burst out laughing.

As far as I know, the cabbage didn't do anyone any harm!

There was quite a lot of entertaining. Lady Constance had three daughters—I don't know if she had any sons—yes, I think she had, but I'm not sure; but they gradually began to give tea parties and dinner parties at their mother's house; and there were cricket teas, with the village cricket team using the "squire's" cricket green, playing a team from a neighbouring village.

It was lovely to sit in a deck chair and listen to the click of the cricket ball in the sunshine, in that summer of 1939.

But before this, just ten days after I got there, I went down with 'flu again! Of course, I was new, and I suppose 'flu can happen to anybody, and it could have happened to me anywhere else, but it made me feel absolutely awful.

Everybody was very kind, and the day nurse came to see me occasionally and took my temperature. One morning I was quite insistent that I could hear a big orchestra—I was delirious, of course, but I didn't know that. It was the night nurse who visited me that day: she was a sweet girl—that was the only time I saw her.

But I was told, many months later, that her Ladyship had said she didn't see why she should pay anyone to lie in bed and have 'flu!

But she paid me, of course.

The meals were, of course, scattered, with such a varied collection of people.

There were her Ladyship's trays—breakfast, lunch, tea, and dinner—always in her sitting-room. She very seldom left it. There was, of course, the invalid Mr. Combe. His food was ordered by his nurse, and it always had to be very tempting and nice. There was the day nurse, who had her meals in her own sitting-room, another tray. There was the night nurse, who had her breakfast when the other nurse had her dinner, and always something left for her to have a meal during her night duty.

Then there was the steward's room, which comprised the butler, the lady's maid, and myself. Then the servants' hall, in which were the two footmen, odd man and hall boy, the four housemaids, and the two laundrymaids.

Then my own girls had a tiny wee room just inside the kitchen, just big enough to hold a table and chairs, where they could have their meals and write their letters, or sew, or be at ease—not that there was room for ease, there were no armchairs in it; but at least it was their own, and they did get time to sit. It had drawers in, too, where they could keep their writing paper and stamps, and books and knitting, and all the odd things one doesn't bother to keep in one's bedroom.

I had the same procedure here as I had had with Mrs. Leonard. I took the tradesmen's books up, with a list of the amounts, plus my own salary and the three girls', with any extras that I had spent during the month. Then she would give me a cheque to cover the full amount. She very seldom made any comment on the books.

Our cooking was always up to first-class standard, and I was very lucky in my girls, so that although we worked hard our work was rewarding and satisfying.

But we couldn't please the staff.

Nobody ever could, so that was nothing new.

But it was mental agony for me to sit in the steward's room with the lady's maid, and especially the butler, when he believed that I carried tales to her Ladyship. Even if I'd been so inclined, I didn't know any tales to carry, my business was in the kitchen.

Sometimes he spoke at meals, sometimes he didn't, and I was still sensitive enough to suffer acutely.

But I was well and comparatively happy. In fact, I was better in health during that year in Surrey than I'd ever been in my life.

I think it was in the early autumn that Mr. Combe died.

We all went to the funeral in the little village church, and her Ladyship watched the solemn procession as it moved slowly up the little hill; she could see the whole length of it from her drawing-room windows. The coffin was carried on a farm cart and all the estate workers, gamekeepers, farmers, farm hands, village men, tradesmen, indoor staff, followed it on foot. I was very deeply touched, as I always used to be by such an emotional ceremony.

But the living went on, and in a few weeks her Ladyship started entertaining. There was more entertaining after the old gentleman died than there had been for many years. The house remained wide open, not a single room had been closed.

But then came a day in September, a sunny Sunday, when we looked up in the sky at an unaccustomed sound, and saw wave after wave of bombers going out to somewhere south.

First a footman left to join the Air Force; then my second kitchenmaid left; then a housemaid, and none were replaced.

Cricket on the lawns stopped. Her Ladyship, under pressure, consented to close one room—one of the spare suite which was never used anyway.

And in spite of all her vindictiveness about the day nurse, she chose that nurse to stay with her after her husband's death. Not to nurse her—she didn't need nursing—but to be a companion to her. That girl was a brilliant nurse, at the top of her profession; and she chose to renounce her calling and waste it on an old woman with too much money, for a salary of seven pounds a week—her Ladyship told me her salary—and she grudged every penny of it.

I don't know whether she found it worth her while to stay till her Ladyship died, but she earned no kudos from the staff who served her. It was one of her habits, which we thought particularly objectionable, that every holiday—Easter, Whitsun, August Bank Holiday, Christmas, as well as her annual holiday—she announced her mother was taken ill and she had to go home.

But to the lighter and brighter side.

I was out one afternoon on my bike, shortly after the war started, just a few days after it, in fact.

Just outside the village pub, although it was well past closing time, or maybe it was nearer opening time, two or three lorries were parked—army lorries, and moving about were some soldiers—*kilted* soldiers!

One of them called to me: "Hey, miss! Can ye tell us whaur's Bridge Manor?"

The accent was pure Glasgow!

I said, "Aye. It's just up 'roon that corner, a wee bit up the road."

There was a hoot of delight, and about six of them clustered round me.

"Where did I come from? What was I doing? Would I tell them where there was a dance hall? Would I go dancing with them?"

They were so gay, so young, so gallant in their dark green tartan kilts—my gallant young countrymen, so soon to be in the forefront of those who went out to die. And one of them, more persistent, more gay, more handsome than the others, insisted that I meet him that night for a walk. And I did.

He was ten years younger than I, and he thought he was in love with me. For the next six weeks we had picnics, we went to the pictures in the town, and once we missed the last bus and then caught an officers' mess car in the blackout. He was handsome, young, in love, passionate, and very conscious that he was going to war.

I was not so terribly old either, and he wanted me. He said he was going to come back and marry me on his first leave, and he wanted me to have a black lace nightdress.

211

I had one letter from France, and then there was—
Dunkirk.

No, I wasn't in love with him, but I was very proud of him.

SIXTY-THREE

I had enough money, even after sending a good bit home,
and I bought clothes again. This time, not off the peg, but
made to fit me. A tailored suit, a black patterned chiffon
blouse, and when I met my Highland laddie I ordered a
Gordon tartan dress. Good shoes, too, and silk stockings and
good silk underwear. I bought, too, a tiny radio set, and had
it plugged into my bedroom, so that on winter nights I could
go to bed early, with a book or some sewing, and a big fire in
my room, and listen to the radio.

My sister spent Christmas with me, and I went to London
and spent New Year with her. I stayed at Mount Royal, and
I walked up Oxford Street on the afternoon of Old Year's
night in a tartan frock and black felt hat with a feather in it,
and a short white astrakhan jacket. I got lots of looks, admir-
ing and otherwise! So *I* wore tartan before the craze for
tartan came in the early fifties.

SIXTY-FOUR

Gradually the staff situation got worse. My head kitchenmaid left to be married; my scullerymaid left to go into a
factory. I had only the help of the woman who used to come
in to do the rough work and our bedrooms.

And in spite of rationing, to which we were very strictly
held, the entertaining went on. And the staff just refused to
accept that I couldn't give them roast beef every day. We had
a lot of eggs, and I bought as many as I could, and about the
beginning of April these eggs put the finishing touch to a
position that was fast becoming untenable. It was already
extremely uncomfortable.

I went up as usual with my menu book, the tradesmen's

books, and the list of their accounts, and my salary. The daily woman was paid by the butler.

Something must have upset her Ladyship—nurse was away—and she had nobody to talk to. She started about the eggs—three dozen eggs in one week! From that to how she suffered in the first war, to her extreme poverty now, to the £60,000 she'd had to pay in death duties, to the laziness of servants, to the food we ate....

She got more and more inarticulate as I stood there, blasted by her tirade, which grew shriller and yet more shrill, till a much-maligned respectable fishwife would have winced at its stridency.

She went on and on about how life used to be, about how the lower classes used to curtsey and bow, and work for love of their betters—and she went on about her being the daughter of this Duchess, and her father, the Duke.

I was getting angrier and angrier, and I wanted to fly back at her, but *she* was the master of words, and I couldn't find any, even if I'd got a chance to use them. She abused everybody and everything, and said cooking was nothing like it used to be, and finally she screamed:

"I'm the daughter of a Duchess! I'm a *Lady*, and don't you forget it!"

She never had allowed anybody to forget it.

My anger suddenly left me, I calmed down. She stopped to get breath from sheer exhaustion. I turned to go, and then looked at her. Then I said very quietly, but my legs were trembling at my unaccustomed rebellion:

"Well, if you're a lady, thank God *I* shall never be one! And," as she opened her mouth to speak, "you can take my month's notice. Good morning," and I turned on my heel and walked out.

SIXTY-FIVE

I never spoke to her again.

That was on the first or second of April 1940, and she was too ill to see anyone. The butler took my book up and she sent it down again without any comment. Of course, nurse

213

gave out that I was the cause of her illness, and I'm sure, if she had died then, I would have stood a very good chance of being accused of her murder—but, even at eighty, she was tough.

What was annoying her most at this time was that her family had finally persuaded her to sell the big house and take a smaller one just outside the village. The thought that *she* would have to go and live in a poky house—she, a *Lady*!—when the Government had taken all her money and left her a poor widow. The house she was going to move to was still large by ordinary standards, but it was certainly much smaller than Bridge House.

She could not see that the past was past; like all the Victorians, she had a touching and insane belief in human permanence, the certainty that things would go on for ever as they were, and she could not, or would not, acknowledge that the era of their greatness was gone for ever.

She sent down next day a cheque for the books and my salary, and things went on as usual; except that the butler decreed that the servants' hall should be shut up and the staff have their meals in the steward's room. The staff was much smaller now—two housemaids, butler and odd man, lady's maid, and myself.

I still had plenty to do, however; there was her Ladyship's trays as usual, and the nurse-companion, but it was all to end soon.

On the 8th April the butler came back with my menu book and said, "Her Ladyship wants me to tell you that she has a cook who can come in to-morrow. Would it inconvenience you to leave then?"

I flew at him.

"What a damned cheek! I haven't got my fare home till I get paid at the end of the month, and I'm going home to be with my mother, I don't care *what* her Ladyship wants!"

He went away and came back, with a personal message from her Ladyship, would I tell her the amount of my fare home? I told him. He came back again, with a cheque for a month's wages, a month's board wages, and my fare home—in all, about eighteen pounds.

Immediately after lunch I dashed into town and paid one or two small bills, and bought a trunk and another suitcase, and hurried back. My grocer changed my cheque. I collected a new dress and a fur fabric coat I had ordered—a very nice coat of what was then a new fabric—it was only five pounds.

I packed quickly and went downstairs to do the dinner and staff supper, dashed upstairs again, and finished packing at two o'clock in the morning.

I was down in the kitchen at six, and put as much ready for the lunch as I could, and left the house at eight o'clock. I had ordered a taxi from the village.

SIXTY-SIX

As my taxi swept away from the back door and took the wide sweep of the back drive, I could see her pink-clad figure at her windows. She missed nothing.

"Yes, you can look, m'lady. I've served you and your kind for the last time...."

My heart was lifted—I felt I had been just released from sixteen years' imprisonment, and as the car left the house behind, I made a vow:

"I swear by everything that's holy, if I starve, I'll never go back to private service. I've done with it—I'll scrub floors or sweep streets—I'll even *walk* the streets—but *I will never go back!*"

And I will never say "m'Lady" again

SIXTY-SEVEN

Euston Station was crowded—uniforms were everywhere. I had never seen it like this before—porters were too busy; the obsequious attention we had had when we travelled up for the Glorious Twelfth was all gone.

There were three ladies in my compartment and five sailor boys; the boys had no money, and we four ladies clubbed together and bought them tea. They didn't know where they were going, but they were told to change at Carlisle. We knew later—it was on that day that Hitler's troops marched into Norway.

I knew not what the future held for me, but it was not

possible, thought I, that it could hold anything as bad as the past had brought. My home was small and cosy and welcoming—my mother's love would surmount the bitterness of all those years that had started on a wee boat down to Tighna-bruaich in the summer of 1924.

APRES PROPOS

The years between have brought me into safe harbour—after a voyage that still had many storms to face.

To-night I am going to the Albert Hall with my husband to hear Malcuzynski play.

I should be going to hear my husband play, but he is another story.

The years, too, brought me a chance in the theatre, by fair means.

I have proved, to a small paying audience, that I can act.

I have proved, to a larger cinema audience, that I can sing.

Last summer I went to a garden party. I bought tickets for a raffle of a bottle of champagne from a lady—still charming, elegant, and beautiful—whom I had not seen for sixteen years.

I remembered it was she who used to say, "Everything is lovely—BUT…!"

I said, "Mrs. Holland? Don't you remember me?"

She looked intelligently puzzled.

"Doris? Kathleen? Ellen? *No*, Mary!"

"Mary's sister—Jean."

She held out her hand and looked sadly and nostalgically reminiscent.

"Oh, Jean!" Her voice was almost a wail—"Jean—the best cook I ever had!"

This time there was no "BUT"!

I am much loved, and I am *needed*.

I am very fortunate.

JEAN RENNIE

16*th May* 1954.

AUTOBIOGRAPHIES AND BIOGRAPHIES
FROM CORONET BOOKS

AL DI ORIO

☐ 20747 7 Little Girl Lost: The Life and Hard
Times of Judy Garland   95p

JOHN COTTREL

☐ 21804 5 Laurence Olivier   £1.25

COLIN COWDREY

☐ 21570 4 MCC: The Autobiography of a Cricketer   85p

JONOTHAN DIMBLEBY

☐ 21308 6 Richard Dimbleby   £1.00

ELIZABETH GOUDGE

☐ 19915 6 The Joy of the Snow   £1.00

DENISE ROBINS

☐ 18877 4 Stranger Than Fiction   75p

JIMMY SAVILE

☐ 19925 3 Love Is An Uphill Thing   60p

All these books are available at your local bookshop or newsagent, or can be ordered direct from the publisher. Just tick the titles you want and fill in the form below.

Prices and availability subject to change without notice.

CORONET BOOKS, P.O. Box 11, Falmouth, Cornwall.
Please send cheque or postal order, and allow the following for postage and packing:
U.K. – One book 22p plus 10p per copy for each additional book ordered, up to a maximum of 82p.

B.F.P.O. and EIRE – 22p for the first book plus 10p per copy for the next 6 books, thereafter 4p per book.

OTHER OVERSEAS CUSTOMERS – 30p for the first book and 10p per copy for each additional book.

Name ....

Address ....

....